Sourcebook

for Older Americans

■ ■ ■

by Joseph L. Matthews
with Dorothy Matthews Berman

Nolo Press ■ 950 Parker Street, Berkeley, CA

Printing History

Nolo Press is committed to keeping its books up-to-date. Each new printing, whether or not it is called a new edition, has been completely revised to reflect the latest law changes. This book was printed and updated on the last date indicated below. If this book is out-of-date, do not rely on the information without checking it in a newer edition.

First Edition: January 1983

Second Printing: August 1983

═══════════════════════IMPORTANT═══════════════════════

Laws and administrative regulations concerning the rules of benefit programs are constantly changing. This book was printed and updated on the last date indicated on this page under "printing history." However, it is impossible to guarantee that all the figures and rules presented herein will still be in effect at the time you read this book. The authors and publishers, therefore, cannot assume responsibility for the accuracy of the information contained herein.

Whenever you seek to rely on rules or benefit amounts described in the book always double-check with the agency or program involved to make sure that the information on which you rely is current and still in effect.

BOOK DESIGN & LAYOUT   TONI IHARA

PRODUCTION   STEPHANIE HAROLDE

ILLUSTRATIONS   LINDA ALLISON

ISBN 0-917316-55-X
Library of Congress Card Catalog Number: 82-073782
© copyright 1983 Joseph L. Matthews

Introduction

■ ■ ■

    Are you 55 or over? Do you help support someone who
is? Are you dependent on someone 55 or over? If so, this
book will help you get the money and other benefits you are
entitled to. Because the rules of the public and private
retirement systems and medical care programs are often over-
lapping and confusing, many older Americans do not receive
all the benefits they have earned. For people who are, or
soon will be, on fixed incomes, this unnecessary loss of
benefits and protection can cause critical problems. It's
hard enough to keep a roof over your head and decent food on
the table these days, let alone a few extras, without having
to get by on less than you are entitled to. With the information you read here, you may well be able to increase your
income and make sure that the medical coverage you receive
is as broad as possible.

    With all the crazy bureaucratic rules the government
has adopted in its program for older Americans, it's a small
miracle that most people actually do receive most of the
benefits they have earned. But the fact remains that many,
perhaps a great many, people do not get the retirement
benefits, disability payments, income for dependents and
survivors, private pensions and health care coverage they
are entitled to. This book can help you make sure that you
are not one of these and that you have done all the many

things in your control to maximize your benefits. To explain what this book can do for you, let me tell you a little story that has a lot to do with how we came to write it.

A friend of mine named Jake, a man 65 years old, had an accident in which he broke his jaw. His doctor set the jaw bone, which healed just fine, and an oral surgeon repaired his gums and the nerves beneath. But Jake soon developed other physical problems. First, he began to have trouble chewing, so he began eating different foods. This change of diet disrupted his digestion and also resulted in his not getting enough vitamins or protein. Because of his poor diet and bad stomach, Jake grew irritable and began losing sleep, energy and weight he couldn't afford to lose. On top of that, because his bite was thrown out of whack, his neck muscles, and soon his whole back, knotted up. To put the matter simply, Jake was a mess.

At the time of the accident, Jake had just retired from his hardware store, and was working part-time as a plumber, earning extra income to supplement his Social Security retirement check. And though his jaw didn't directly interfere with his work, his neck and back began hurting so much that he couldn't handle his plumbing chores. Without his extra income, it was a struggle just to pay the rent.

To make matters worse, when Jake submitted his medical bills to Medicare, they notified him they would not pay any of one of the two doctors' bills. Because an oral surgeon rather than an M.D. had worked on the nerves and gums, Medicare ruled this was "dental" work, and Medicare doesn't pay for dental work. Jake did have some supplemental private health insurance, but his company gave him the same story as Medicare. Not only was Jake stuck with a huge bill, but without his plumbing income, he couldn't hope to make a dent in it.

Soon Jake went back to his own doctor to see about his other medical problems, especially his back. The doctor told him misalignment of his teeth and jaw were probably responsible for his pain and referred him to a clinic which specialized in non-surgical remedies for just such problems.

"Dentists, not doctors?" Jake asked.

"No, they're not M.D.'s, Jake. They're oral surgeons," the doctor told him, "and they're the very best at this. They'll fix you right up."

I stopped by to visit Jake the next morning and found him pretty glum. He explained the oral surgeons could help him, but they needed some guarantee of payment on what would be a hefty bill. Since Medicare and his private insurance probably wouldn't pay, for the same reasons they had refused to pay his first bill, Jake would have to come up with the money himself. And he simply couldn't swing it. His Social Security didn't pay enough, and because his neck and back were still all knotted up, he couldn't work to make the extra money. He was in quite a bind.

All day I kept thinking about Jake's problem. It seemed there should be some way out of the vicious circle that held him, but I didn't know what. So, I did what a good private eye would do when faced with a sticky problem and no leads--I called my mother. In this case, it made even more sense than usual, since my mother had worked for several years as a site director at a senior center and was familiar, both from her job and her own experience, with the workings of Social Security and Medicare. We put our heads together and started making calls. I went to the Social Security office and got their printed information and finally spent some time in several libraries. After several days, during which I felt like the proverbial rat in the maze, Jake, my mother and I discovered that there were, indeed, several ways for Jake to deal with his problem. In the process of learning this, I also learned something more fundamental: given the labyrinth of rules and regulations controlling our senior programs, and the fact that complete and easy-to-understand information is almost impossible to come by, there are very often benefits to which people are entitled which they simply never know about. But before I sacrifice the story to the moral, let's find out what happened to Jake.

When I dug out the Medicare regulations, I found that although Medicare does not cover dental work, it does cover work done by dentists or oral surgeons if the same work would have been covered if a doctor had done it. We asked Jake's oral surgeon and doctor to write letters to Medicare explaining that the work was not "dental," but rather medical, having to do with repair of Jake's trigeminal nerve and gums. They were happy to do this. Medicare eventually paid for a large portion of the original oral surgery.

In addition, we learned something about Social Security retirement rules. Social Security retirement benefits are reduced if you have earnings over a certain amount. Because of his plumber's income, Jake had been receiving a reduced check since his retirement. But because his illness had prevented him from working, we found out he was eligible to receive higher benefits under a special first-year-of-retirement rule for any month he was out of work. Jake applied for those benefits and received them, not only for the next couple of months while he was recovering, but also back payments for the months he had already missed.

In the midst of all these hassles over rules and regulations, Jake remarked: "I feel like I'm back in the Army." That led to our checking on veterans' benefits. It turned out that even though Jake's medical problems were not service-connected, he still qualified for free treatment at the nearby Veterans Administration Hospital, which, just to make a good ending better, happened to have a maxillofacial surgery clinic with the best jaw people in the state. In no time Jake was fitted for a bite device, which he wore at night, to realign his jaw. Within a few weeks his chewing became more comfortable, his eating improved, his neck and back loosened up and he was as good as new. Just in time, too--one of my bathroom pipes sprung a leak and I'm nothin' but a fool with a wrench in my hand. I suppose I could have called my mother, but . . .

I learned several things from Jake's situation.*
First, I learned even intelligent, organized people can
easily miss out on benefits to which they are entitled. The
complex of public and private retirement and health benefit
programs presents a series of numbers and regulations heavy
enough to stagger an accountant. Even if people manage to
find their way without losing any entitled benefits, many
encounter pitfalls that could have been avoided and suffer
bureaucracy-induced trauma to which they need not have been
exposed. On the other hand, I learned that if you understand the rules and regulations of each program that might
apply to you, you can not only get the full benefits you
know you've got coming, but you may very well receive income
and other coverage to which you didn't even realize you were
entitled.

Understanding these programs, and how to apply for
their fullest benefits, would be considerably less difficult
if all the relevant material was collected together and set
out in plain language. Unfortunately, one of the things I
learned first from digging into cases like Jake's is that
there is no such simple, direct, down-to-earth explanation
of how all this works. Public information, disseminated by
the various governmental agencies, is generated in fits and
starts--a pamphlet here, a booklet there, none of it complete, much of it out-of-date, and most of it hard to read.
Not surprisingly perhaps, the people who hand out the money
also hand out documents that help guarantee they will give
out as little money as possible. The library and bookstores
had a ton of books and articles about older Americans, but
virtually all of them try to tell you how you can live a
"fuller" life without ever explaining the nuts and bolts of
how to collect income and benefits to help you survive in
this inflationary world. It seemed time for someone to put
those nuts and bolts together. This book is the result.

In the following chapters you will find a clear, complete explanation of how various benefit programs work.
With the information provided, you should be able to gauge
how much in benefits you can receive, how and when you
should file your claims, and how to make employment plans so
you can maximize your benefits income while protecting your
right to keep working during "retirement" years. This material should also help you handle the increasingly serious
problem of soaring health care costs, explaining both government (Medicare/Medicaid) and private health insurance
programs. Armed with this information, you may find that,
like Jake, there are things you can do to make sure you
receive all the rights and benefits to which you are entitled.

---

* In reality, Jake is a composite of several people whose battles with public and private
benefit regulations my mother and I had encountered.

Just about everyone is aware that virtually all government benefit programs for older Americans are under siege these days. The proposals for change are referred to as "saving" or "attacking" the programs, depending on who's talking. I hope that once you have a fuller understanding of how these entitlement programs work, you will be better equipped to see through the various political smokescreens which are all too often thrown up around proposed changes in benefit programs. This is not primarily a "political" book, but after reading it, it will be obvious to you that government programs need to provide more, not less, protection to older Americans, and that entitlement programs are not the place to cut corners off the federal budget.

One final note--"entitled" is a key word in this book. Almost all the benefits discussed herein are paid to you because you <u>worked</u> for them, <u>earned</u> them through your entire working life. These are <u>not</u> handouts; even the government's own bureaucratic language refers to these as "entitlement" programs. If you are an older American facing retirement and a fixed income, you need all the financial support these programs are supposed to provide--<u>you</u> <u>are</u> <u>entitled</u> <u>to</u> <u>it</u>.

And if you ever wonder whether a particular benefit is really meant to apply to you, or whether you should insist on a right that is not at first made available to you, just think of the casserole my mother often makes. When I ask if I can have a helping, she always gives the same reply: "That's what it's there for."

HOW TO USE THIS BOOK

This book is divided into chapters, each of which explains a different benefit program or set of laws designed to protect the rights of older Americans. It explains how each particular program works, and also how it may relate to the other programs discussed in the book. Not all of these benefits will apply to you. However, even if you don't think you are eligible for a particular benefit, at least take a look at the general requirements discussed in that chapter; you may be surprised to find that an entitlement program, or some part of the program, applies to you in ways you had not previously realized.

When you have taken a look at each of the benefit programs, return to the chapters which cover the rights and benefits you think might apply to you. If you examine

these chapters carefully, you will discover exactly how and
when to apply for income or other benefits to which you
might be entitled. At the beginning of each chapter is a
separate section pointing out some of the "Highlights" from
that chapter. These "Highlights" include both benefits you
might not have known about and pitfalls to watch out for so
you do not lose any benefits to which you are entitled. Pay
special attention to the explanations in the chapters of how
your income or your participation in one benefit program
might affect your rights in another program; a simple example of this is understanding how much outside income you
can earn before your Social Security benefits would be
reduced. The "Highlights" will draw your attention to these
double-program situations. Then you will be best able to
choose which benefits to claim in order to maximize your
income and coverage.

Here is a checklist of some things you will want to
consider as you read what follows. It is not a complete
list of every detail of every program discussed in the book.
It is, however, a reminder of the major categories of benefits to which you may be entitled.

■If you are age 55 or over and not yet retired, check
    the rules regarding the age at which you are eligible
    for retirement benefits, the amount those benefits are
    reduced for "early" retirement, and how much outside
    income you can earn while collecting benefits for:

        Social Security retirement, if you have worked
        for any private employer since 1936.

        Civil Service retirement, if you have ever
        worked for federal, state or local govern-
        ment or any public institution (school system,
        library, public health facility, etc.).

        Private pension benefits if you worked for any one
        private company for five years or more (remember
        to check with each company you worked for), or if
        you belonged to any union more than five years.

■If you are within six months of your 65th birthday,
    check the rules of Social Security retirement, civil
    service retirement and private pension plans regarding
    "normal" or "delayed" retirement, and check the rules
    regarding eligibility for Medicare and supplemental
    health insurance.

■If you are currently retired, check the rules of your
    retirement plan--Social Security and/or other public or

private retirement programs--regarding permissible
outside income.

■If you are under 65 but unable to work for long periods
of time because of a physical condition, check the rules
regarding Social Security disability, your private pension
plan's disability program, and, if you were ever in the
armed forces, Veterans Administration benefits.

■If you ever served in the armed forces, check the
benefits available for veterans, including free medical
care.

■If you are the spouse of a retired or deceased worker,
check the rules of Social Security and public and private
pensions regarding various categories in which you may
qualify for dependents' or survivors' benefits.

■If you are age 65 or over and require any medical
treatment, carefully review Medicare rules to insure
that the maximum amount of your medical care will be
covered, and check to see if you are eligible for your
state's Medicaid assistance.

■If you are age 40 or over and you believe that some employment opportunity has been denied you, or you have suffered
discrimination of any kind in your employment because of
your age, read the chapter on age discrimination in employment.

A NOTE ON KEEPING RECORDS: In a sense, the benefit and
pension programs which provide you with retirement income
and protection make up the "business" you're in during your
later years. Your contact with these programs should be run
like a business. The more organized you are, the easier it
will be for you to show a "profit." Keep your personal
papers and records in order. Do things in writing whenever
possible, keeping copies of all correspondence and arranging
papers by subject and date. When you have a conversation
with someone which may have some bearing on a benefit or
other program, make notes of what was said, by whom, when
and where, and who else was present. Get your papers in
order well before you have to present them in making a
particular claim. Decide which benefits you want to claim,
and when and where to claim them, well in advance of the
time you become eligible to claim them. And regarding
medical treatment, know in advance whether your doctor
accepts Medicare and/or Medicaid payment in full; also make
sure your doctor knows that referrals should be made only to
other doctors who accept Medicare/Medicaid payment.

You will save yourself a lot of aggravation if you take the simple steps required to keep your papers in order. If the old saying is true that an ounce of prevention is worth a pound of cure, in dealing with bureaucracies it's worth a ton. Or to paraphrase some other famous words of advice, "Don't moan, organize!"

◆◆◆◆◆

A Word About Unofficial Marriages and Benefit Programs

As you go over the rules of the specific programs discussed in this book, you will notice that eligibility for many benefits depends on the marital status of the person making the claim. In some situations, the amounts of any given benefit may vary depending on the marital status of the claimant. Social Security and other programs provide a number of benefits to the spouse of a worker, but make no provision for people who live together without the benefit of formal marriage. On the other hand, eligibility for and benefit amounts of some benefit programs depend on the combined amount of income and assets of a claimant and his or her spouse. So, if you're not married, your partner's income and assets would not be counted "against" you. Of course, most people decide whether or not to marry for reasons that have nothing to do with Social Security or other benefit programs. But since getting married can affect these benefits, you should be aware of what is, and what is not, an official marriage.

Many people live together in the belief they have a "common law marriage"--a legal marriage--even though they never went through a formal ceremony, took out a marriage license or filed a marriage certificate. Many people believe that if they have lived together for a certain number of years, they automatically have one of these "common law marriages." In most states, however, this is just not so. And if you're not considered married in the state in which you live, you're not married as far as Social Security and most other benefit programs are concerned. How do you know whether you qualify as having a common-law marriage? First of all, common-law marriages are only recognized in the following states: Alabama, Colorado, Georgia, Idaho, Iowa, Kansas, Montana, Ohio, Oklahoma, Pennsylvania, Rhode Island, South Carolina and Texas. If you don't live in one of these states, you don't have a common-law marriage.

If you do live in one of the common-law states, how do you know whether your relationship qualifies as a common-law marriage? There are no hard and fast rules. There is no magic number of years living together which confers married status on you. It all depends on whether or not your living situation indicates that you both <u>intend</u> to have a common-law marriage. This can be shown in a number of ways, including living together as husband and wife for several years, using the same last name, referring to your-selves as married, owning property in common, etc. Anything that shows you intend to enter into a common-law marriage, or that you consider yourselves married, can be considered as evidence that you do, indeed, have a common-law marriage. You can even write out an agreement that says you regard yourselves as being in a common-law marriage. Unfortunate-ly, there is nothing you can count on to absolutely prove the existence of your common-law marriage, and for that reason nothing guarantees that Social Security will consider you married when making a decision about your benefits.

One final note on this subject. No matter how much evidence you have that you intend to have a common-law marriage, no matter what state you live in, if either you or the person you live with is still lawfully married to someone else, there can be no common-law marriage.

Your Social Security: How Secure Are You?

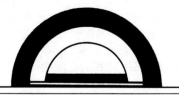

■ C H A P T E R   1 ■

HIGHLIGHTS

If you work for a state or local government agency or institution, or for a non-profit institution, or you will begin work for the federal government after December 31, 1983, check the new rules to see whether your work is or will be covered by Social Security (see Section C, "What is Covered Employment?").

If you have income from self-employment or from domestic or agricultural work, you must make sure that your income is counted by the Social Security Administration in order for that income to raise the level of your Social Security benefits (see Section C, "What is Covered Employment?").

Regularly check your earnings record with Social Security to make sure that there are no errors in your record and that all your income is being reported. This also permits Social Security to give you estimates of what your retirement bene-fits would be before you actually retire (see Section E, "How Does Social Security Figure Your Earnings Record?").

■ ■ ■

A. Introduction

For most working Americans, the notion of "Social Security" is a little like the notion of sex to a teenager: you've heard about it, and you know it will arrive in your life someday, but you don't know exactly how it works; and when it does finally get there, you find out that while it isn't bad, you can't live on it.

Social Security isn't even a very accurate term. In fact, Social Security has become a general term for a number of related programs--retirement, disability and dependents' and survivors' benefits. All these programs are designed to operate together to provide workers and their families with some income when their normal flow of income shrinks because of the retirement, disability or death of a wage earner. But while the Social Security system does provide a supplement to income, savings and other assets, it does not, standing alone, provide adequate financial "security" for older Americans. And despite its name, the Social Security system was never intended to provide the sole means of support for retired or disabled workers and their families. It was intended, though, to provide older citizens with enough supplemental financial support to compensate for limited job opportunities made available to them by our society. Unfortunately, today even this modest goal is increasingly remote. The combination of rapidly rising living costs and reductions in coverage and benefits have made the amount of support offered by Social Security more inadequate with each passing year. This, of course, makes it even more important that you get every benefit to which you are entitled.

The purpose of this first chapter is to give you a feel for how Social Security operates in general. Don't worry about the details. It is helpful to know how the whole system works before you start to figure out the rules for a particular benefit program. When you're familiar with the terms used by Social Security, as explained in this chapter, you'll be well-equipped to understand the details of getting the fullest benefits possible from Social Security programs.

B. Social Security: What Is It?

Let's start with a riddle. Who is 45 years old and gets an allowance from nine out of ten workers in America? You need another hint? Who is it that sends money from home every month to one out of every six people in the country? Give up? It's the Social Security Administration, of course.

All right, time to get down to work. Let's start by defining Social Security. As mentioned above, it's actually a series of different, but related, programs--retirement, disability, and dependents'/survivors' benefits. Each part of Social Security has its own set of rules and payment schedules. But all of the programs have one thing in common: benefits are paid--to the retired or disabled worker and/or the worker's dependent or surviving family--based on a worker's average wages in jobs covered by Social Security over his or her working life. In other words, the amount of your benefits under any Social Security program is not directly related to "need," but rather to what you have earned through your years of working.

There are three basic categories of benefits under Social Security:

Retirement Benefits: You may choose to begin receiving your retirement benefits at any time after you reach age 62, with the amount of your benefits going up for each year you wait to retire. And as the following chapter explains, official "retirement" does not preclude you from continuing to work and earn some extra income.

Disability Benefits: If you are under 65 but have met the work requirements (number of quarter-years of employment) for your age, and, under the rules of the program, are considered "disabled," you can receive benefits roughly equal to what your retirement benefits would be.

Dependents'/Survivors' Benefits: If you are the spouse of a retired or disabled worker, or the surviving spouse of a deceased worker who would have qualified for retirement or disability benefits, you and your children [under 18 or disabled (and in some instances, under 19)] may be entitled to benefits based on the worker's earning record.

IMPORTANT: You may qualify for more than one type of Social Security benefit. For example, you might be eligible for both retirement and disability, or you might be entitled to benefits based on your own retirement and that of your retired spouse. Social Security rules state, however, that you can collect only one of the benefits, whichever is larger.

C. How Do You Qualify For Social Security Benefits Generally?

The specific requirements vary for qualifying to receive retirement, disability or dependents'/survivors' benefits. Within each program they also vary depending on the age of the person filing the claim (or on the age of the worker if you are claiming as a dependent or survivor). However, there is a general requirement that must be met in order for anyone to receive any Social Security benefit. The worker must have worked in "covered employment" for a sufficient number of years (measured in quarter-years of work credit) to reach "insured" status, based on when he or she reaches age 62, becomes disabled, or dies.

D. What Is "Covered Employment"?

Any job, or self-employment, from which Social Security taxes are reported is "covered employment." Over 90 percent of all American workers now work in covered employment. The three largest category of workers who have not been covered by Social Security are people who have worked for the federal government, some state and local governments and some non-profit organizations. People who work for the federal government, or for those state and local agencies which have not participated in Social Security, are covered by civil service retirement systems.*

The Social Security reform bill passed into law in April, 1983, however, has changed some of the rules pertaining to coverage of these previously uncovered categories of workers. Beginning January 1, 1984, all newly hired workers for the federal government will be required to pay into the Social Security system; they will no longer be included in the federal civil service retirement program. If you were already working for the federal government on December 31, 1983, though, you will continue to participate in federal civil service retirement; you will not be required to switch to Social Security.

---

* Civil Service retirement is discussed in Chapter 10, "Government Employment, Railroad Worker and Veterans Benefits."

If you have been working for a non-profit organization, you may have been paying into the Social Security System, into a private company pension system or into no retirement system at all (check with your employer if you're in doubt as to what your coverage has been). Beginning January 1, 1984, however, all employees of non-profit organizations must begin having Social Security taxes taken out of their paychecks. A special qualification schedule will allow these employees to qualify for Social Security benefits without having to contribute very long to the Social Security system.

Finally, those state and local government agencies which do not participate in Social Security will be permitted to remain outside the Social Security system. But, no state or local government agency will be permitted to withdraw from the Social Security system if they have not already done so by April, 1983. If you're in doubt about whether you are participating in Social Security through your government job, check with the personnel office where you work (or used to work).

Self-Employed: If you work for yourself, you are now covered by Social Security. The self-employment earnings you report when you file your federal income tax return are credited to your Social Security record. However, self-employed persons have only been covered by Social Security since 1951; self-employment earnings before then were not applied to your Social Security record and do not help you achieve enough quarters of coverage to reach insured status. Similarly, if you fail to pay self-employment taxes on self-employment income, or do not report that income at all, you will not get credit for the income in your Social Security record. This might not only affect your initial eligibility, but also might reduce the amount of your Social Security benefits if you do reach insured status. As the following section explains, the amount of your benefit check from Social Security depends on your "earnings record," which is the amount of money you earned over the years in covered employment. This means if much of your working life was spent in self-employment before 1951, your earnings record will most likely be low and the benefits you receive will also be relatively modest.

Domestic Workers: In theory at least, if you have been a domestic worker you have been covered by Social Security for that work since 1951. It's only "in theory," though, because you only get credit for your work if you or your employer reports your earnings and pays Social Security or self-employment taxes. As a lot of domestic work is paid for in cash, it is commonly not reported to the government.

And if no Social Security tax is paid, no Social Security credit is earned. Domestic workers--housekeepers, cooks, gardeners, etc.--can be given credit for covered employment for each quarter-year in which they earn $50 in wages from any one employer, if that income is reported. So, if you work regularly for one or more employers, earning $50 a month or more from any one employer, and you want to receive credit for these earnings with Social Security, make sure that either your employer withholds and reports Social Security taxes or else you report your earnings as self-employment income and pay the self-employment tax when you pay your federal income tax. If you or your employer need help figuring out how to withhold and report the Social Security tax, call the local office of the Internal Revenue Service or your local Social Security office and ask for assistance [the number is listed in your local phone directory, in the white pages, under "United States Government, Internal Revenue Service (or Social Security Administration")].

Farmworkers: Since 1954, farmworkers have been covered by Social Security. If you do agricultural work, you must be paid $150 cash in one calendar year from the same employer, or work 20 or more days for the same employer in one year (piecework is not included in this formula), in order to be covered by Social Security for that year. But you get credit for this work only if your earnings are reported to the Social Security Administration. It is the employer's responsibility to withhold, report and pay to the government your Social Security taxes. So, if you want to make sure your farm work is counted toward your Social Security record (meaning, though, that Social Security taxes will be taken out of your pay), make sure your employer is reporting and paying your Social Security tax. If you are unsure whether your employer is paying the tax or not, ask your local Social Security office to find out. They are able to do so without using your name.

E. How Do You Earn Social Security Work Credits?

In order to receive any kind of Social Security benefits, you must have accumulated enough work credits from covered employment to reach "insured" status for the benefit you are claiming. Work credits are measured in "quarters" (January through March is the first quarter of each year, April through June is the second, etc.) in which you earned more than the required minimum amount of money (explained below) in covered employment. The number of work credits you need to be fully "insured" (meaning you are eligible for benefits) depends on the benefit you are applying for and your age at the time you apply. The requirements for each program will be explained in the separate chapters on each particular program.

Whether you gained a work credit for a particular quarter-year depends on the required minimum income for the year in which you worked. This is really simpler to understand than it sounds at first:

■Between 1936 and 1978, you received credit for one
  quarter of credit for each quarter-year in which
  you were paid $50 or more in wages in covered
  employment.

■Between 1951 and 1978 you could receive credit
  for four quarters of coverage for each year in which
  you earned and reported $400 or more from self-
  employment.

■Beginning in 1978, you were credited with one quarter
  of coverage for each $250 per year of earnings from
  covered employment. Since then, this amount has increased
  each year, as follows:

  1979 - $260   1981 - $310   1983 - $370
  1980 - $290   1982 - $340

These amounts will increase in the years to come.

IMPORTANT NOTE: Under these rules, the maximum you can receive credit for in any one year is four quarters, no matter how much money you earn.

EXAMPLE #1: In 1938, Ulis was paid $180 between January and March, nothing between April and July (after he hurt his back), $340 in August, and $600 in cash from self-employment in October and November. How many quarters of credit would he get? The answer is two. He would get a quarter of credit for the first quarter in which he was paid $180 (over the $50 minimum); he earned nothing in the second quarter, so he got no credit; in the third quarter he only worked one month, but earned well over the $50 minimum for the whole quarter; he got no credit for the last quarter, though, because in 1938 self-employment was not covered by Social Security; also, he got no credit because Ulis did not report the money to the Social Security Administration by paying income tax on it.

■■■

EXAMPLE #2: Under the current rules, Eve was paid
$1,360 in January 1982, but didn't earn anything the rest of
the year. Since she gets one quarter of credit for each
$340 per year of earnings, she would receive credit for four
quarters for 1982 based on her earnings of January alone
($340 x 4 = $1,360).

EXAMPLE #3: If Tom is paid $115 a month every month in
1982 at his part-time job, he would have total earnings for
1982 of $1,380 per year of earnings. Since his $1,380
divided by $340 is more than 4, he receives credit for the
maximum 4 quarters for 1982.

EXAMPLE #4: Big Julie makes about $10,000 per month in
earnings from his poolroom. How many quarters of coverage
does he earn in one year? No matter how much money he
earns, he can only get the maximum of four quarters credit
for each year, the same as Eve and Tom earned.

NOTE: Remember, although you can only earn four quarters of work credits in any calendar year toward Social
Security eligibility, no matter how much money you make, the
amount of the benefits you ultimately receive will be higher
or lower depending on your total earnings over the years.
The way in which your total earnings are figured is explained in the next section.

F. How Does Social Security Figure
  Your Earnings Record?

As you are now aware, the question of whether you are
eligible for Social Security benefits depends on how many
work credits you have earned and whether those credits are
enough, given your age, to qualify you for the particular
benefit you are seeking. The next thing to understand is
that if you are eligible, the amount of your benefit is
determined by your Social Security record. Your earnings
record is the history of all your reported earnings in
covered employment since you began working (after 1936).
The amount of your benefits will depend on an average of
your reported income. The way the "average" of your earnings is figured differs depending on your age. People who
reached age 62 or became disabled on or before the last day

of December, 1978: the actual dollar value of a worker's total past earnings is used to calculate their average earnings. People who turn 62 or become disabled on or after January 1, 1979: workers who fall into this category have their average earnings calculated in a more complicated way.* Here's how it works. If you reached age 62 or became disabled on or after January 1, 1979, your earnings are divided into two categories. Earnings from before 1951 are credited with their actual dollar amount up to a maximum of $3,000 per year. From 1951 on, yearly limits are placed on earnings credits as shown below, no matter how much you actually earned in those years:

1951 - 1954	$ 3600/yr.	1977 -	$16,500
1955 - 1958	4200	78 -	17,700
1959 - 1965	4800	79 -	22,900
1966 - 1967	6600	80 -	25,900
1968 - 1971	7800	81 -	29,700
1972	9000	82 -	32,400
1973	10,800	83 -	34,500 (estimated)
1974	13,200	84 -	36,900 (estimated)
1975	14,100	85 -	39,600 (estimated)
1976	15,300		

The Social Security Administration then applies one of two computation methods, one beginning with 1936, the other beginning with earnings from 1951. Depending on the benefit you are seeking, and your age when you claim your benefit, different formulas are applied to your average income from these years to determine your benefit amount.

All this sound very complicated? Luckily, Social Security keeps a running account of your Social Security earnings and does all the figuring for you on a computer. The long explanation above is so you can double-check your official record, something you should do every couple of years. How do you find out what your official earnings record is so that you can check it? Easy. Your local Social Security office has a short form (No. 7I004) called "Request for Social Security Statement of Earnings." Fill out the request form, making sure your name is exactly the same as it is on your Social Security card, and either return it to your local Social Security office or mail it directly to the Social Security Administration. Remember to fill in your Social Security number accurately.

---

* Under either method, veterans receive extra earnings credit; an extra $160 per month for active duty between September 1, 1940 and December 31, 1956; an extra $300 per quarter for active duty from 1957-1977; after 1977, veterans receive $100 of credit for each $300 of actual military pay, up to a maximum credit of $1200 per year.

It takes several weeks for the Social Security Administration to process your request, so be patient. A copy of your earnings record will be mailed to you. A sample earnings record is reproduced below:

Social Security
Summary Statement of Earnings

From: Office of Central Records Operations
Baltimore, Maryland 21235

We are glad to send you this statement of the earnings shown on your social security record. Included are wages you have had for covered employment after 1936 and any earnings from covered self-employment after 1950. This statement does NOT show social security contributions paid.

The statement does not include your earnings for this year (to be reported after the end of the year) and may not include some or all of your earnings for last year because of the time needed to process annual earnings reports. Generally, the statement also does not include earnings over the yearly maximum that can be counted for social security purposes and military service pay before 1957.

If some of your earnings are missing or incorrect, contact any social security office promptly. It is important that your record be correct because entitlement to monthly benefits and Medicare will depend on it. If you wait more than 3 years, 3 months, and 15 days after the year an error occurs, correction may not be possible. Most errors can be reported by phone. If you write or visit an office, submit this statement and furnish proof of the earnings in question (such as a form W-2, pay-slips, or Federal income tax return).

The enclosed leaflet explains further what to do if you disagree with the statement and tells about benefits payable. If you have any questions after reading the leaflet, the people at any social security office will be happy to help you.

Social Security Number   573-62-6516

Years	Covered Earnings (Not Social Security Contributions)
1937 THRU 1950	18,959.00
1951 THRU 1977	129,647.74
1978	17,700.00
1979	18,284.98
1980	19,087.40
1981 NOT YET COMPLETED	16,282.80
TOTAL - 1937 THRU 1981	$ $219,961.92

Enclosure

Department of Health and Human Services   Form OAR-7014 (3-80)
Social Security Administration

Notice that the earnings for 1981 on the sample is marked "NOT YET COMPLETED." This is because the Social Security Administration computers are a year (and sometimes two years) behind in record keeping. If you look at your income tax forms or W-2's for the missing year or years, you can add that income to the totals given in your earnings record. Remember, though, that if you turned 62 or became disabled after January 1, 1979, you can only add in your earnings up to the maximums of $29,700 for 1981, $32,400 for 1982, and an estimated $34,500 for 1983. When your earnings record is up-to-date, your local Social Security office will be able to figure out for you the amount of any specific benefit before you actually apply for it. This prior knowledge may help you to decide which type benefit you want to claim or whether it's better to wait to claim a benefit at a later time when the benefit amount would be higher.

What happens if you don't agree with the figures you're given on your official statement of earnings? What!! Disagree with the computer? Yes, it happens. The first thing to do is to check the Social Security number of the earnings statement to see if it is, in fact, your earnings that are being stated. Then check the amounts with your own record of earnings, remembering the limits that can be credited to your record for years after 1950. If you find a discrepancy, bring it to the attention of your local Social Security office. Bring in copies of your tax records or W-2's for the year or years in question and ask that they correct your earnings for you. This is done by filling out a form called "Request for Correction in Earnings Record." Note, however, that you may not be able to correct mistakes in your earnings record more than three years, three months and 15 days after the end of the year you are complaining about. That's why it's important to check your earnings record every couple of years, so you'll have time to correct any errors that do appear.

Social Security Retirement Benefits

■CHAPTER 2■

HIGHLIGHTS

Even if you have not worked for many years, and your earnings from those early years of work were very low, you may still be eligible for retirement benefits (or near enough that a short while of part-time work will make you eligible). [See Section B, "How Much Work Credit Do You Need to be Eligible for Retirement?"]

Request an estimate of what your retirement benefits would be if you were to retire at age 62 or wait until you are older. Make the request about six months <u>before</u> you turn 62. [See Section D, "How Much Will Your Retirement Check Be?"]

The minimum benefit for retirees has been eliminated for anyone first retiring in 1983 or later, <u>but</u> a special minimum benefit rule still protects those who have over 10 years of work in Social Security covered employment. [See Section D, "How Much Will Your Retirement Check Be?"]

A special first-year-of-retirement rule permits you to collect your full retirement benefits for any <u>month</u> in which your income is under certain limits, no matter how much you earn the rest of the year. [See Section E, "Can You Work After You Retire?"]

If you intend to continue working full-time after you reach age 62, resist the temptation to claim your retirement benefits until you are ready to cut down on work. [See Section F, "When You Should Retire".]

■■■

A. What Is Retirement?

Many of us look toward retirement as a time of content-edness and quiet, new time for old friendships, a period of calm sufficiency. We imagine we will be able to do the things we always wanted to do but couldn't because we were always working and tending to the needs of others. And while this may be true for some, many people find a far different reality. Indeed, it is difficult to enjoy retirement life without the financial resources to cope with a high-priced world. In a society that has forgotten how to revere and succor its older human resources, retirement has become just another, more difficult seige in the same old battle for survival. Like Othello's revenge, the need to keep laboring "Ne'er feels retiring ebb, but keeps due on, . . . with violent pace." The truth is that after "normal" retirement age is reached, more and more Americans have to continue working hard to make ends meet.

In the real world of work, retirement too often means merely moving from one level of employment to another-- usually down to a position of less responsibility, less time and less pay. Unfortunately, it is as much society's false image of older people as it is the wishes and physical limitations of older Americans that conspires against our ability to earn substantial income in our later years.* The Social Security retirement benefit programs, as well as other retirement plans, are intended to take up some of the financial slack of our retirement years. The current version of the Social Security law both guarantees that many people must continue to work after reaching "normal" retirement age and, to a certain extent, makes benefit adjustments for the retirement income which is earned.

Under Social Security rules, "retirement" doesn't necessarily mean you have reached a certain age or even that you have stopped working altogether. Retirement merely refers to the time (after reaching at least age 62) you claim and start collecting your Social Security retirement benefits. You may continue to work while receiving your

---

* See Chapter 12 for information on age discrimination in employment.

benefits, though the amount of your benefits may be reduced if you earn more than a prescribed amount of income. The following sections explain how Social Security figures your eligibility for retirement benefits, when you may and when you should claim the benefits, and discuss the rules regarding outside income after you have "retired."

B. How Much Work Credit Do You Need To Be Eligible For Retirement?

As with other Social Security benefits, in order to be eligible for any amount of retirement benefits, you must have reached a certain "insured" status, meaning you must have earned enough work credits over your working years. The way you earn work credits for Social Security was explained in Chapter 1, Section D. How many quarters of work credits do you need to qualify for retirement? You are fully insured and eligible for retirement benefits if, at the time you apply for retirement, you have:

- Either a total of 40 quarters (ten years) of work credit from covered employment; or

- At least one quarter of work credit for every year beginning with 1951 (up to the year you reach age 62). Thus, if you reached 62 in 1983, you would need 32 work credits (one quarter for every year between 1951 and 1983). Another way of looking at it is that if you worked eight full years (32 quarters) in covered employment, you would be eligible.

This graph is yet another way of showing how many work credits you'll need:

■ ■ ■

If you reach age 62 in:	You need this many quarters:
1980	29 (7.25 years)
1981	30
1982	31
1983	32 (8 years)
1984	33
1985	34
1990	39
1991 or later	40 (10 years)

IMPORTANT: Even if you haven't worked for many years,
and you didn't make much money in the few years you did
work, check your earnings record. You may be surprised to
find you have quite a few quarters of credit from years gone
by. Remember, the rules for getting quarters of work credit
were pretty easy before 1978. As we discussed in detail in
Chapter 1, Section D, through 1977 you only needed to make
$50 to get credit for a quarter of coverage. And even if
you find you don't have enough work credits to be fully
insured now, you may be able to work part-time for awhile
and earn enough extra quarters of credit to put you over the
line into "insured" status. And once you qualify for retirement benefits, you are eligible to receive them for the
rest of your life. That could mean a lot of money for you
over the years to come. It's worth doing a simple check of
your earnings record, isn't it?

EXAMPLE: Let's take a look at how Millicent Moss
handled her retirement. When she got out of school in 1936,
Millicent married Timothy (known to his classmates as Timid
Timmy), her high school sweetheart. They moved from Moline
to Chicago to make their fortune. Millicent worked hard in
a millinery shop while Tim parlayed his trash wagon into a
scrap iron business. After several years of hard work, they
began to prosper. Unfortunately, as soon as things picked

P L A N N I N G   A H E A D ?

The 1983 Third Edition of attorney Denis Clifford's <u>PLAN YOUR ESTATE: WILLS, PROBATE AVOIDANCE, TRUSTS & TAXES</u> is out with information on the latest changes in federal estate tax laws and an explanation of how the repeal of the California Inheritance Tax affects you. <u>PLAN YOUR ESTATE</u> shows you how to reduce death taxes, reduce probate fees, provide prompt cash for your survivors and transfer your estate in exactly the way you choose. Written specifically for Californians, Clifford's book is detailed and accurate. Also included: joint tenancy, California community property laws, writing your own will, savings bank trusts, funeral rights (cremation rules, etc.). Comes with tear-out will form. *"Like the other do-it-yourself manuals from Nolo Press,* Plan Your Estate *is particularly helpful to the layperson who does not want to consult a lawyer - a clear, comprehensive and even charming book, focused specifically on California law and tax regulations."* - Los Angeles Times. $15.95

Are you 55 or over? Do you help support someone who is? Attorney Joseph Matthews' <u>SOURCEBOOK FOR OLDER AMERICANS: Income, Rights & Benefits</u> (with Dorothy Matthews Berman, Program Director, L.A. Senior Center) is the first comprehensive, easy-to-understand resource guide for older Americans. <u>SOURCEBOOK</u> can help save you money over retirement years by unravelling the mysteries of Medicare, Medicaid, and private health insurance; retirement benefits and pension options; age discrimination; Social Security, SSI, Civil Service, Veterans Administration, and Railroad Retirement System benefits. *"Matthews tells you what the laws that affect you mean, avoiding labyrinthian circumlocutions that only lawyers, supposedly, can unravel."* - San Francisco Examiner. You need this book to get the maximum in benefits and health protection. $10.95

                 * To order, please see form in back of book *

up, Timid Timothy turned into Terrible Tim the Tycoon; he divorced Millicent in 1940. Millicent was awarded $250 a month alimony. When the war came, she got a job in a private agency that promoted war bonds, not so much for the money--they paid only $10 a week--but because she wanted to help the war effort. She worked there four years, off and on. When the war ended, Millie quit work and lived frugally on her alimony check, concentrating on developing her love of painting.

As prices rose over the years, though, Millie's alimony of $250 per month was barely able to sustain her. In 1977 Tim died and the alimony stopped. Millicent no longer had any income. As she hadn't worked in over 30 years, she had a terrible time finding full-time employment. Then someone suggested she check her Social Security record and Millicent found she had 36 quarters of coverage (four-and-one-half years--equal to 18 quarters--from her years at the millinery shop, just after the Social Security law went into effect in 1936, and another four and-one-half years, or 18 quarters, during the war. Even the $10 a week she got selling bonds added up to well over the $50 per quarter she needed to earn to get credit). With 36 quarters, she needed only four more quarters to reach insured status (40 quarters total). Millie found a part-time job in an art gallery and in only a year was able to qualify for Social Security retirement benefits.

The lesson to be learned? No matter how long ago (after 1936) you worked, check your Social Security record; you may be pleasantly surprised to find you are closer to qualifying for retirement benefits than you thought.

C. When Can You Claim Your Retirement Benefits?

Remember, when the term "retire" is used by the Social Security Administration, it only refers to the time you claim your retirement benefits. It does not necessarily mean you have reached a particular age or that you've stopped working.

1. Retirement At Age 62

You first become eligible to claim retirement benefits when you turn 62. But if you have just had your 62nd birthday party, don't reach too fast for your application form. Why not? Well, if you do retire at 62, your monthly benefit payment will be considerably less than if you wait until age 65 or later. You see, Social Security considers 65 to be "normal" retirement age. Although the law permits you to retire as early as 62, if you do, you will receive a lower monthly amount, one that Social Security figures will total, over your lifetime, the same amount you would have received if you retired at 65. This means that monthly benefits for retirement at age 62 are about 20 percent less than if you wait until age 65 (about 13 percent less if you retire at 63, 6.6 percent less at age 64). The reduction in monthly benefits is permanent; they do not increase to the full amount when you turn 65.

2. Retirement After Age 65

Not only do you have the option of claiming "early" retirement, you can also wait until after age 65 and claim a higher delayed retirement benefit. Your benefits will be permanently higher than if you retire at age 65.

If you reached age 65 before January 1, 1982, your monthly benefits are one percent higher for every year after age 65 you wait to claim retirement benefits. The one percent per year adds up until you reach age 72. In other words, if you wait until age 72 to claim retirement, your benefits would be 7 percent higher than if you retired at age 65.

If you reach age 65 between January 1, 1982 and December 31, 1989, your benefits will increase three percent for each year you delay your retirement. This increase continues only until you reach age 70. If you wait until age 70 to claim your benefits, then, they would be 15 percent higher than if you retired at age 65.

The Social Security Reform Act of 1983 makes this delayed retirement even more attractive. If you reach age 65 on January 1, 1990 or after, your benefits will be even higher, rising from three percent per year to eight percent a year for those who turn 65 in the year 2008.

If your benefits will only go up a small amount for each year you delay, why wait? Well, one other Social Security rule reduces your monthly benefit if you earn over a certain amount of outside income, and a 1983 change in the law will require that you pay taxes on Social Security benefits if your total income is over certain levels. So many people who continue to work at good paying jobs after they reach age 65 wait to claim their retirement until after 65 when they stop working. In that way, they get several more years of good pay followed by increased benefits when they retire. (The rules regarding outside income and taxes on benefits are discussed in Section E of this Chapter.)

D. How Much Will Your Retirement Check Be?

Since the amount of your retirement check depends on your earnings record, we can't tell you exactly what your monthly benefit will be. But your local Social Security office can. Once you or the local office have received a copy of your statement of earnings record (see Chapter 1, Section E for instructions on how to get a copy of your records), and you have brought that record up to date by bringing your tax returns or W-2 forms for the past year or two, a Social Security worker can and will figure out what your retirement benefit would be. Several months before your 62nd birthday you should ask for an estimate of what your benefits would be if you retired at age 62, age 65 or any age in between. Don't be bashful about asking the Social Security worker to do this for you; it's the job of the local office to give you these estimates and you are entitled to them. Just remember to give the worker time to figure out the numbers; you have a right to know, but nothing happens too fast in a government bureaucracy office. So ask well in advance of when you need to make a decision and be patient waiting for an answer.

Although the Social Security Administration puts out a pamphlet on how to make your own estimate of your retirement benefits, it's an almost hopeless task. The process is _very_ complicated, the pamphlet's explanation only makes it worse, and the figures given in the pamphlet are usually out of date. But even more important than the difficulty of doing the figuring yourself is the fact that the actual amount of your check will not depend on the figures you come up with, but rather on the official figures the Social Security Administration arrives at. You might as well find out what _their_ figures are from the beginning.

While we can't tell you exactly what your retirement check will be, we can give you an idea of what average retirement benefits are, as well as the maximum and minimum amounts permitted under current Social Security guidelines. These figures should help you get a pretty good initial sense of the amounts you can expect from Social Security retirement.

1. Average And Maximum Benefits

For the last half of 1982 and the first half of 1983, the average retirement benefit check for an individual is slightly above $400 a month. For a couple, the average retirement benefit (the retiree and one dependent) runs about $700 a month. If you had a very high earnings record and qualified for the maximum retirement benefit when you retired in the first half of 1983, as an individual you would receive about $730 per month. If you reached age 62 in 1982 or the early part of 1983 and chose to retire, the maximum you could receive as an individual was about $580 per month.

2. The Minimum Benefits Rule

Since retirement benefit amounts are determined by figuring your average income over all the years you worked, many people who had enough earnings to qualify for retirement would nevertheless have an average income so low that their benefits would be almost nonexistent if it weren't for the minimum benefits rule. Our friend Millie, for example (remember Millie, from the example in Section B of this chapter?), never earned very much in any one year either at the millinery shop back in the mid-thirties, when wages for shopgirls were miniscule, or at the war bond office. If it weren't for the minimum benefits rule, her total income would probably only qualify her for a couple of dollars a month in retirement benefits under the regular figuring process. Fortunately, however, the minimum benefits rule recognizes that people who did most of their work in the years when wages were so very low should not be forever penalized regarding retirement benefits. The rule provides that no matter how low your average earnings were, if you qualify at all for Social Security retirement, you will receive a certain minimum amount, currently set at $122 per month (for those retiring at age 65). This may seem a very meager amount, but it's more than what many people would receive under the regular figuring process.*

IMPORTANT NOTE ON ELIMINATION OF MINIMUM BENEFITS: Though the minimum benefits rule continues in effect for all those people who were collecting a minimum benefit through the end of 1981, there will be no minimum benefit amount for those people who first become eligible for Social Security benefits January 1, 1982 or later. For people who first become eligible for benefits after January 1, 1982, their benefit amount will be based solely on their earnings record, no matter how low their benefits turn out to be.

———————————————————— ■ ■ ■ ————————————————————

3. The Special "Over 10" Minimum Benefit Rule

In addition to the minimum benefits rule described above, special consideration is given to you if you worked for more than 10 years in covered employment. This rule can give you a higher minimum benefit if you spent many productive years working for low wages--even "good" jobs paid next-to-nothing in the late 30s, 40s and 50s if you measure the wages against today's dollar--and then you either stopped working or worked in jobs not covered by Social Security.

---

* This amount increases automatically with the cost of living.

In deciding if you qualify for this special "over 10" minimum benefit, Social Security looks at the years you worked and the amounts you earned. Here is how it is figured: your total amount of wages from 1937 through 1950 is divided by $900, with a maximum amount of 14 years of coverage under this special rule credited to that period. For example, if your total wages from covered employment for that period was $4,500, that $4,500 is divided by $900, which equals five years of coverage ($4,500 divided by $900 is 5). After 1950, you receive a year of coverage for each year in which you earned at least 25 percent of the maximum covered by Social Security (take a look at these maximum amounts again, listed in Chapter 1, Section E). Thus, in this example, if you continued working in covered employment from 1951 through 1968, you would add eighteen years of special credit to the five years earned pre-1951, for a total of 22 years credit.

EXAMPLE: Millie won't mind if we use her as an example one more time. Let's say that her ex-husband, Tim, died soon after they split up and Millie never received any alimony. Instead, she had to stay in the millinery shop for six years before moving on to a department store for five more years, where she worked until 1949. Her total wages for that period of eleven years was $5,400. Divided by $900, as the special rule provides, Millie qualified for five years of credit for those working years. After 1950, Millie worked steadily in clothing stores and department stores until her retirement in 1978. Though her wages were always low, she did earn at least 25 percent of the maximum earnings that Social Security would credit for each of those years (for example, in 1951 the maximum income credited was $3,600 per year; though Millie earned only $1,000 that year, that's more than 25 percent of $3,600). Thus Millie got credit for all 27 years between 1951 and 1978. When her five early years of credit were added, Millie qualified under the special rule for 32 years of credit.

How much is the minimum benefit under this special rule? Social Security takes the number of years of special credit over 10 years and multiplies them by $17.50.* Thus, if you have 20 years of credit under this rule, you would receive a special minimum benefit of $175 a month (10 years over 10, multiplied by $17.50). If, like Millie, you have 32 years of credit (22 years over 10 years), your benefit would be $385 a month (22 multiplied by $17.50).

If your regular monthly retirement benefits are less than these amounts and you think you might qualify under the special "over 10" way of figuring, bring it to the attention of your local Social Security office and ask them to check your records to see if you qualify.

---

* This amount increases automatically with the cost of living.

4. Cost-of-Living Increases

Whatever the amount of your retirement benefit, you will receive an automatic cost-of-living increase on January 1 of each year.* This cost-of-living increase is tied to the rise in the Consumer Price Index (the cost of basic goods and services). In the late 1970s and early 1980s, this Consumer Price Index rose more than 10 percent a year, meaning that Social Security cost-of-living benefits rose more than 10 percent each year. In 1981-82, though, the cost-of-living increase was only 7.4 percent, and for 1983 it is expected to be only around 3 percent. Thus you cannot be sure that your benefit amounts will increase at any set pace. And Congress may change the rules regarding cost-of-living increases at any time. For example, the 1983 Social Security reform bill provides that if the Social Security "trust fund" (a bookkeeping fiction having to do with the total amount of money on Social Security's books) falls below certain levels, the cost-of-living increase will be limited to the rise in consumer prices or in average wages, whichever is <u>lower</u>. The government believes the cost-of-living provision is one of the easiest, politically, to tinker with; the rules may well be changed again in the next few years.

E. Can You Work After You Retire?

Perhaps the title of this section should be "Can You Afford <u>Not</u> to Work After You Retire?" Remember, for purposes of our discussion, the term "retire" only means claiming your retirement benefits; it does <u>not</u> necessarily imply giving up your work. Since the combination of Social Security and private pension retirement benefits, plus savings, is often not enough to live on, many people keep working, full or part-time, for at least a few years after they "retire." And in addition to the need for more income, lots of people keep their jobs or take new ones so that they can stay active and involved in the world of work. But if you do plan on working after retirement, you must be aware that the money you earn may cause a reduction in the amount of your Social Security retirement benefits.

---

* Before 1983, the COL increase was made each July 1. The Social Security reform act of 1983 delayed the increase of July, 1983 to January, 1984 and each January thereafter. In effect, there was no cost-of-living increase for 1983.

Until you reach age 70, the Social Security Administration will subtract money from your retirement check if you have a substantial "earned income." This term refers only to money you receive for work you are currently doing. Social Security does not count as earned income any money you receive from such things as interest on savings, insurance premiums, investments, royalties, rental income or pensions. Of course, this rule favors the well-to-do who have significant income from such non-earned sources, do not need to work, and have less need for their Social Security benefits. Those who need and want to keep on working, on the other hand, may be penalized by having their retirement benefit reduced.

How much can you earn before your retirement benefits are reduced? Currently, the rule is that if you are under 65 you are allowed $4,920 per year of earned income without having your benefits reduced; if you are between 65 and 70, the limit is $6,600 per year. (These dollar limits go up periodically). After reaching the dollar cut-off level, you will have one dollar of your retirement benefits taken away for each two dollars you earn over the amount allowed.* Once you reach age 70, though, you may earn as much as you are able to without losing any benefits.

How does Social Security know how much you earn? You tell them, that's how. Well, you're supposed to tell them, anyway. Each year you are obliged by law to report to Social Security any earnings over the allowable limit. And if you know in advance that you will be earning over the limit, it's best to report this fact in advance to avoid receiving over-payments and later having to repay them. You have no obligation to report your earnings until you go over the maximum, however. Once you report your earnings, Social Security will make a periodic request that you report any changes. If you fail to report income over the limit, and you're caught--through your tax returns, for example--you could be required to pay back to Social Security all over-payments they made to you.

SPECIAL FIRST-YEAR RULE: During the first year you retire, there is a special rule that permits you to get the full amount of your retirement benefits for any month you don't earn more than the maximum allowable ($410 per month if you are between 62 and 64, $550 a month if you are 65 to 69)--instead of at the normal yearly frequency. If you are self-employed, you may receive your full benefits for any month in which you did not perform "substantial services," the usual test for which is whether you worked in your business more than 45 hours during the month.

---

* Beginning in 1990, a retiree will only lose one dollar for every three over the allowable limits.

TAXES ON YOUR BENEFITS: A NEW RULE: For most people collecting Social Security retirement benefits, those benefits are tax-free. In other words, they are not considered "income" by the Internal Revenue Service and you do not have to pay income tax on them (though you do have to pay income tax on any interest you earn from saving your benefits). But a new rule passed by Congress in April, 1983 provides that " . . . if your adjusted gross income plus one-half of your year's Social Security benefits adds up to $25,000 or more ($32,000 for a couple), then you must pay income tax on one-half of your Social Security benefits. 1984 federal income tax forms will include an explanation of how to report this income."

F. When You Should Retire: Make A Benefits Checklist

The decision about when to stop working--or at least, greatly reduce your workload--is a very personal one. Many factors enter into your decision: your health, financial position, family responsibilities, interest in your work, opportunity to do something different, etc. Maximizing your retirement benefits is only one element in this decision, but for many people it is a very important one. The following checklist reminds you of the most important things to consider--not necessarily about when to stop working altogether, but rather, when to claim your retirement benefits so that you get the highest possible amounts:

■If you claim your retirement benefits at age 62 instead of waiting until 65, your monthly checks will be significantly lower, even after you reach 65. If you are still working, you should probably resist the temptation to retire at 62 unless the income you currently earn is small enough that you will not lose much, if any, of your already reduced benefits.

■If you do retire and continue working part-time, you can often maximize your combination of earnings and benefits by keeping your earned income under the maximums allowed for your age ($4,920 per year under 65; $6,660 per year from 65 to 69; no limit from age 70 on).

EXAMPLE: When Charlie Gage turned 62, he went to his local Social Security office; they estimated his retirement benefits for him: about $450 a month at 65, less twenty percent (to $360 a month) if he retired at 62. Since Charlie was only working part-time, making $450 a month, his total yearly earnings of $5,400 would only be $480 over the allowable limit for earned income by a person retiring at 62. Thus his retirement benefits would only be reduced by $240 (one dollar for every two dollars over the limit) for the whole year. By retiring at 62, Charlie would receive an average of about $340 a month from Social Security plus his

$450 a month paycheck.* For Charlie, it wasn't a bad idea
to retire at 62. If he waited until 65, his Social Security
check would be twenty percent higher, but he would have
missed out on three years of benefits at $340 per month, or
$12,240. It would take him a lot of years of twenty percent
higher benefits after 65 to get even, especially if he
invested some of the early retirement money in a money
market fund or other high interest savings plan.

■Once you reach age 65, there is no great advantage in
delaying retirement unless you are continuing to work
and you earn considerably more than the allowable
limit (currently $6,600).

■If you intend to continue working full-time at a comfortable salary, it is often best to delay your retirement
claim as long as possible. This not only prevents your
retirement checks from being eaten up by the excess earned
income rules, but it also allows you to continue building
up your earnings record so that when you do finally claim
your retirement, your benefits will be higher.

EXAMPLE #2: If our friend Charlie from the previous
example intended to keep his job as a "salter" at the Cosmopolitan Potato Chip Factory, making $12,000 a year, he would
be foolish to claim retirement at age 62. If he claimed
retirement at 62, his benefits would be reduced by one
dollar for every two dollars he earned over $4,920 per year.
Subtracting $4,920 from $12,000, Charlie would lose half of
$7,080, or $3,540, from his yearly retirement benefits.
Since he was only entitled to $360 a month in benefits
before this offset, or a total of $4,320 for the year, his
benefits would be almost totally wiped out by his earned
income. No dice, Charlie.

If Charlie were 65, the prospect for retirement benefits would be somewhat better. He would lose one dollar of
benefits for every two dollars over $6,600 a year of earned
income; that would mean losing one-half of the $5,400 dif-
ference between the exempt amount of $6,600 and his yearly
income of $12,000. Thus Charlie would lose $2,700 from his
benefits. He would be entitled to $450 a month in retire-
ment benefits, or $5,400 a year; this would be reduced by
the $2,700 earned income offset, leaving Charlie with actual
benefits of about $2,700 for the year if he retired at 65
while still working.

---

* Social Security would not actually reduce Charlie's monthly check by $20, but instead
would probably withhold one entire monthly check and then make an adjustment at the end of
the year after Charlie had filed his official annual report of his earnings.

EXAMPLE #3: For Charlie's sister-in-law, Mazine, there
would be no point to claiming retirement benefits at age 65
if she intends to keep her job. She works for Cosmopolitan,
too, earning $22,000 a year as a quality control officer
("taster," really). At age 65, Mazine would lose one dollar
of benefits for each two dollars she earned over $6,600 a
year. That would mean she would lose half of $15,400, or
$7,700, from her yearly benefits. At 65, if Mazine were
eligible for $650 a month, or $7,800 a year, in retirement
benefits, these benefits would be completely eaten up by the
$7,700 offset from her earned income. If Mazine continues
to work at that high a salary, she should delay her retirement until age 70, when there is no longer any offset from
earned income.

■Once you reach age 70, there is little point in waiting
to claim retirement. There is no limit on the amount of
outside income you can earn without penalty, so go for it!
You are entitled to it.

Social Security Disability Benefits

CHAPTER 3

HIGHLIGHTS

If you are a disabled widow or widower age 50 or over, you may be able to collect disability benefits even if you did not work enough in your lifetime to qualify on your own record for Social Security Benefits (see Section F, "What Conditions Does Social Security Consider Disabling?").

You may be permitted to earn a little money-- usually up to about $300 in a month--without losing your disability status (see Section G, "How Much Are Your Disability Benefit Payments?").

Even though you receive Workman's Compensation, state disability, private insurance disability or other compensation for your disability, you may also be able to collect Social Security disability benefits (see Section H, "Can You Collect Social Security Disability and Other Benefits, Too?").

If you have been receiving disability and want to try to return to work, you can do so under a "trial work period" during which you can collect both your disability benefits and any income you earn; if you are unable to continue with the work, you will remain on disability (see Section J, "Termination of Your Disability Benefits").

"Gold that buys health can never be ill spent
Nor hours laid out in harmless merriment."
                                              John Webster, *Westward Hoe*

■ ■ ■

A. Introduction

One out of every four regularly employed workers in America can expect to become disabled for a period of at least a year before reaching age 65; three-and-one-half million workers and their families currently draw Social Security disability benefits. Many injuries and illnesses are obviously disabling. There are others, however, such as chronic illnesses which become acute with age, or residual conditions which deteriorate over time, that become disabling though they were not initially too severe. For example, an older worker may have had an injury years before, or an illness which has been dormant, under control or merely "livable," but which has become aggravated through the years to the point where work is extremely difficult or impossible. In such cases, an older worker may become eligible for disability benefits though the original illness or injury was not disabling. If you have had difficulty working over a period of time of several months because of a physical condition, examine the following disability rules carefully. Though you are short of retirement age, you may be able to qualify for disability benefits of roughly the same amount as your retirement benefits would be. And though the requirements for Social Security disability are fairly strict, it is somewhat easier for an older worker to qualify than for a younger worker.

B. What Are The Work Requirements For Disability Benefits?

Just as with other Social Security benefits, disability benefits are only paid to workers and their families when the worker has enough work credits to qualify. Work credits for disability benefits are calculated in exactly the same way as for retirement benefits (see Chapter 1, Section D). Just to refresh your memory, you currently accumulate one quarter of work credit for each $370 per year you earn in covered employment, up to a maximum of four quarters per year.

Now that you remember how you earn work credits, how many work credits do you need to qualify for disability benefits? As usual with Social Security, there is no simple answer. The number of work credits needed to qualify for disability benefits depends on your age when you become disabled. Here are the rules:

If you were born before 1930, and you became disabled in:	You need this many quarters of work credit:
1980	29
1981	30
82	31
83	32
84	33
85	34
87	36
89	38
1991 or later	40

If you were born after 1929, and you became disabled at age:	You need this many quarters of work credit:
42 or younger	20
44	22
46	24
48	26
50	28
52	30
54	32
56	34
58	36
60	38
62 or older	40

In addition to the requirement of a certain total number of work credits, depending on your age, you must have earned at least 20 quarters of the required credit within the 10 years immediately preceding the time you became disabled (unless you qualify under one of the special rules explained immediately below).

Special Rules for Younger Workers

If you were disabled when still young, you are required to have fewer work credits. This is because you obviously did not have the opportunity to acquire many quarters of work. So, if you were disabled between the ages of 24 and 31, you only need work credits for half of the quarters between age 21 and the time you became disabled. In other words, if you became disabled at age 29, there were eight years between age 21 and the time you became disabled; you would need credit for half that time--four years (16 quarters). If you were disabled before age 24, you only need credit for six quarters in the three-year period immediately before you became disabled.

Special Rules for Blindness Disability

If you are disabled by blindness, there is no requirement that any of your work credits were earned within the years immediately preceding your disability. Your work credits can be from any time after 1936 (the year the Social Security law went into effect). The only requirement is that you have enough work credits, based on your age, as shown in the charts above.

C. What Constitutes Being Disabled?

In order to receive Social Security disability benefits:

■You must have a physical or mental impairment;

■The impairment must prevent you from doing any "substantial gainful activity;" and

■The disability must be expected to last, or has lasted, at least 12 months, or is expected to result in death.

Of course, these terms are subject to different interpretations. There are guidelines developed by Social Security and the courts regarding qualifications for disability. We'll examine each of these terms in more detail in the following sections, using these guidelines. But remember, every person's physical and mental state is different, unique. Proving a disability is often a difficult task, even if you seem to "fit" into one of the categories you will find in the next few pages. In preparing your claim for a disability, examine these guidelines carefully, discuss the matter with your doctor or doctors, and plan your claim thoroughly using the step-by-step guidelines provided in Chapter 5 of this book, "How to Apply for Your Social Security Benefits."

D. What Is A Physical or Mental Impairment?

The basic rule regarding disability is that the condition which prevents you from working at gainful employment must be a "medical" one, meaning that it can be discovered and described by doctors. To prove this, when you file your disability claim you should bring with you letters from your doctors, or from hospitals or clinics where you have been treated, describing the medical condition that prevents you from doing any substantial gainful activity. The letters should also state that your disability is expected to last for 12 months (or is expected to result in death).

E. A Disability Must Be Expected to Last One Year

41

No matter how serious or completely disabling an illness or injury is, it will not qualify you for disability benefits unless it has lasted, or is expected to last, for 12 months, during which time you are unable to perform substantial gainful work. The disability will also qualify if it is expected to result in death. Even though the disability must be expected to last 12 months, you don't have to wait for the 12 months to apply. As soon as the condition is disabling and a doctor can predict that it is expected to last a year, you may qualify for disability benefits.* And if, after you begin receiving benefits, it turns out that your disability does not last 12 months, Social Security cannot ask for its money back. You are not penalized for recovering sooner than expected, as long as the original expectation that the illness would last 12 months was a legitimate one.

EXAMPLE: Ladonna Sanders fell down some stairs and dislocated her hip. Luckily, the hip wasn't broken. She was placed in a body cast and was told by her doctor to stay in bed for three to four weeks. The cast would stay on for four months. After that, Ladonna would need a cane for another two or three months. In six to nine months, she would be walking normally again, though a little bit more carefully, particularly around stairs. She would be off work about seven or eight months. Can Ladonna claim Social Security disability benefits? The answer is no. Although she had a serious, painful and totally disabling injury, she could not receive Social Security disability payments because her disability was not expected to last for 12 months. (On the other hand, she might qualify for her company's disability benefits, if the company provides them, or for unemployment disability compensation through her state's employment or disability office.)

F. What Conditions Does Social Security Consider Disabling?

Any medical condition which prevents you from performing "substantial gainful activity" may be considered disabling. To simplify things a bit, the Social Security Administration has developed a list of conditions which they usually consider disabling without giving much of an argument. In other words, if you prove, through medical records and/or doctors' reports, that you have one of the condi-

---

* There is a waiting period of five full months from the outset of the disability before you receive your first check. This rule is discussed more fully in Section I, later in this chapter.

tions--say, paralysis of an arm and a leg--on Social Security's Listing of Impairments, you will probably be considered disabled without having to convince Social Security that you cannot perform substantial gainful activity. They will simply assume you cannot.

1. Listing of Impairments

The following is the list of major conditions which Social Security normally considers disabling. But remember, each claim for disability is considered separately; having a condition on this list does not <u>automatically</u> qualify you for disability benefits.

<u>IMPORTANT</u>: The fact that your medical condition is not on this list does <u>not</u> mean you won't be eligible for disability benefits. It only means that you will have to work a little harder to prove that you are, in fact, disabled. This process is described in the sections following the Listing of Impairments.

a. Diseases of the heart, lung or blood vessels which have resulted in a serious loss of heart or lung reserves as shown by X-ray, electrocardiogram or other tests; and, in spite of medical treatment, there is breathlessness, pain or fatigue.

b. Severe arthritis which causes recurrent inflammation, pain, swelling, and deformity in major joints so that the ability to get about or use the hands is severely limited.

c. Mental illness resulting in marked constriction of activities and interests, deterioration in personal habits and seriously impaired ability to get along with other people.

d. Damage to the brain or brain abnormality which has resulted in severe loss of judgment, intellect, orientation, or memory.

e. Cancer which is progressive and has not been controlled or cured.

f. Diseases of the digestive system which result in severe malnutrition, weakness, and anemia.

g. Progressive diseases which have resulted in the loss of a leg or which have caused it to become useless.

h. Loss of major function of both arms, both legs, or a leg and an arm.

i. Serious loss of function of the kidneys.

j. Total inability to speak.

"For all your ills I give you laughter."
Rabelais

2. "Substantial Gainful Activity"

If your medical condition is not on the Listing of
Impairments, Social Security will require more proof from
you that you are unable to work. But remember, you need not
be <u>completely</u> unable to function or do any work in order to
qualify for Social Security disability benefits. However,
you must be unable to perform any "substantial gainful
activity." How is "substantial gainful activity" defined?
To Social Security it means, basically, any job for pay.

If your condition is not on the Listing of Impairments
(and sometimes even if it is on the list), Social Security
will first consider whether it prevents you from doing the
job you had at the time you became disabled, or the last job
you had before becoming disabled.* If your disability prevents you from performing your usual job, Social Security
will next decide whether you are able to do any other kind
of substantial gainful work. As part of this determination,
they will consider your age, education, training and work
experience. Social Security will determine whether you are
able to perform any kind of work for pay existing anywhere
in the entire economy, whether or not there are actually any
such jobs available in the area in which you live. However,
it is up to Social Security to prove that there is gainful
employment you can perform. It is not up to you to prove

---

* The special disability office which makes these decisions is discussed in Chapter V,
Section B, which explains how to apply for disability benefits.

there is no work you can do. Once you show that you are unable to do your usual work, the shoe is on Social Security's foot.

EXAMPLE #1: Arnold Meeks has been a longshoreman for most of his life. He had a back injury in his twenties which kept him off the job for a couple of months, but he went back to work on the docks and has not had any other serious physical problems. Unfortunately, his back has grown slowly, but steadily, worse over the past ten years. Arnold is now 58 years old. In the past two years, he has missed several months of work--a few days here, a few days there--because of his back. Lately, he has been off work more than on. His doctor has told him that his back will not get better, and that continuing to do longshore work, even the easier jobs he can get because of his seniority in the union, will not be possible much longer. He decides to apply for disability. What are his chances?

In the first place, there is no question that Arnold's back problem is a medical one, nor is there any question that his condition will last more than a year. But does it prevent Arnold from performing any substantial gainful employment? When Arnold checks the Listing of Impairments, he doesn't find "bad back" listed anywhere. Does that mean he can't qualify as disabled? Nope. As we have said, each case is unique, and being on the List of Impairments is not an absolute criterion for eligibility. Social Security will first check to see if Arnold can still do his usual job.

Assuming both his doctor and work record indicate he can no longer do longshore work, Social Security will next ask if he can do some other substantial work. Any work at all. That will depend on how bad his back has become. As Arnold's back prevents him from standing for long periods of time, and restricts the movement of his arms, let's assume Social Security determines he is unable to do any physical labor. The next question would be whether he was able to do any other kind of work. It's possible that his back would be too bad for him to do even a job which required him to sit at a desk; if so, and Arnold proved this to Social Security through his doctor or by trying and being unable to do a desk job, he would probably get his disability payments. On the other hand, if his back were not quite that bad, he might be forced at least to try other work. But because Arnold had only done physical labor all his life, the question would now be "Does he have the training, work experience or education to do a desk job?" Assuming he doesn't, and considering his age, Social Security would probably not require that he learn the job skills necessary to start a new job in an office somewhere. Based on the facts set out above, Arnold would stand a good chance of qualifying for disability benefits.

EXAMPLE #2: Ernestine Williams has been a music teacher for many years; she is 60 years old. Ernestine has been losing her hearing gradually over the past several years; she has also developed phlebitis, an inflammation of the blood vessels of the leg, which makes it difficult for her to walk very far or to stand for long periods of time. She has to elevate her legs for awhile every few hours. Her loss of hearing has finally made it impossible for her to continue teaching music. Can she qualify for disability benefits? Or must she find another job?

Again, of course, the answer would depend on how severe her hearing loss was and how bad the phlebitis had become. Much would depend on what her doctors said about her legs. Although neither of her conditions is on the Listing of Impairments, the combination of conditions may make her unable to perform any gainful employment. Why? She would have to find a job which did not require either good hearing or standing up, and where she would be able to put her legs up for a half hour or so several times a day. Since it would probably be extremely difficult to find such a job, Social Security would very likely allow Ernestine's disability claim, particularly in light of her age. You see, Social Security is aware they are not committing themselves to as great an outlay of money when they grant disability to persons nearing retirement age as they would be in granting it to younger workers. Since older workers could collect retirement benefits anyway as soon as they turn 62, and since no one can collect more than one benefit at a time, Social Security is not really committing itself to pay much more money to an older worker than they would have without granting the disability. For this reason, and because it is more difficult for older workers to find new employment, older workers tend to have their disability claims approved without as great a struggle.

EXAMPLE #3: Rebecca Burney is 52. Her doctor recently told her she has a mild heart condition and she should be a bit more careful in her activities and diet. He placed her on low doses of medication and told her she could return to her job as a security guard in a large department store. After awhile, though, Rebecca returned to her doctor complaining of intermittant fatigue and shortness of breath, especially after dealing with shoplifters. The doctor told her he could increase the level of her medication, but it would be much better if she could find less stressful work. Rebecca said, "Oh, don't worry. I'll just go on disability. My condition is on the Listing of Impairments, right up at the top."

Not so fast, Rebecca! While it's true that Rebecca's condition--disease of the heart leading to breathlessness and fatigue despite medication--is on the Listing of Impairments, it's not true that she would be automatically eligible for disability. Her condition is mild enough and she is young enough that she could give up her stressful, and sometimes physically difficult, job as a security guard and work at something else, perhaps even in the same store. If Rebecca had training or experience doing any other kind of work, she would almost certainly be required to look for a job elsewhere. Even if she had no other highly developed job skills, because of her relatively young age and good health, she probably would be required to train for some other type of work.

EXAMPLE #4: Winston Woo is the office manager for a large office of doctors. He is 55. In the fall, while playing tennis, Winston smashed his kneecap, dislocated his hip and wound up in the hospital. He was placed in a body cast and remained in the hospital, and then in bed at home, for two months; the cast will stay on for another three months after he is up and about. He is unable to sit, except in a semi-reclining position in a special chair set up at home. There is no way he can perform his job. Can he get disability payments? This is a test--what do you say?

The answer is a simple no. If you didn't get it right, you'd better review the last few pages. The reason Winston is not eligible for disability is that although he is severely disabled and obviously unable to work at his, or any other, job, his disability will not last for more than a year, and, despite the fact that Winston complains of feeling like the end may be near, the doctors assure him that he will make a full recovery. Sorry, Winston.

Of course, Winston is not completely out of luck. He may be eligible for unemployment benefits, health insurance benefits (if he is covered by a private health insurance policy), Workman's Compensation benefits for loss of wages, or private disability payments if he or his office carries such an insurance policy.

3. Special Provisions for Blind People

If your vision is not better than 20/200 even with glasses, or if your field of vision is limited to twenty degrees or less, you are considered "blind" under Social

Security rules. Assuming that you have worked long enough
to have earned the required work credits for your age, you
and your family can receive disability benefits. This is
true even though you may actually be working, under special
Social Security rules which apply to blind persons
who work, which state:

■You can earn up to $550 per month (in 1983) before
your earnings are considered "substantial gainful
work" which would disqualify you from benefits.

■If you are between age 55 and 65, you can receive
disability benefits (and Medicare) if you are
unable to perform work requiring skills or abilities
comparable to those required by the work you did
before you turned 55, or before you became blind,
whichever is later. Checks will be withheld, however, for any month in which you do perform substantial gainful work.

IMPORTANT: If you are legally blind but are earning
too much money to qualify for disability benefits, you may
want to apply for them anyway if your earnings are significantly lower than they were before the onset of your blindness. Why? If you would qualify for disability were it not
for your earnings over the limit (but which are still much
lower than you were making before), the Social Security
Administration can put a disability "freeze" on your earnings record. How does this help? Remember, the amount of
your ultimate retirement benefits (or of your disability
benefits if you later qualify) is determined by your average
income over the years (see Chapter 1, Section E). If, after
your disability, you are making considerably less than you
were before, the years of those earnings would pull your
average income lower, which could result in a lower ultimate
Social Security payment. The disability "freeze" permits
you to work and collect your lower income without having it
figured into your lifetime average earnings.

4. Special Rule: Disabled Widow or Widower

If you are a widow or widower, age 50 or over, and
disabled, you may receive disability benefits even though
you don't have enough work credits of your own to qualify if
your deceased spouse had enough work credits for his/her age
at the time of death. The rules are as follows:

a. You must be disabled (under this rule your age, work experience and training are not considered in whether you are disabled);

b. You must be age 50 or older;

c. Your spouse must have been fully "insured" (meaning he or she had enough work credits considering his/her age) at the time of death.

d. Your disability must have begun before your spouse's death or within seven years after the death.

e. If you already receive Social Security benefits as a surviving widow or widower with children*, you will be eligible for these special disability benefits if you are age 50 or older and you become disabled before those payments end or within seven years after they end.

f. Even if you were divorced before your ex-spouse died, you may still be eligible for these benefits if you had been married to your ex for 10 years or more.

The amount of these special benefits will depend entirely upon your spouse's work record and average earnings.

NOTE: These special disability benefits may end if you remarry.

G. How Much Are Your Disability Benefit Payments?

Like other Social Security benefits, the amount of your monthly disability check is determined by your age and earnings record. The amount of your benefits will be based upon your average earnings for all the years you have been working, not just on the high salary you were making most recently.

Monthly payments for those persons first qualifying for disability benefits currently range up to about $768. The average disability payment for a disabled worker with a spouse and two children under 16 is about $1,152 a month. There is also a yearly cost-of-living increase (if the Consumer Price Index rises over three percent for the year).

---

* See Chapter 4 for a discussion of survivors' benefits.

Unfortunately, for those who first become disabled in 1982 or later, there is no minimum benefit amount; your monthly check will be based entirely on your earnings record, with no consideration given to a minimum amount needed to survive. If you receive only a small disability benefit, however, and you do not have a large amount of savings or other assets, you may be eligible for some Supplemental Security Income Benefits (SSI) in addition to your Social Security disability benefits. SSI is discussed in Chapter 6.

If you are disabled, your spouse and children under age 18 may also be eligible for dependents' benefits, which are explained in Chapter 4. If so, your combined "family benefits" (the total amount you, your spouse and your children receive) will be limited to a maximum of either 85 percent of what you were earning before you became disabled, or to 150 percent of what your monthly individual benefit would have been, whichever is <u>lower</u>.

<u>EXAMPLE</u>: Juan Barojas was making $2,200 a month when he was disabled. At the time he became disabled, Juan's total Social Security earnings record would have given him an individual disability benefit of $600 a month. But Juan's wife, Theresa, and their two teenage children, Angela and Bobby, were also eligible to collect dependents' benefits. How much would their total family benefits be? The amount would be the lower of 85 percent of Juan's $2,200 monthly salary, which comes out to $1,870, or 150 percent of what Juan's individual disability benefit ($600) would be, which comes out to $900. The Barojas family would receive $900 a month, the lesser of the two amounts.

H. Can You Collect Social Security Disability and Other Benefits Too?

Since disability payments are often not enough to live on, it is important for you to collect all the other benefits to which you may be entitled, and even try to supplement your income by working a little if you are able to.

1. Disability and Earned Income

There is no rule which reduces the amount of your disability benefits by amounts of income you earn while on disability (as there is with retirement benefits). But, if you earn any regular income, you might not be considered disabled any longer and you could lose your disability eligibility altogether. Remember, you are only officially disabled if you are unable to perform any substantial gainful activity. So, if you are earning money, you are performing "gainful" employment. It is possible, though, to earn a little money and still remain "disabled." Social Security usually permits you to earn up to about $300 a month before they consider you to be performing substantial gainful work. But this $300 is not a fixed rule, and a review of your disability status to see if your work is substantial can also take into account your work duties, the number of hours you work, and, if you are self-employed, the extent to which you run or manage your own business. In deciding how much you are earning, though, the Social Security disability review people can deduct from your income the amounts of any impairment-related work expenses such as medical devices or equipment (a wheelchair, for example), attendant care, drugs, or services required for you to be able to work.

2. Disability and Other Social Security Benefits

Let us remind you again that you are not permitted to collect more than one Social Security benefit at a time. If you are eligible for more than one monthly benefit--disability and retirement, for example, or disability based on your own work record and also as the disabled spouse of a retired worker--you will receive the higher of the two benefit amounts to which you are entitled, but not both. For the purposes of this rule, though, Supplemental Security Income (SSI) is not considered a Social Security benefit; you may collect SSI in addition to a Social Security benefit. See Chapter 6 for more on SSI.

3. Social Security and Other Disability Benefits

You are permitted to collect Social Security disability payments and, at the same time, private disability payments from an insurance policy or coverage from your employer. You may also receive Veterans' Administration disability coverage at the same time as Social Security disability benefits (Veterans' Benefits are discussed in Chapter 10). And you may collect Workman's Compensation benefits at the same time as Social Security disability benefits. However, the total of your disability and Workman's Compensation payments cannot be greater than 80 percent of what your average wages were before you became disabled. If they are, your disability benefits will be reduced to the point where the total of both benefits is 80 percent of your earnings before you became disabled. If you are still receiving Social Security disability benefits when your Workers' Compensation benefits run out, you can again start receiving the full amount of your Social Security benefits.

EXAMPLE: Maxine Czazsy became disabled with a lung condition while working for the telephone company in their computer analysis department. At that time she was making $1,400 a month. Her Social Security disability benefits were $560 a month; she also applied for and began receiving Workman's Compensation benefits of $625 a month. Because the total of the two benefits was more than 80 percent of her prior salary (80 percent of $1,400 is $1,120, and she would be getting $1,185), her disability benefits were reduced by the extra $65 down to $495 a month. If Maxine were still disabled when her Workman's Compensation benefits ran out, her Social Security disability benefits would go back up to $560 a month, plus whatever cost-of-living increases had been granted in the meantime. If Maxine also had private insurance which paid disability benefits, she could receive all of these as well as all of her Social Security.

4. Social Security Disability and Supplemental Security Income (SSI)

If your savings and assets are not too high, you may be able to receive both SSI benefits and Social Security disability benefits. The requirements for SSI eligibility are discussed in detail in Chapter 6.

5. Social Security Disability and Medicare

After you have been collecting disability benefits for 24 months (not necessarily consecutive months), you become eligible for Medicare coverage even though you are not old enough to be covered by Medicare under the regular Medicare rules. Medicare hospitalization coverage is free (after you pay a $304 deductible). Like everyone else, though, you must pay a monthly premium if you want to be covered by Medicare medical insurance. Medicare is explained in great detail in Chapter 7.

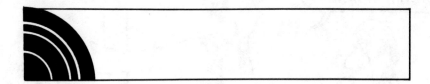

I. When Can You Start Collecting Disability Benefits?

If you think some of the rules and regulations we've gone over so far are a little confusing, you haven't seen anything yet! For sheer dizziness, those that follow take the cake. They are best dealt with slowly; read them over several times. If they still seem confusing to you, you are not alone. When you apply for disability benefits, the best way to cut through all these rules is simply to ask the disability eligibility worker: "When will I actually receive my first check?"

- You must wait five full months from the date your disability begins before you will receive any payment at all. You will receive your first payment for the sixth full month following the beginning of your disability. (If you become disabled in mid-May, for example, your first check will arrive in December.)

- Ordinarily, your first check will be for one month only. In other words, there is a waiting period of five months not only for receiving your check, but also for being <u>entitled</u> to a check.

- If your disability began (and you were unable to work) more than six months before you applied for disability, you may be eligible for some months of "back benefits." There is a limit, however, of 12 months on these back benefits.

<u>EXAMPLE</u>: If our friend Maxine Czazsy in the phone company became disabled in May and applied for disability before the end of that month, her first check would be for the month of November received in early December.

If Maxine had become disabled (and stopped working) in
May but did not apply for disability until December, she
could receive her first payment as soon as she was determined to be eligible.

If this still confuses you a little, just remember one
rule: as soon as you think you may be disabled, file a
claim for disability at the local Social Security Administration office, or if you are unable to file the claim
yourself, have someone file the claim for you. Social
Security will then figure out for you when you were first
entitled to disability benefits and how much your first
check will be. Applying for disability benefits is explained in more detail in Chapter 5.

J. Termination of Your Disability Benefits

If your medical condition improves and you go back to
work your disability eligibility will end. Even if you don't
go back to work voluntarily, Social Security will review

your case periodically--or at least once every three years--to determine whether, in their opinion, your condition has improved enough for you to go back to work. From time to time, therefore, Social Security may ask for updated medical evidence from your doctor, or may even require that you be examined by another doctor, or undergo additional medical tests (arranged and paid for by Social Security). You must cooperate with these periodic reviews or run the risk of losing your disability benefits. You certainly have the right, though, to insist on being given enough time to gather necessary information from your doctor, and enough notice to meet the appointment for the examination or test. If you're going to be unable to keep an appointment scheduled for you by the Social Security office, do not hesitate to ask for a rescheduling. Simply call your local office, or the office that sent you the notice of the appointment, and explain that you will be unable to make the examination or testing on the date or time they have arranged. They will reschedule and notify you of your new appointment date.

1. Adjustment Period

Even if Social Security decides to end your disability benefit, you may continue to receive your regular payments for an adjustment period of up to three months. This is a cushion to give you income while you find new work or go back to your old job, where you may have to wait awhile for your paycheck. You must request this adjustment period from your disability worker. It is not given automatically.

Remember, the decision that your disability has ended, like most other eligibility decisions, may be appealed through the proper Social Security appeal procedures.   If you feel that your disability continues to make it impossible to work, file your appeal right away. The appeal procedures are explained in detail in Chapter 5.

2. A Trial Work Period

   Most disabled persons would rather work than not, and
many attempt to find ways of working despite their disabling
conditions. Social Security encourages people to try to
work despite their disability, particularly if their condition has improved somewhat. This encouragement takes tan-
gible form in a device called the "trial work period."
During this period you may try out some kind of gainful
employment while still getting your full disability benefits. Of course, your medical condition must still technically qualify you as disabled in order for you to take
advantage of this trial period. You may use up to a total
of nine months during this testing of your ability to work.
During these months, you may keep both the income you earn
and your full disability benefits. The nine months need not
be consecutive; you may try one job for a month or two and,
if it doesn't work out, you may attempt another sometime
later, up to a total of nine months. And any months in
which you do not earn more than $75, or spend more than 15
hours in self-employment, do not count as trial months at
all.

   After a trial work period, Social Security will review
your case to see if, based on your trial work period, you
have become able to perform substantial gainful work. The
first thing they will look at is your earnings: if you are
regularly making over $300 per month in gross wages ($500
per month if you are blind), you are usually considered to
be doing substantial gainful work. There are other things
which may be considered, though: if you are putting in long
hours or have significant responsibilities, you may be considered as doing substantial gainful work even though your
"gain" is not over $300 a month.

   EXAMPLE: Let's return again to Maxine, the computer
operator for the phone company, whose lung problems forced
her onto disability. After awhile, one of her doctors
suggested she might breathe easier if she moved into the
country where the air was clean. Taking his advice, she did
just that, and, sure enough, her lungs improved. When she
visited her doctor again a few months later, she suggested
to him that the airless computer room where she had worked
might have contributed to her lung problems. The doctor
suggested that if she felt up to it, Maxine might try to
find some not-too-strenuous work outdoors, or in a well ven-
tilated place.

   When Maxine spoke to her disability benefits caseworker
at the local Social Security office, the caseworker told her
to give it a try, and said she could continue to collect her
disability benefits while in a trial work period. Maxine

found a job working in the accounts department of a small
factory near the little town in which she now lived. She
was delighted to be working again, even though she received
a much smaller salary than she had earned at the phone
company, and she was still getting her disability check.
Unfortunately, after a couple of months her lungs started to
get bad again and she realized that the air in the office
where she was working, plus the stress of the job, were
getting to be too much for her lungs. She had to give up
the job. She continued to collect her disability.

A couple of months later, Maxine found a little newspaper in a neighboring town that was putting in a small
computer and was looking for someone with experience who
could operate the new machine. City-slicker Maxine was just
the one for the job. She explained her health problem to
the newspaper folks and they agreed to set the machine up in
a loft above the main newspaper room--a spacious place with
lots of high windows that could be kept open most of the
time. Maxine went to work for them under the trial work
period, collecting both her pay and disability benefits.
This time she made it. After collecting disability for
several more months, Social Security decided Maxine should
go off disability altogether. Maxine found herself heal-
thier than she had been in a long time; not only was she
making a good salary again, but several other staff members
at the paper had moved into the loft too, and Maxine found
herself having a high old time up there with all that sun-
light, fresh air and friendly co-workers.

If you are on disability and feel you would like to try
returning to work but don't want to risk losing your disability benefits if it turns out you are unable to stay on
the job, contact your caseworker at the Social Security
office and ask to be given a trial work period. Who knows--
you might "move up" just like Maxine.

3. Reinstatement of Disability Benefits

Some people return to work when their medical condition
improves, or when they find a way to work around their
condition, but then later become unable to work again when
the condition worsens or they find they are simply unable to
continue on the job. If you go off disability because you
have found work (though you still have the medical condition
which led to your disability), and then within one year
after the disability benefits stopped, you again become unable to work, your monthly disability benefits can begin
again immediately, without your filing a new claim and
without going through another five-month waiting period.
Just notify your local Social Security office that you are
no longer working (because of the disability) and they will
start your checks again.

4. A Second Period of Disability

If you once received disability benefits and you again become disabled and unable to work <u>within 5 years</u> after your benefits stopped, you may begin receiving disability payments again without going through another five-month waiting period. This is true whether your payments were originally stopped because your medical condition improved or because you returned to work. Your new period of benefits starts with the first full month of your "new" disability. This provision also applies if you had received benefits as a disabled widow or widower and have become disabled again within seven years after your benefits ended.

Under these rules, if you had been entitled to Medicare during your earlier disability period, your Medicare coverage will automatically resume when your new benefits start. If you had not yet been on disability for 24 months (thus qualifying for Medicare), the months you were on disability in the earlier period will be added to your new disability period until you qualify for Medicare coverage.

5. Continuation of Medicare

If your medical condition continues, but you lose your disability benefits because you have returned to gainful employment, you may continue your Medicare coverage (if you had qualified for it) for up to three years after your monthly disability benefits have stopped.

6. Vocational Rehabilitation Services

When you apply for Social Security disability benefits, you may be referred to your state's vocational rehabilitation agency for them to determine if any of their services would be of benefit to you. These services may include counseling, medical help, job training and placement. Cooperation with the vocational rehabilitation agency may be a requirement for you to receive your disability checks. Of course, if you have good reasons not to participate in particular rehabilitative services offered to you, you don't have to participate. But remember, if you absolutely refuse even to consider the vocational rehabilitation services, your benefits may be denied.

Social Security Dependents' and Survivors' Benefits

CHAPTER 4

HIGHLIGHTS

If you receive Social Security retirement or disability benefits and your grandchild(ren) live with you and are dependent on you for support, they may be eligible to collect their own Social Security dependents' benefits (see Section B, "Dependents' Benefits: Who is Eligible?").

If you are eligible for a pension from your work in public employment, you may lose much or all of your Social Security dependents' benefits; however, there are a number of exceptions to this "offset" (see Section E, "Public Employee Pension Offset").

If you are a widow or widower age 50 or over and you have become disabled, you may be eligible for special survivors' benefits even though you do not have enough of your own work credits to be eligible for disability benefits based on your own work record (see Section F, "Survivors' Benefits: Who is Eligible?").

You may be eligible for survivors' benefits if you are at least age 62 and you were dependent for at least half of your support on your child who has died (see Section F, "Survivors' Benefits: Who is Eligible?").

If you are a widow or widower age 60 or over, you may remarry without losing your survivors' benefits (see Section F, "Survivors' Benefits: Who is Eligible?").

A. Introduction

Bureaucracies don't tend to pay much attention to folk wisdom. And in many cases, the organizational "wisdom" they substitute has more to do with the needs of the bureaucracy than of the people it is intended to serve. But in rejecting the old adage that "two can live as cheaply as one," Social Security regulations make a lot of sense. For the simple truth is that a retired or disabled worker with a family--either a spouse, a spouse and children, or just children--cannot live on the same benefit amounts as a retired or disabled person living alone. These "dependents" need financial support above what would be sufficient to help support an individual worker. Hence, the Social Security law provides for <u>dependents' benefits</u>, paid to the spouse and to children under 18* of a retired or disabled worker.

The Social Security laws also recognize that a worker's family will continue to need financial support after the worker dies. Even if the surviving spouse has always worked, the loss of the deceased spouse's income will almost surely be a severe economic blow to the family. And if the surviving spouse did not work, or worked much less than the deceased spouse, the loss of the deceased worker's income can be a devastating financial blow. Consequently, the Social Security laws provide for <u>survivors' benefits</u> to be paid to the surviving spouse and children under 18** of a worker who has died.

Finally, if you are nearing retirement age and are about to check with Social Security about the amount of your own retirement benefits, also ask what your benefits would be if you claimed dependents' or survivors' benefits based on your spouse's work record instead of claiming retirement on your own record. As with other Social Security benefits, you are not permitted to collect both your own retirement or disability benefits and dependents' or survivors' benefits. But if your own earnings record is low and your spouse's earnings record is high, you may find that you are entitled to higher benefits as a dependent or survivor than you would

---

* Children may receive dependents' benefits until age 19 if they are still in elementary or high school. Children of any age may receive such benefits if they were disabled before age 22.

** Same rule as described in previous footnote.

be as a retired worker collecting retirement benefits on your own work record. To repeat, you can't collect both, but you are entitled to collect whichever benefit is higher.

B. Dependents' Benefits: Who Is Eligible?

Certain dependents of a retired or disabled worker are eligible for monthly dependents' benefits if the worker is eligible for retirement or disability benefits. In other words, the right of dependents to collect benefits exists only if the worker has enough work credits to qualify for his or her own retirement or disability benefits. Similarly, the amount of benefits paid to dependents is determined by the worker's earnings record. Here is a list of the types of dependents who are eligible for dependents' benefits, assuming of course that the worker is eligible for retirement or disability benefits.

IMPORTANT: Being a "dependent" for Social Security purposes does not necessarily mean that you are, in fact, dependent on the worker or on the worker's benefits for your support. In order to be entitled to benefits, you do not have to prove that you are actually dependent; you only need to prove that you "fit" one of the following categories:

- A spouse age 62 or older.

- A spouse under age 62 if he or she is caring for the worker's child who is under age 16 or who is disabled before age 22.

- A disabled spouse under age 62 (see Chapter 3 for an explanation of what constitutes being "disabled"). Remember, though, that your own benefits as a disabled worker may be higher than the benefits you would be entitled to as a dependent. It all depends on the earnings records of you and your spouse.

- A divorced spouse age 62 or older, if your marriage to the worker lasted 10 years or more.

- Unmarried children under age 18. Though benefits to the parents end when the child turns 16, the child continues to receive benefits until age 18.

- Unmarried children of any age if they were severely disabled before they reached age 22, as long as they remain disabled.

■In a few cases, grandchildren of the worker qualify for benefits if they live with, and are under the actual care and custody of, the worker. Proof of actual dependent status is required.

EXAMPLE: Fred Astello has just claimed his retirement benefits at age 62; Fred's wife, Ginger, is 56. Their youngest child, Maria, is 15. Is Ginger entitled to dependents' benefits? How about Maria? And for how long?

Ginger is entitled to dependents' benefits because she and Fred are still caring for their child under 16. But as soon as Maria turns 16, Ginger's benefits will end; Maria, on the other hand, will collect dependents' benefits until she turns 18. Five years from now, though, when Ginger turns 62, she will again be eligible to collect dependents' benefits.

C. How Much Are Your Dependents' Benefits?

The amount of your dependents' benefits is based primarily on the earnings record of the worker upon whom you are "dependent." One dependent will normally receive about one-half of the worker's retirement or disability benefits. If there is more than one dependent, however, the benefits paid to the worker and dependents are combined into a "family benefit" which is less than the total would be if the worker's benefits and individual dependent benefits were added together. The amount of the family limit varies depending on the amount the worker is entitled to: the current maximum family benefit amount is about $1,050 per month.

D. Can You Work and Also Receive Dependents' Benefits?

The rule is the same as for a worker's own retirement benefit: a dependent's benefit will be reduced by $1 for every $2 of income earned by the dependent over the yearly maximum. The current limits, which vary depending upon whether you are under or over 65, are explained fully in Chapter 2, Section E. Note, though, that if a family is receiving a "family benefit" amount, one dependent may earn more than the income limits without affecting the total amount the family receives (see the example below).

EXAMPLE: George and Gracie Kamenos and their two children receive a family retirement benefit of $1,050 a month. Gracie's portion of the family benefit is about $150 a month. Gracie is offered a job for a year as a substitute teacher at $12,000 per year. What happens to the family's benefits if she takes it?

Since her own benefit amount is reduced $1 for every $2 Gracie earns over $4,920 (Gracie is 63), her benefit would be reduced by half ($1 out of $2) of $7,080 ($12,000 minus $4,920). Her benefits would thus be reduced by $3,540, which works out to $295 per month. Since her own benefit is only $150 per month the question arises as to whether the remaining $145 a month is taken out of the family benefit. The answer is no. The family benefit would only be reduced by the $150 a month Gracie would have been entitled to. When this is done, a new family benefit is figured, which must be at least as high as the old benefit minus Gracie's share ($1,050 minus $150 = $900), and probably will end up being close the same $1,050. Take the job, Gracie!

■ ■ ■

E. Public Employee Pension Offset

This rule can be a little complicated so be prepared to read this paragraph a couple of times. If you receive Social Security dependents' benefits and also a public employment retirement pension--federal, state or local government or civil service employment--based on your own work record, your dependents' benefits will be reduced dollar for dollar by the amount of your pension. But, and this is the part that sometimes seems a little confusing, this rule does not apply if you are receiving a dependents' benefit rather than your own retirement benefit from the public employment pension plan. In other words, if your spouse is collecting a public pension as well as Social Security and you collect dependents' benefits from both programs, your Social Security benefits are not affected by the dependents' benefits provided by the pension and you can receive both.

IMPORTANT: None of these rules apply to pensions paid by private employers. You are entitled to all of your Social Security as well as your private pension benefits, unless the private pension plan provides otherwise (see Chapter 11).

EXAMPLE: Eugene Chenier is retired and collects both Social Security retirement benefits from his years as a structural engineer in private industry and a retirement pension from his years working for the United States Commerce Department. Lucinda, his wife, collects dependents' benefits based on Eugene's Social Security retirement; she wants to know about collecting either retirement or dependents' benefits from the civil service pension plan. She and Eugene met at the Commerce Department, you see, while she was working there as an economist. Lucinda is eligible for a good retirement pension of her own from civil service, and a smaller amount as a dependent on Eugene's pension. Which should she claim?

Even though her own civil service pension would be higher than the amount she would get as a dependent on Eugene's pension, she might not want to claim her pension. Why? Well, if she accepts the dependents' benefits from Eugene's pension, this money will not be subject to the offset against her Social Security. However, if she accepts her own pension, her Social Security dependents' benefits could be reduced, dollar for dollar, by the entire amount of her pension. Lucinda might be better off to take the pension dependents' benefit and keep her entire Social Security dependents' benefits as well. Of course, if her own pension is much higher than the two dependents' benefits, she'll want to claim her own pension.

IMPORTANT EXCEPTIONS: There are some large exceptions to the public pension offset rule:

■The offset does not apply if you were eligible for Social Security dependents' or survivors' benefits before December 1, 1977.

■If you began receiving or were eligible to receive (meaning you did not have to have actually applied for) your public employment pension before December 1, 1982 and you meet the requirements for dependents' or survivors' benefits in effect in January, 1977, you can collect both dependents'/survivors' benefits and your public pension. What rules were different in January, 1977? For a divorced woman, her marriage must have lasted 20 years rather than the 10 year requirement today. And for a man, he must prove actual dependence on his deceased or divorced wife for at least one-half of his support.

Though a rule requiring actual dependence by men only is obviously discriminatory, and was changed after January, 1977, its last gasp remains in this exception to the public offset rule. Since the rules in January, 1977 did not require proof of actual dependence for women, most women who were eligible for their public pension before December 1, 1982 are not affected by the public pension offset rule. In other words, most women can collect both Social Security dependents'/survivors' benefits and their own public pension.

F. Survivors' Benefits: Who Is Eligible?

(1) Minimum Earned Credits by Worker's Record: Surviving family members of a deceased worker may be entitled to survivors' benefits if the worker had enough earned work credits at the time of his or her death. The number of earned credits on the worker's Social Security record needed for survivors to collect benefits are set out just below:

If the worker was born after 1929, and died or became disabled at age:	If the worker was born before 1930, and died or became disabled before age 62, in:	Years of work credit needed:
28 or younger		1.5
30		2
32		2.5
34		3
36		
38		4
40		
42		5
44		
46	1975	6
48	1977	
50	1979	7
52	1981	
54	1983	8
56	1985	
58	1987	9
60	1989	
62 or older	1991 or later	10

IMPORTANT! Even if the deceased worker did not have enough work credits according to this chart, benefits may still be paid to the surviving spouse and children if the worker had at least one-and-one-half years of work in covered employment in the three years immediately before he or she died. So, if the deceased worker in your family worked for at least a year-and-a-half in the three years before he or she died, make sure you apply for survivors' benefits. Remember, the worst Social Security can do is say "No." And if they say "Yes," you may be entitled to receive benefits for many years.

(2) Who is Considered a "Survivor?" Not every surviving family member can collect survivors' benefits. If the worker had enough work credits, the following family members are eligible for survivors' benefits:

- Surviving spouse (widow or widower) age 60 or over. If you were divorced, your marriage must have lasted for at least 10 years in order for you to collect survivors' benefits.

- Surviving spouse under age 60 if caring for the worker's child under age 16. This benefit is often called the "mother's benefit," or "father's benefit." It is also payable to a surviving divorced spouse.

- Surviving spouse age 50 or over who becomes disabled within 7 years of the worker's death or within 7 years after "mother's benefits" or "father's benefits" end. Here the term "disabled" is defined more strictly than for disability benefits: a disabled surviving spouse must be unable to perform <u>any</u> gainful activity (rather than no <u>substantial</u> gainful activity) before benefits will be paid. If you were divorced, you can collect these survivors' benefits only if your marriage had lasted at least 10 years.

- Unmarried children under 18 (benefits may continue to age 19 if the child remains a full-time high school student).

- Unmarried children of any age who were severely disabled before age 22 and are still disabled.

- Parents of the worker who are at least age 62 and who were actually dependent on the worker for at least one-half of their financial support.

(3) Length of Marriage Rule: In order to collect benefits as a surviving spouse, your marriage must have lasted at least 9 months before the worker's death, unless you had or adopted a child with the worker, or the worker's death was caused by an on-the-job accident.

(4)   Remarriage: As of January 1, 1979, a widow or
widower age 60 or over who collects dependents' benefits
does not lose those benefits if he or she remarries, no
matter how much income the new spouse may have. If you are
under age 60 and you remarry, however, you will lose your
dependents' benefits (though your children will still collect their benefits).

EXAMPLE: Akiko and Yosh Suehiro were divorced ten
years ago after being married 25 years. Three years ago,
Yosh died. Akiko and Ben have been together for the past
year and are now considering marriage. But one of the
things Akiko is concerned about is the effect their marriage
would have on her right to collect Social Security
survivors' benefits. Akiko is 59 and next year she would be
eligible for survivors' benefits based on Yosh's work record
(despite the fact they were divorced ten years before, their
marriage had lasted more than the required ten years).
Akiko realizes that if she waits one more year before she
and Ben get married, she can collect survivors' benefits and
also be able to remarry without losing those benefits. Ben
will just have to wait.

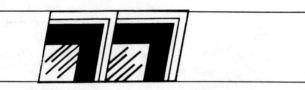

G. How Much Are Survivors' Benefits?

The amounts of survivors' benefits vary according to the category you fall into, and according to how much the deceased worker was entitled to:

- A surviving spouse age 60 or over, if there are no children receiving benefits, will receive 71.5 percent to 100 percent of what the worker would have been entitled to.

- The "mother's benefit" is usually about 75 percent of what the worker would have been entitled to.

- A surviving child will usually receive about 75 percent of what the worker's benefits would have been.

- A surviving parent may be eligible for about 75 percent of what the worker's benefit would have been; for both surviving parents, the total is 82.5 percent.

Family Benefit Limits

As is the situation with other Social Security benefits, when several members of a family receive survivors' benefits, they do not all get the same amount they would each receive if they were receiving benefits alone. Instead, a "family benefit" total is arrived at which is less than the sum of what all the individual benefit amounts would have been. If you and your child or children receive survivors' benefits based on your deceased spouse's work record, you will receive benefits only up to a family benefit maximum. This maximum is a percentage of what the worker would have been entitled to and varies depending on the worker's level of earnings.

∎∎∎

H. Lump-Sum Death Benefits

In addition to the monthly survivors' benefits to which many family members are entitled, some members of the family may also receive a one-time only payment, currently $255, intended to defray funeral or burial expenses. Only one claim for a lump-sum death benefit may be paid, usually to the eligible surviving spouse, or to a surviving child if there is no surviving spouse. A claim for the death benefit must be filed within two years of the worker's death with your local Social Security office.

∎∎∎

I. Can You Work and Collect Survivors' Benefits?

The same rules apply to survivor's benefits as to retirement or dependents' benefits: the amount of your benefits will be reduced by $1 for every $2 of income earned by the survivor over the maximum yearly limit. The current limits are explained in more detail in Chapter 2, Section E.

∎∎∎

J. Can You Receive A Public Employment Pension and Also Survivors' Benefits?

Your survivors' benefits are reduced by any <u>public</u> employee pension you receive based on your own work record. See Section E in this chapter for a complete explanation. Private pensions, on the other hand, do not affect your right to collect survivors' benefits.

How to Apply for Your Social Security Benefits

CHAPTER 5

HIGHLIGHTS

You will make the application process for any
Social Security benefit go more quickly and
smoothly if you gather together the necessary
papers before actually filing your claim (see
Section B, "Steps to Follow," Steps 5 and 6).

Always file a claim in writing and insist on
receiving a decision on your claim in writing;
then you will be able to appeal any decision you
disagree with (see Section C, "How Will You Find
Out What Happens to Your Claim?").

Most banks and savings associations can arrange
for your Social Security check to be sent directly
to the bank and deposited directly into one of
your accounts (see Section D, "How Do You Get Your
Benefit Check?").

You don't necessarily need a lawyer to appeal a
Social Security decision; free assistance may be
available to you from many sources (see Section E,
"What if Your Claim is Denied?").

"For age is opportunity no less
Than youth itself, though in another dress,
And as the evening twilight fades away
The sky is filled with stars, invisible by day."

Longfellow, *Morituri Salutamus*

■ ■ ■

A. Introduction

The three "P's" of dealing with the Social Security Administration are Preparation, Patience and Perseverance. You have to remember that this enormous government bureaucracy, like most others, is often poorly organized. Unfortunately, there is no particular reason or incentive for the organization itself to see to it that your claim is processed quickly and efficiently. And although individual workers are often helpful, polite and well-versed in the various regulations that govern Social Security programs, the maze of Social Security rules, when added to normal human fallibility, inevitably makes for some mistakes. So, it's up to you to decide to help yourself to the greatest extent possible, even if this occasionally means having to put your foot down--politely, of course--to insist on your rights. The best way to begin the Social Security process, of course, is to know your rights, organize the details of your claim, and start any application procedure early enough to give yourself, and the local Social Security workers, plenty of time to process your claim.

B. Steps to Follow in Making Your Claim

This chapter is arranged in steps for you to follow in getting yourself and your claim organized and ready to bring to the Social Security office.

How to Apply for Social Security

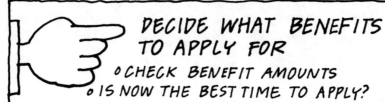 DECIDE WHAT BENEFITS TO APPLY FOR
o CHECK BENEFIT AMOUNTS
o IS NOW THE BEST TIME TO APPLY?

 GATHER DOCUMENTS, INFORMATION (SEE STEP 5.)

LOCATE SOCIAL SECURITY OFFICE o CHECK THE PHONE BOOK UNDER "UNITED STATES GOVERNMENT"

 IF YOU'RE APPLYING FOR DISABILITY SEE (SEE STEP 6)

VISIT THE SOCIAL SECURITY OFFICE
o BRING DOCUMENTS
o YOU WILL MEET WITH A WORKER

 BE SURE TO KEEP COPIES OF EVERYTHING!

PUT YOUR SOCIAL SECURITY NUMBER ON EACH DOCUMENT

 DURING THE INTERVIEW
o FILL OUT THE FORMS.
o SOME MAY BE COMPLETED AT HOME

 WAIT
o 6-10 WEEKS FOR SOCIAL SECURITY NOTIFICATION
o 3-6 MONTHS FOR A DISABILITY DECISION

 A CHECK WILL BE SENT IN THE MAIL.

Step 1. Know Your Rights

By reading this book, you are making a good start at
satisfying this requirement and getting an overview of the
various types of Social Security benefits you can apply for.
You're only part-way through Step 1, though, because you
will probably want to refer back a number of times to the
sections that particularly apply to you and to double-check
the information you read there with your local Social Security office.

■

Step 2. Plan Your Benefits

It may be a good idea, after going through the book, to
write out a list of all the various benefits and rights to
which you might be entitled--Social Security benefits plus
other benefits and rights discussed in other chapters of the
book. Then compare the rules for each program to see
whether claiming one benefit may affect your right to collect others. Also, double-check any rules concerning the
time in which you have to claim benefits. Only after you
have an idea of all the benefits and rights to which you are
entitled will you be able to make the best decision about
what Social Security and other benefits to claim, and when
to claim them. Perhaps Social Security benefits and Medicare will be the only benefits or rights discussed in the
book which apply to you. Or perhaps you will have to figure
out how your Social Security, private pension, public pension, veterans' benefits and right to keep working all
relate to one another. In any event, take the time to look
carefully at all the various benefits and their rules before
you decide which benefits to apply for. Remember, the more
organized you are in dealing with these benefits and rights,
the more likely you are to ensure you will get all the
benefits and rights to which you are entitled.

■

Step 3. Check Your Benefit Amounts Before Filing Your Claim

As we've mentioned several times now, you may be eligible for different benefit amounts, depending on when you
claim your benefit and on which benefits you and your spouse
claim. Your decision about when, and which benefits, to
claim can be best made when you know what the amounts would
be for the various benefits to which you would be entitled.
As explained in Chapter 1, Section E, you may request a copy

of your earnings record and ask that your local Social Security office give you estimates of what your various benefits would be if you claimed them at different ages. Do this advance checking several months before you would become eligible for a particular benefit. This will both give the Social Security workers plenty of time to figure out what your benefits would be and give you plenty of time to make an informed decision about which claims to file and when to file them.

■

Step 4. Find Your Local Social Security Office

To talk to the people at your local Social Security office, you first have to find it. Fortunately, that's not so hard to do: there are lots of them. Every medium to large city has one or more local Social Security offices and in major urban areas there are several local offices to choose from. You can find the address and telephone number of the office closest to you by looking in the white pages of your telephone directory under the listing for United States Government, Social Security Administration (or sometimes under United States Government, Department of Health and Human Services, Social Security Administration or just under "SSA.")

Many general questions you may have about Social Security claims or benefits, as well as Medicare coverage, can be answered over the phone. Most areas have a sort of Social Security "hotline" over which workers answer general questions about benefits and rules, including how to fill out a form, when to file a certain paper, etc. But specific questions about your particular claim can best be answered by the Social Security worker who is assigned to oversee your case.

How do you get a worker assigned to your case? When you file a claim for benefits, you are usually assigned a "service worker." You will want to write this person's name down and keep it with your other Social Security papers. When you file your claim, the claim will be assigned a number (usually just the worker's Social Security number). Should you have a question about your claim, call or go to the local office and ask to speak with your particular service worker; always refer to you claim number as well as giving your full name.

Although many papers and forms can be sent to the local office through the mail, it is best to deliver important papers in person. That way the papers will get to your service worker in the shortest possible time and you will avoid the adventures that sometimes befall anything entrusted to your postal service. There are two things always to remember when you submit papers to the Social Security office: always attach your claim number to each paper you submit; and always keep a copy of every form, paper or document you submit. Things have a way of getting lost in big government offices, so you'll want to keep copies of all your papers in case you need to file a replacement. If you are filing more than one claim, organize your papers according to the claim they relate to, and try to keep them in some kind of chronological order. The more organized your papers are, the easier it will be for you to find them if Social Security needs to see them in processing your claim.

■

Step 5. Gather the Information Needed to Take to Social Security

The waiting time for service in most local Social Security offices is longer than one would like. A number of people have suggested the most important things to take with you to Social Security are a sandwich and something to read. But personal needs aside, you will want to bring the following. Again, remember to keep copies of everything at home.

■Your Social Security card (or your Social Security number if you have lost your card).

■If you are applying as a dependent or survivor, then you must bring the card or Social Security number of the person on whose work record you are applying.

■Proof of your age: this could be a birth or baptismal certificate, a passport, a census record,* school records, marriage certificate, life insurance policy, family bible with birth dates, or any other document that tends to establish your age. If there is some question about your age, bring as many of these documents as possible.

---

* You may write to the United States Department of Commerce, Bureau of the Census, Washington, D.C. and request an "Application for Search of Census Records." They will send you an application and will do a search of the records to find your birth date (cost is $8.00).

■ Your marriage certificate, if you are applying as a dependent or surviving spouse. If you are not legally married but believe you have or had a "common-law marriage," read Chapter 1, Section F.

■ Your children's birth certificates, if you are applying for them as dependents or survivors.

■ Your W-2 forms (or federal income tax returns if you are self-employed) for the previous two years (or the forms for the person on whose earnings record you are claiming benefits) so that the earnings record can be brought up to date.

■ Proof of military service, if any; extra work credits may be given for active military duty.

■ If applying as a dependent parent who was receiving support from your son or daughter who has died, take a recent tax return from your deceased child which shows you as a dependent, or take proof of expenditures by your deceased child showing how much support was given to you.

REMINDER: Even if you are having trouble getting these papers together, don't delay in filing your claim. After the claim process is started you will have time to collect and file the rest of the required documents; your Social Security caseworker may assist you in getting the papers you need.

■

Step 6. Special Information Needed for Disability Applications

If you are thinking of applying for disability benefits, don't wait to gather all the information and doctors' reports (the information you need to gather and the procedures to follow are discussed in detail below) before you file your claim. File the claim as soon as you suspect your medical condition may prevent you from working for anything close to a year. Disability claims take three to six months to be processed, so get things moving as soon as a medical condition forces you off work.

Because disability eligibility depends upon your physical or mental condition, and your inability to work because of that condition, the application process is much more complicated and time-consuming than it is for other Social Security benefits.

When you file an application for disability, take with you to the Social Security office the following papers:

- Your Social Security number and proof of age for each person eligible for dependents' benefits;

- Names, addresses and phone numbers of doctors, hospitals, clinics and institutions that have treated you and the approximate dates of treatment;

- A summary of where you have worked in the past 15 years;

- A copy of your W-2 forms (or your federal income tax returns if you're self-employed) for the past two years;

- The dates of your military service, if any;

- If your spouse is applying as a dependent, the dates of any prior marriages;

- The claim number for any other check you receive or are scheduled to receive because of your disability;

- If you are applying as a disabled widow or widower, the death certificate of the worker on whose earning record you are applying; and

- If you are applying as a disabled surviving divorced husband or wife, bring proof that your marriage lasted ten years (marriage certificate and divorce papers).

NOTE: If you are unable to get to a Social Security office in person, some or all of your claim may be filed through the mail and over the phone. And if you are physically unable to complete the forms or meet other filing requirements, your application can be completed by your spouse, parent, other relative, friend or legal guardian.

■

Step 7. File All Your Claims in Writing

Always file a formal, written claim for every benefit to which you believe you may be entitled. Don't accept an "Oh, I can save you the trouble--you are not eligible for that one" from a well-meaning Social Security worker who doesn't think you will qualify for a particular benefit. The only "trouble" is the extra work for the Social Security worker; for you, if there is even a remote possibility that you would qualify for a benefit, it's worth it. Insist on your right to file a claim. The only way to fully protect your right to claim a particular benefit, or to appeal the wrongful denial of a benefit, is to file a written claim for that benefit and to receive a written decision. Be polite--remember, you may need the worker's assistance at some point, and Social Security workers have a lot of other cases to deal with besides yours. But don't take "Don't bother" for an answer.

■

Step 8. Cooperate With the Disability Determination Services

If you apply for disability benefits, when your claim has been completed and the local Social Security office has checked to see that you meet all the general requirements, they will forward your claim to a special Disability Determination Services (DDS) office in your state. The DDS people will decide whether or not you are "disabled" under the rules of the Social Security law. A doctor and a disability evaluation specialist for DDS will examine your medical records. They may request more information from you, your doctors or your employers and in some instances they will request that you undergo further medical examination or testing. The cost of these additional reports, examinations or tests are paid by the government; if travel expenses are involved, the government may pay for some of these, too. Even though you may not be thrilled by the idea of going through more medical examinations by strange doctors or having to be put through more medical testing, you'll have to put up with a certain amount of it; cooperation with the DDS is essential for a speedy and successful processing of your disability claim.

■

Step 9. Relax and Take A Deep Breath

In fact, take a few deep breaths. Understanding your rights may not have been easy, but it will definitely be worth the effort. Assuming you have followed the steps set out here and the instructions given by the Social Security people about filing your claim, you should receive all the benefits to which you are entitled as soon as you are entitled to them.

C. How Will You Find Out What Happens to Your Claim?

Social Security will notify you in writing whether or not your claim or claims have been approved, how much your benefits will be and when you'll get your first check. It may take from six to ten weeks for retirement claims to be approved.* Disability claims take three to six months.

If your claim has been denied, or if your claim has been accepted but for less benefits than you think you are entitled to, you have a right to appeal the decision. The written notice of denial will normally state the reasons why the claim was denied. The appeal process must be started within 60 days from the date you receive written notice of the denial or other decision. The appeal process is explained in full in Section E of this chapter.

---

* If you do not receive action on your claim for survivors' benefits after 90 days, you are entitled to make a demand for immediate payment; if you appear to be eligible for benefits and the delay is causing a hardship, a check must be issued to you within 15 days of your demand.

Remember, always make sure you get a written notice of any Social Security decision. Only by receiving a written decision will you have something concrete from which to appeal if you have been denied some benefit to which you believe you are entitled. Even if your claim is approved, get the decision in writing; it may turn out later that it was not approved for the right amount, or that it began later than it should have. If you've got written proof of the date and content of the decision, you'll have a much easier time correcting any mistakes that were made.

D. How Do You Get Your Benefit Check?

All Social Security checks, from all the benefit programs, are sent through the mail at about the same time, close to the third of every month. If your check does not arrive on or near its usual day, call your local Social Security office right away to report it lost. Be ready to give your name as it usually appears on your check, your Social Security claim number, the amount and type of check you receive and the day you usually receive it. The local office will start the process of getting you a replacement check. This usually takes 20 to 30 days.

1. Direct Deposit

If you don't want to count on the mails and would like to save yourself a monthly trip to the bank, you can have your bank arrange with Social Security to deposit your check automatically in your checking or savings account. Most banks provide this direct deposit service and will supply you with the necessary form to fill out. A bank officer will help you complete the form if you find it confusing.

2. Substitute Payee

If a person entitled to Social Security benefits is unable to care for him or herself, a family member or friend who cares for the person, or a legal representative, may be appointed as substitute payee and receive the benefit checks on behalf of the recipient. Anyone proposing to be a substitute payee must bring medical proof (letter from the payee's doctor) that the payee is unable to care for himself. In addition, the substitute payee must sign a sworn affidavit at the Social Security office stating that he or she will use the Social Security check for the benefit of the payee. If you have already been appointed by a court to serve as the payee's legal guardian or conservator, proof of that court appointment is all that is required.

The rules require that a substitute payee deposit and keep the money belonging to the person entitled to Social Security in a separate bank account. A periodic accounting is made by Social Security to determine how the substitute payee has spent the money to care for the beneficiary. Bills, receipts, etc. should be kept in a systematic and organized way so they can be produced easily for this periodic accounting.

3. Protected Benefit Status

Social Security benefits are not subject to state or federal income taxes. And in general, they may not be attached by creditors or persons having obtained a legal judgment against you. If Social Security benefits are kept in a separate bank account that is attached, they can be returned to you under exemption laws. You will probably need the help of a private lawyer or the legal aid society to accomplish this, however.

E. What If Your Claim Is Denied?— Your Right to Appeal

No matter how carefully you follow Social Security rules and regulations, you may wind up being denied eligibility for a benefit to which you believe you are entitled. But that doesn't end the matter--far from it. Virtually any decision of the Social Security Administration can be appealed. Whether your new benefit or Medicare claim has been denied entirely, or your existing benefits are to be reduced or ended, you may appeal the decision as long as you follow some fairly simple rules. Those rules are outlined in the following section, step by step.

The first question that may occur to you when considering an appeal is "Is it worth the effort?" The answer is almost always, "Yes." The decision that you think is incorrect may affect your rights for many, many years. If you can get the decision partially or completely reversed, you will almost surely have an easier time making financial ends meet. Seen in this light, almost any effort is worth it. You should know, too, that appealing a Social Security decision is far from hopeless. A substantial percentage of decisions are changed on appeal. Disability claim appeals are particularly likely to result in a favorable change; almost half of all disability benefit denials are modified at some point in the appeal process. And appealing a Social Security claim need not be as difficult as you might imagine. If you have properly organized for and prepared your original claim, most of your work for the appeal is already done. In many situations the appeal will require little more from you than giving you another opportunity to explain why the information you already presented should qualify you for a benefit. Certainly the thousands and thousands of people who have successfully appealed Social Security decisions would tell you--"It's worth the effort."

"As if old age were never kindly as well as frosty; as if it had no reverend graces of its own as good in their way as the noisy impertinence of childhood, the elbowing self-conceit of youth, or the pompous mediocrity of middle life.!"

James Russell Lowell, *A Good Word for Winter*

■ ■ ■

How to Appeal a Social Security Decision

IF YOUR SOCIAL SECURITY CLAIM IS DENIED...

ORGANIZE YOUR PAPERS
o CONSIDER GETTING ASSISTANCE

FILE A FORMAL APPEAL
- DO THIS WITHIN 60 DAYS OF DENIAL
- YOUR FILE WILL BE CHECKED FOR MISTAKES
- DECISION IS BY MAIL

REQUEST AN ADMINISTRATIVE HEARING
o WITHIN 60 DAYS OF DENIAL
o CONSIDER ASSISTANCE

HEARING DATE ASSIGNED

HEARING
o A-NOT-TOO-FORMAL AFFAIR OFTEN AT A SOCIAL SECURITY OFFICE.
o DECISION SENT BY MAIL IN ABOUT 30 DAYS

DECIDE TO GO TO COURT
o GET A LAWYER

FILE AN APPEAL WITH NATIONAL APPEALS COUNCIL, WASHINGTON D.C.
o WITHIN 60 DAYS OF DENIAL
o A FORMALITY IF YOU FILE SUIT.

FILE A LAWSUIT IN FEDERAL COURT

Here is how to file your appeal:

Step 1. Organize Your Papers

Gather all the papers you have concerning your claim and put them in chronological order, including the written notice of decision from Social Security. Assuming that you have kept a neat file, this should be easy. Make sure you have copies of each of the papers. If you get any additional information for the appeal, keep it in a separate file from the papers you actually submitted during the original claim. This just helps you keep it straight as to which information was originally submitted and which information is "new."

■

Step 2. Consider Getting Some Assistance

In many cases, assistance in preparing or presenting your appeal is not necessary, particularly in the early stages of the appeal. But if your appeal is complicated, and particularly if it involves medical issues, you may well want to get some advice or even formal legal representation early in the appeal process. Such advice or representation can range from simply talking over your appeal with a knowledgeable friend or relative, to having a person who specializes in Social Security problems go over your papers with you, make suggestions, and assist you at hearings, to having a lawyer prepare and present the appeal on your behalf. Whether to use some kind of formal representative--lawyer or not--depends on:

- How complicated your case is

- How much money is at stake

- How comfortable you feel in handling the matter yourself

- How far along in the appeals process you go

- Whether or not such representation is available to you

Many senior centers have regularly scheduled sessions during which trained Social Security advocates can give you advice on your Social Security and Medicare problems. If the senior center near you has no such program, or the program cannot handle your particular problem, or you cannot make it to the center to get the advice they offer, referrals to Social Security advocates (people trained to assist in Social Security matters) are usually available. Such advocates are also available at or through the offices of legal services for seniors which exist in many large cities.

Each state also has its own agency or department which handles problems regarding aging. They are referred to, variously, as the Office, Department, Bureau, Division, Agency, Commission, Council, Administration or Center . . . on Aging. In most cases, this state agency will be able to refer you to someplace close to your home where you can obtain assistance in preparing and presenting your Social Security appeal. You can find your state's agency on aging by looking in the white pages of your local telephone directory under the listing for your state government offices; the agency on aging will either be listed under its own heading, or there will be a listing for a department or agency of Human Services, Social Services, Health and Human Services, Civil Rights or something similar, a sub-agency of which will be the agency on aging. Call them and explain that you are looking for someone to assist you with a problem concerning Social Security. They will usually steer you to a Social Security advocate or legal aid office which handles Social Security matters. And don't forget that your church, social group, business association or union may also have a referral service which can put you in touch with Social Security advocates.

Finally, you may want to contact a private attorney regarding your appeal. But be wary, here. Lawyers tend to cost a lot of money, and many know very little about Social Security. There are lawyers, however, who do specialize in Social Security claims, and although they cost money, there are times when their help may be worth it. You are entitled to a lawyer or nonlawyer representative at all stages of your Social Security appeal.* But if you get to the point where you are considering taking your appeal to court (see Step 6), then consultation with a lawyer is strongly advised. Through federally funded legal services offices (sometimes listed in the phone book under legal aid), you may be able to obtain legal advice and representation for little or no money. Because of budget cutbacks, however, these services can be difficult to obtain. That doesn't mean you shouldn't try to get a legal services lawyer, however. They are often extremely knowledgeable when it comes to Social Security questions. Remember, your claim probably involves benefits which, if granted, will involve a lot of money over the years. It may well be worth some money now

---

* If you are going to be represented in your appeal process, you must fill out a Social Security form which officially designates this person as your representative.

to seek and obtain legal advice and perhaps representation. If none of the senior referral offices can put you in contact with a lawyer who specializes in Social Security appeals, and you can't get help from legal services, call the state or local bar association. They will refer you.

■

Step 3. File A Request for Reconsideration

The first formal step in the appeal process is to file, or have your representative file, a written request for reconsideration of the "initial determination" of your claim (the decision denying benefits). Your local Social Security office has the form necessary for your request for reconsideration, or you can make the request by letter. Remember to include the date, your Social Security number, and your claim number on all appeal papers filed with the Social Security Administration. Your written request must be filed with a Social Security office within 60 days from the date you receive the written decision denying your claim. Remember, keep a copy of your "reconsideration request," as you should keep a copy of all papers filed with Social Security.

What does a Social Security reconsideration consist of? Your claim and all the evidence in your file will be re-examined by someone in the Social Security office other than the person who made the decision on your claim the first time around. You may present additional written information and should do so if you feel you have any information not already in the official file. In addition, the person doing the review may ask you for more information.

At this stage, there is no formal hearing or opportunity to make a formal appeal in person to the Social Security worker doing the reconsideration, nor can you present witnesses to attest to your eligibility for the particular benefits you are seeking. You or your representative can, however, ask to speak informally with the person who is doing the reconsideration. Though they are not required to do so, some Social Security workers will be willing to speak with you informally about the reconsideration; others, unfortunately, will refuse to do so.

You should receive a written notice of the decision made on your request for reconsideration. If you do not receive a written notice within 30 days after you have completed information regarding reconsideration, you should demand one from the local Social Security office. Only by having a written decision can you move on to the next stage of the appeal process, if necessary.

■

Step 4. Request An Administrative Hearing

If after reconsideration your claim is again denied, you may request a formal administrative hearing. This hearing is actually your best chance to have the denial of your claim reversed. You must file a written request (on a Social Security request form or in a letter) for an administrative hearing within 60 days after you receive written notice of the denial of your claim after reconsideration. The hearing will not take place for several months, so you will have plenty of time to prepare for it. However you should use your time wisely, as you may only receive notice of the exact date of the hearing about two weeks before it is to be held. So don't wait to the last minute to get organized--gather your materials, meet and discuss your claim with the attorney or advocate who will assist or represent you at the hearing, if you choose to use one, and discuss the case with any witnesses you may need to have testify at the hearing. You also have a right to examine your file at the Social Security office to see that all the papers you have filed have found their way into the file. It is an excellent idea to do this, as it will allow you to review all of both the positive and negative information that Social Security has.

If you will be unable to attend the hearing on the date that has been scheduled, you can reschedule it by calling your local Social Security office. Do this as soon as you receive notice of the date. Remember, though, that if you do reschedule, you will probably have to wait another several months before the next hearing is scheduled. Even if you do not have all the evidence (papers, documents, etc.) collected by the time of the hearing, it may be best for you to go ahead with the hearing, explain the situation to the hearing judge, and ask that the judge's decision be delayed until you have had the opportunity to submit these additional papers. This is not an unusual procedure, and as long as you have a good reason for not having the evidence at the hearing (other than "I didn't get around to it"), the judge will most probably grant your request for a delay in the decision.

The hearing itself will be conducted in a style some-where between the formality of a courtroom and the infor-mality of discussions with your original service worker. An administrative law judge will preside, and everything that is said or done in the hearing will be recorded. You may be represented or assisted at the hearing by a lawyer or other advocate, or by a friend or relative. You may present any evidence you would like the judge to consider, including documents and reports, and you may present the testimony of any witnesses you would like to have help prove your claim. If there are witnesses who will not appear voluntarily, you may have them subpoenaed (ordered by the judge) to appear at the hearing. If you need any witnesses subpoenaed, you must notify the judge's office at least five days before the hearing. And, finally, at the hearing itself you will be given an opportunity to explain, in your own words, why you think your claim should be upheld.

The administrative law judge who presides at your hear-ing is a lawyer who works for the Social Security Adminis-tration, but has taken no part in the original claim deci-sion or in the reconsideration of your claim. The judge will follow certain rules of procedure and may ask you some difficult questions about your claim, but in general the hearing will be run in a relaxed way. If you are not sure how to go about presenting certain information to the judge, just explain your problem and the judge will help you get the information into "the record" of the case.

The judge will issue a written decision on your appeal, usually within a few weeks of your hearing. If your claim has been denied by the administrative law judge, you will have 60 days from the date you receive written notice of the denial to file a further appeal. If your claim is approved, you may be entitled to receive benefits dating all the way back to the time you filed your original claim.

■

Step 5. File An Appeal With the National Appeals Council

If your appeal has been denied after an administrative hearing, your next recourse is to file a written appeal with the Social Security Administration Appeals Council in Wash-ington, D.C. A written request must be filed within 60 days from the date you receive the notice of the administrative law judge's decision. Forms for requesting this appeal are available at your local Social Security office.

Unfortunately, your appeal to the Appeals Council is not likely to meet much success. The Appeals Council rarely accepts a case for actual hearing, and when it does, the Council meets only in Washington, D.C. If you want to appear at the hearing, you've got to go--or send a representative--to the hearing in Washington. Most people don't even request to appear, and instead send a written statement to the Appeals Council. The Council then decides the case based on the papers in the file and on the written statement submitted. With or without an actual hearing, the success rate of people filing claims with the Appeals Council is very low. Nonetheless, filing the appeal is important. For only by filing this appeal will you have fulfilled the procedural requirement for moving on to the next real step, which is filing a lawsuit against the Social Security Administration in federal court.

■

"Age takes from the intelligent man no qualities except those which are useless to wisdom."

Joseph Joubert, *Pensees*

Step 6. File A Lawsuit in Federal Court

If you feel your claim has been unjustly denied, and you have unsuccessfully exhausted all the Social Security Administration appeals procedures, you are entitled to bring a lawsuit against the Social Security Administration in federal district court. You must file the initial papers of this lawsuit within 60 days of the mailing of the Appeals Council's decision. Though a federal court lawsuit is a complicated and expensive procedure, it may be worth it for you if the benefits you are seeking would be considerable. When you add up the total amount of benefits you might receive in your lifetime should your claim be approved, you may find that there is a lot of money at stake. If the amount seems worth the time and effort to you, then you should at least investigate the possibility of filing a lawsuit.

While you may want to get legal assistance at some earlier stage of the appeal process, you will certainly want to get trained legal assistance if you intend to file a lawsuit in federal court. Consult with a lawyer as to your chances of winning a lawsuit based on the facts of your case. And make sure that you have found a lawyer who specializes in doing Social Security appeals. (As with selecting a doctor, it's sometimes a good idea to get a second opinion from a different lawyer before you take any action.) The main things to weigh in deciding whether actually to file a lawsuit are your chances of winning, the money it will cost you to fight the legal "battle," and the amount of money in benefits that you stand to gain. If, when you balance all these things, it still seems like a good idea to go ahead with the lawsuit, good luck.

HIGHLIGHTS

Even if you are not eligible for any Social Security benefits, you may be eligible for free Medicare hospitalization coverage if you are 65 or over [see Section D].

A prolonged hospital stay is only partially paid for by Medicare hospital insurance, but the much less expensive alternative of recuperation in a skilled nursing facility is covered by Medicare hospital insurance after you leave the hospital [see Section H(3) and Section J(5)].

Medicare pays for an unlimited number of visits to your home by a home health care agency if you are confined to your home and need some part-time nursing care or physical therapy; you do not need to have been hospitalized to take advantage of this Medicare coverage [see Section H(5) & Q].

You can save yourself a large amount of money in doctor's bills if you make sure before you receive treatment that your doctor accepts "assignment" of Medicare's "approved charges" as the full amount of your bill [see Section N(2) and R(a)(2)].

Medicare medical insurance will pay 100 percent of doctor's bills, instead of the normal 80 percent, for surgery performed on an outpatient basis [see Section O(3)].

Routine physical examinations are not normally covered by Medicare, but if your doctor gives you a complete physical as part of attempting to diagnose and treat symptoms you have, Medicare may pay 80 percent of the reasonable cost of the examination [see Section P(1)].

"Your Money or Your Life" Health Coverage Under Medicare

C H A P T E R   6

■ ■ ■

"Well, the doctor comes around with
    his face all bright;
And he says in a little while you'll
    be all right.
All he gives is a humbug pill,
Dose of dope and a great big bill.
Tell me how can a poor man stand such
    times and live?"

Alfred Reed, *How Can a Poor Man Stand Such
    Times and Live?*

A. Introduction

The United States and South Africa are reported to be the only industrialized nations in the world without a national health insurance program. And the United States is perhaps the world's only so-called developed nation in which virtually all medical services--hospitals, clinics, pharmacies, drug companies, doctors, nurses--are operated for profit. The resulting horrendous expense for medical care, coupled with the lack of comprehensive national health insurance, rightfully has been termed a national disgrace.

Regardless of the amount of their retirement savings, almost all Americans on fixed incomes fear the financial jaws of any serious medical crisis. If you've ever been faced with even a brief stay in a hospital or the need for a doctor's care, you know that getting sick or injured can be an economic catastrophe for you and your family. Since 1950, the cost of a hospital stay has risen more than 1,000 percent, eight times greater than the rise in the overall Consumer Price Index. In 1980, the average hospital stay cost more than $3,000; when the final figures are in for 1982, it is expected the average cost will be well over $3,500. What about 1983? And what about total medical costs? In 1970, Americans spent about $75 billion on medical care; in 1982, it is estimated the figure was close to $300 billion. How much is $300 billion? It's over one-tenth of our entire gross national product. What do these figures mean for you? In 1980, the average out-of-pocket medical costs for the year for persons 65 or over was more than $2,100; in 1983, that average may well reach $3,000 on top of whatever medical insurance coverage you may have.

In 1965, Congress made the first inroad into this growing "national disgrace" by passing a law creating what is now called Medicare. During 1982, almost 30 million Americans--most aged 65 or over--were covered by Medicare. But "covered," when applied to what Medicare recipients actually receive in reimbursement for medical costs, is a very misleading term. Although Medicare does pay for much of the cost of hospitalization and some of the cost of medical care when you have a serious illness or injury, there are many costs which are not covered at all. In fact, when all types of medical costs for those 65 and up are totalled, it turns out that Medicare pays for only about 40 percent. In an era of skyrocketing medical costs, that uncovered 60 percent can prove to be a financial nightmare for you and your family, particularly if you are living on a fixed and limited income. Indeed, there are some people who contend that considering the astronomical increases in medical costs, particularly hospitalization, it may actually cost more out-of-pocket today for a Medicare recipient to receive adequate medical care than it did for the same level of care in 1964, before Medicare. Nevertheless, Medicare is now an important part of the lives of older Americans, and for many it is the difference between being able to afford decent medical care and going without.

If you want to take maximum advantage of Medicare, and protect yourself against the gaps in Medicare's coverage, you've got to be well-informed about precisely how Medicare does, and does not, work. The following sections of this chapter explain in detail what Medicare pays for and what you must pay for. Our effort has been, as far as possible, to do this without technical medical or bureaucratic language. This chapter gives you the information necessary to make sure your health care providers (doctors, hospitals, nursing facilities, physical therapists, et. al.) are paid by Medicare for as much of their bills as possible. It explains step-by-step how to prepare and file your Medicare claims. And finally, the two following chapters explore what additional types of coverage are available--Medicaid, private insurance, health maintenance organizations--to protect you against the medical costs Medicare does not pay for.

"Give me health and a day and I will make the pomp of emperors ridiculous."

> Emerson,
> *Nature, Addresses & Lectures: Beauty*

■ ■ ■

B. Medicare: What Is It?

Medicare is a federal government program to assist senior and some disabled Americans to pay for their medical costs. It is run by the Health Care Financing Administration, part of the Department of Health and Human Services, in cooperation with the Social Security Administration. The program is divided into two parts: Part A is "hospital insurance," covering most of your bills for a stay in the hospital or skilled nursing facility; Part B is "medical insurance," paying some of the cost of doctors and out-patient medical care. Since it is a federal program, Medicare's rules are the same in every state. Medicare's daily business, however, is run by private companies, called "carriers" or "intermediaries," operating under contract with the government. Most of your direct contact with Medicare comes with the company--usually Blue Cross/Blue Shield or one of the other large insurance companies--which administers Medicare in your area.

IMPORTANT: Remember that Medicare is <u>not</u> welfare or charity. Eligibility is not tied to individual need. Rather, Medicare is medical protection you have earned as a result of your contributions over the years to the common economic good of the country. Like most of the other programs discussed in this book, Medicare is an <u>entitlement</u> program; you are entitled to it because you have earned it. Medicare is also the result, at least in part, of the recognition that older citizens have medical bills significantly higher than the rest of the population, while our society makes it much more difficult for seniors to continue to earn enough money to cover these higher medical bills.

About one out of every eight Americans is entitled to Medicare coverage. If you are one of the almost 30 million Americans who has earned Medicare coverage, it is essential that you know what your rights are under the program in order to be sure you receive everything you are <u>entitled</u> to.

C. Medicare and Medicaid: Which Is Which?

Sometimes people get a little confused as to the differences between the two programs called Medicare and Medicaid. Medicaid is a federal-state program for low-income and needy people, administered differently in each state. Though you may qualify and receive coverage from both Medicare and Medicaid, there are separate eligibility requirements for each program; being eligible for one program does not necessarily mean you are eligible for the other. Medicaid is explained in full in Chapter 7. But for now, take a quick look at the differences between the two programs as indicated by this chart. It will help you keep straight in your mind what each program covers.

1. Medicare is for almost everyone 65 or older, rich or poor, for certain people on Social Security disability, and for some people with permanent kidney failure.

2. Medicare is an insurance program; people are entitled to Medicare from their Social Security contributions and payment of premiums.

3. Medicare is a federal program. Medicare rules are the same all over the country. Medicare information is available at your Social Security office.

4. Medicare Hospital Insurance (Part A) provides basic coverage for inpatient hospital stays and post-hospital nursing facility and home health care. You must pay a deductible and a share of the costs for a hospital stay over 60 days.

Medicare Medical Insurance (Part B) helps pay the cost of doctors, out-patient hospital and laboratory work, medical equipment and supplies, home health care, therapy, etc. Part B pays 80 percent of what it determines are "reasonable" charges, Part B charges a monthly premium (currently $12.20).

1. Medicaid is for low-income and needy people--over 65, the blind, the disabled, and in some states, others.

2. Medicaid is an assistance program for those eligible as "needy."

3. Medicaid is a federal-state cooperative program. Rules vary widely from state to state. Medicaid information is available at your local social services, welfare or Department of Human Services office.

4. Medicaid can pay for the Medicare deductibles and for the portion of the "reasonable charges" not paid by Medicare (20 percent). In many states, Medicaid will cover a number of services and costs Medicare does not cover, including prescription drug costs, dental care, diagnostic and preventive care, eyeglasses, etc. Medicaid can also pay for the Medicare premium.

D. Who Is Automatically Eligible for Medicare Part A (Hospital Insurance Coverage)?

1. If you are 65 or older and eligible for Social Security retirement benefits or for Railroad Retirement benefits (Railroad Retirement is explained in Chapter 10), you are automatically eligible for Medicare Part A, sometimes referred to as "hospital insurance," coverage. "Automatically" simply means you do not have to pay a monthly premium for Part A coverage. You will receive your Medicare Part A Coverage when you apply for retirement benefits at the local Social Security office. And you are eligible for automatic Medicare coverage even if you do not begin collecting your retirement benefits at 65, as long as you are eligible to collect retirement. In other words, if you wait to retire until after 65, you may still begin Medicare coverage at 65 if you apply for it. (If you begin collecting retirement benefits before age 65, you must still wait until 65 to get Medicare coverage.)

2.   If you are 65 and eligible to collect Social Security benefits as the dependent or survivor of a worker, you are automatically eligible for Part A of Medicare. If you are already receiving Social Security benefits, you will receive your Medicare card from Social Security in the mail by your 65th birthday. (If you don't receive it, contact your local Social Security office and make sure they send you one or know the reason why not.)

3.   Even if you are not eligible for Social Security benefits, you are eligible for Medicare Part A coverage if you reached age 65 before 1968. You must be either a U.S. citizen or have been lawfully in the United States for five consecutive years immediately before you apply for Medicare.

4.   There is a special transitional category of automatic eligibility for Medicare Part A for a few people who reached 65 before 1975 (before 1974 for women) but who are not eligible for Social Security benefits. If you reached 65 before 1974 (before 1975 for a man) and have three quarters of credit for work in covered employment for each year after 1966 before you reached age 65, you may be automatically eligible for Medicare Part A coverage (see Chapter 1, Section D, for an explanation of how "quarters" of credit are earned).

EXAMPLE: Marguerite Ray was born in Montreal, Quebec, Canada. Her father was French-Canadian, her mother was from Louisiana. Marguerite lived in Canada until 1968, when her husband died. Then she moved to New Orleans to be near two of her three children, her grandchildren and the rest of the family. She was 61 when she moved. Marguerite immediately got work teaching French and continued to work, part-time, until she retired at age 65 in 1972. Even though Marguerite did not have enough quarters of work credit in the U.S. to qualify for Social Security, she did qualify for Medicare Part A coverage because she had at least three quarters of work for each year after 1966 before she turned 65, and her 65th birthday was before 1974.

If you believe that this transition provision could apply to you, check with your local Social Security office for details.

5.   If you are under 65 but have been entitled to Social Security disability benefits for 24 months, you become eligible for Part A hospital insurance. (You do not actually have to have received disability payments for 24 months, you only need to have been entitled to them for that long).

6.   If, at any age, you, your spouse or any of your dependents has permanent kidney failure requiring either a

kidney transplant or maintenance dialysis, that person may be eligible for Part A hospital insurance, depending on whether you have worked a certain amount at jobs covered by Social Security. For details of this coverage, check with your local Social Security office.

E. Can You Obtain Medicare Part A Coverage If You Are Not Automatically Eligible For It?

If you are 65 or over but not automatically eligible for Part A hospital insurance coverage under any of the provisions described in Section D above, you can still enroll in the Medicare hospital insurance program at your local Social Security office. However, unlike those automatically eligible for Part A coverage, you will have to pay a monthly premium ranging from $113 up, depending on how long after your 65th birthday you wait to enroll. (The premium increases by 10 percent for each year after your 65th birthday during which you are not enrolled.)

Enrolling in Part A hospital insurance also requires that you enroll in Part B medical insurance, discussed in detail in the following section, which costs an additional $12.20 per month. You may enroll in Part B without Part A, but not vice-versa.

NOTE: If you are considering enrolling in and paying for Part A hospital insurance, it might be worth your time to compare several private insurance plans first. You may already belong to a plan, or be able to find one that has a premium in the same range as the Medicare premium but which provides better coverage than Medicare Part A.

F. How Do You Apply for Part A Hospital Insurance Coverage?

Application for Medicare coverage is made at your local Social Security office. You should apply about three months before your 65 birthday to make sure your coverage begins as soon as you turn 65. Often, people apply for Social Security retirement and Medicare at the same time. If you do, you will receive your Medicare card in the mail.

If you apply for Part A of Medicare within six months after you turn 65, your coverage will date back to your 65th birthday. But if you apply after that, your coverage can only date back 6 months from the month in which you apply.* If you have been receiving Social Security or Railroad Retirement benefits before you reach age 65, you do not need to fill out a separate application for Part A Medicare coverage. Your Medicare card will be sent to you, automatically, by your 65th birthday. Likewise, if you are receiving Social Security disability benefits, your Medicare card will be sent to you automatically after your twenty-fourth month on disability. In either case, if you do not receive your Medicare card in the mail immediately, report that fact to your local Social Security office so that you don't lose any period of coverage.

■■■

G. What To Do If You Are Denied Medicare Part A Coverage

Like any other decision of the Social Security Administration, a decision denying eligibility for Medicare Part A hospital insurance coverage can be appealed. The appeal process is described below, step by step; the process is explained in greater detail in Chapter 5, Section E. If you are considering an appeal, read Chapter 5 thoroughly.

Step 1

Discuss the matter informally at your local Social Security office. They may prove very helpful, and, in some

---

* If your Medicare eligibility is based on disability or kidney failure, your coverage can date back one year from the date you apply.

instances, may encourage you to appeal and help you organize your papers to get ready for the appeal. In other situations, however, you may find yourself confronted with an unsympathetic Social Security worker who simply can't or won't understand your situation. If this is the case, don't let yourself be talked out of or discouraged from filing your appeal. You should know that thousands of people who have been turned down initially in their application for Medicare have eventually won on appeal their right to receive full Medicare coverage.

Step 2

Within 60 days of the date you receive written notice that you have been denied Medicare eligibility, you must file a written request for reconsideration at your local Social Security office. The office will provide you with the form to use, or you can make your request by letter. Social Security will then review your file; this reconsideration is made by someone who was not involved in the original decision. You are not given any opportunity to make your appeal in person as part of this review. Nonetheless, you must go through with this step in order to be permitted to go on to the next steps of your appeal.

Step 3

Within 60 days of the date you receive written notice of the decision after reconsideration, you may request a hearing in front of a Social Security Administration administrative law judge. This semi-formal hearing is discussed in full in Chapter 5, Section E.

Step 4

If you disagree with the decision made at the hearing, you have 60 days from the date you receive notice of the decision to request a review by the Social Security Administration Appeals Council in Washington, D.C. (see Chapter 5, Section E).

Step 5

As with all other decisions of the Social Security Administration, once you have "exhausted" (and it is often exhausting) all these appeals procedures, you may file a lawsuit in federal court within 60 days of the Appeals Council decision, to enforce your rights to Medicare coverage (again, see Chapter 5, Section E).

Assistance in organizing and processing your appeal may be available from several sources; representation by a lawyer is almost certainly needed if you plan to file a lawsuit in federal court. Sources of this kind of assistance are discussed in Chapter 5, Section E, Step 2 ("Consider Getting Some Assistance").

H. What Type of Care Is Covered by Medicare Part A Hospital Insurance

1. General Requirements for Part A Coverage

In general, Part A hospital insurance pays for most of the costs you incur directly from a hospital, skilled nursing facility or home health care agency because of a medical condition requiring inpatient treatment.* But before the details of Part A coverage are explained, it is important for you to understand two basic rules which apply to all claims under Part A hospital insurance coverage:

a. Medically Reasonable and Necessary

In order to have your stay in a hospital or nursing facility, or your treatment by a home health agency, covered by Part A, the care you receive must be "medically reasonable and necessary." That means that Part A will not normally cover the cost of hospitalization for cosmetic or elective surgery and will only cover you if the care you do need can only be provided to you if you are in a hospital or nursing facility. In other words, if the condition could be treated at the hospital with you as an outpatient, or at the doctor's office or at your home, Part A will not cover you if you actually check in and become an inpatient for that medical condition.

b. Custodial Care

Part A hospital insurance will not pay for a stay in a hospital or nursing facility or for care from a home health agency when the services you receive from them are primarily to make life more comfortable for you--to help you with dressing, eating, bathing, moving around, etc.--rather than

---

* Doctors' bills are not included in Part A coverage; they are covered under Medicare Part B, which is discussed later in this chapter.

providing skilled medical care for treatment of the condition. Of course, this can often be a grey area and as you will see as you read on, one that sometimes results in disputes between Medicare and patients.

2. Specific Requirements for Part A Coverage

a. Inpatient Care Must be Medically Necessary

As explained above, it must be that the medically necessary treatment you receive in the hospital or skilled nursing facility can <u>only</u> be provided if you are an inpatient at the hospital or nursing facility.

b. The Hospital or Skilled Nursing Facility Must Be an Approved Facility

Always find out in advance if the facility to which you are being admitted as an inpatient is approved by Medicare and accepts Medicare payment. That can be done by checking with the admissions desk or the hospital administrator's office. There is an exception made for emergencies: if the hospital to which you are admitted in an emergency does not participate in Medicare, you will be reimbursed by Medicare for your bills there if that hospital was the closest to you at the time of a genuine emergency.

c. Your Treatment Must be Doctor-Prescribed

The specific care and treatment you receive in the hospital or skilled nursing facility must be prescribed by a doctor. In other words, there must be a physician who determines that you require certain medical care or service <u>and</u> that you must be in the hospital or nursing facility to receive that care.

3. Part A Coverage for a Stay in a Skilled Nursing Facility

The much less expensive alternative of skilled nursing facility care is getting increasing attention as hospital costs go through the roof. Since Medicare does not pay for all the costs of inpatient hospital care, you may want to consider saving quite a bit of money by moving to a skilled nursing facility for any fairly long period of convalescence after an initial stay in a hospital. Unfortunately, Medicare coverage for a stay in a skilled nursing facility is not automatic; you must meet two special requirements, in addition to the standard conditions, for all inpatient coverage discussed just above in Sections H (1 & 2). And there are limits on how much Medicare will pay for a stay in a skilled nursing facility [see Section J(5)].

a. Prior Hospital Stay Required

Your stay in the skilled nursing facility must come after you have spent at least three consecutive days (not counting the day of discharge) in a hospital. Also, you must be admitted to the nursing facility within 30 days of your discharge from the hospital. This 30-day grace period gives you a chance to find room in an appropriate facility and also lets you see if you are able to convalesce at home instead of in a nursing facility. If you leave the nursing facility to try to make it at home (or in the home of a friend or relative), but must be readmitted to the nursing facility within 30 days, you do <u>not</u> need another hospital stay to qualify for Part A Medicare coverage.

b. Daily Skilled Nursing Care Required

Your doctor must certify that you require daily skilled nursing care or skilled rehabilitative services for the same condition or combination of conditions for which you were hospitalized. In other words, you must be in the nursing facility so that you can daily receive actual skilled nursing treatment--injections, changing of dressings, the monitoring of vital signs, the administering of medicines or treatments, etc. which cannot be performed by untrained personnel--or rehabilitative services by professional therapists. If you are in the nursing facility only because you are unable to feed, clothe, bathe or move yourself, even though these restrictions are the result of your medical condition, you are not eligible for Part A coverage since you do not require "skilled nursing care" or skilled rehabilitative services. (If you only require occasional part-time nursing care, you may be eligible for what is called Home Health Care coverage under Part A or Part B of Medicare. Home Health Care coverage is explained in detail later in this chapter.)

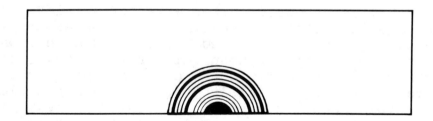

4. Coverage for a Stay in a Foreign Hospital

Generally, Medicare does not cover you outside of the United States, Puerto Rico, the Virgin Islands, Guam and American Samoa. There are, however, three minor exceptions to this rule:

a. If you are in the United States when an emergency occurs and a Canadian or Mexican hospital is closer than any U.S. Hospital to provide the emergency services you need, Medicare will help pay for your care at that foreign hospital.

b. If you live in the United States and a Mexican or Canadian hospital is closer to your home than the nearest U.S. hospital providing the care you need (and if, of course, you choose to go there), Medicare can cover your care there even if there is no emergency.

c. If you are in Canada while traveling directly to Alaska from one of the other states, or from Alaska directly to one of the other states and an emergency arises, you will be covered for your care at a Canadian hospital. This does not, however, cover you if you are vacationing in Canada.

CAUTION: Since there is no protection for you through Medicare while you are traveling outside the United States, it might be wise for you to look into "traveler's insurance." These short-term policies are available for a one-time only premium and cover you (under various terms and conditions) while you are abroad. A travel agent should be able to provide you with one of these policies or give you information on where to obtain such coverage.

5. Home Health Care Coverage Under Part A Hospital Insurance*

In the past several years, there has been a nationwide move by consumers and progressive health care professionals to encourage people to get out of hospitals and into their own homes while recovering from injury or illness. In response to this move, home health care agencies have expanded considerably. There are more of them, available to more people in more areas, providing virtually all of the services required by patients who no longer need surgical or

---

* Home health care coverage is also available under Medicare Part B medical insurance. See Section Q of this chapter.

intensive care in a hospital but who still require part-time skilled nursing care and/or physical therapy.

The benefits of properly administered home health care can be enormous. In the first place, the friendly surroundings of your own home, or a friend or relative's, are often more conducive to a speedy recovery than the impersonal and sometimes frightening environment of a hospital. You have familiar things around you, your friends and family can come and go as you and they please and they can lend a hand with your care. You have greater privacy and are free from dreadful hospital routines which are often more disturbing than preventive or curative. The other obvious advantage of home health care is that it is far, far less expensive than a stay in the hospital or in a nursing facility.

If you are interested in home health care as a way of shortening your stay in the hospital or as an alternative to any stay at all in a hospital or nursing facility, you can contact a home health care agency directly or have your doctor or the hospital discharge planner contact an agency for you. Help in locating home health care agencies can also be obtained through a local Social Security office, community health organization, visiting nurses association, United Way, Red Cross or neighborhood senior center.

Of course, Medicare places certain conditions on coverage under Part A for home health care services.

a. The agency providing the care must "participate" in Medicare, meaning it must be approved by Medicare and must accept Medicare payment. Since not all agencies participate in Medicare, make sure you double-check before you make any arrangements for care.

b. You must be confined to your home by an injury, illness or other medical condition. If you need nursing care or other medical services but you are able to leave home on a regular, daily basis, you might not be eligible for home health care coverage under Part A hospital insurance.

c. You must require part-time skilled nursing care or physical or speech therapy. Part A coverage will not pay for full-time nursing, however. Once home health care coverage has begun, Medicare can continue to pay for it even if you only need occupational therapy, though occupational therapy alone cannot justify home health care coverage in the first place.

d. Your doctor must determine that you need home health care and must help set up a plan for the care in cooperation with the home health care agency. Though some doctors still resist the idea of home health care, if you make your wishes known to your doctor, he or she will most likely cooperate with the home health care agency and give the required okay (the "prescription") for home health care.

e. _Important!_ Medicare Part A coverage no longer requires any stay in the hospital before you can receive home health care.

"The old are always young enough to profit from learning."
Aeschylus, _Agamemnon_

■ ■ ■

I. What Specific Services Does Part A Coverage Pay For?

It's all well and good for you to know that you are eligible for Part A of Medicare, and it definitely helps to know whether care in a particular health facility is covered by Part A. But now it's time to get down to brass tacks: just what kinds of services does Part A coverage pay for? The following lists give you a good idea of the kinds of things Medicare Part A does, and does not, pay for during your stay in a participating hospital or skilled nursing facility. (Remember, though, even the things that Part A "pays for" have significant financial limitations which are explained in the following section).

Medicare Part A hospital insurance pays for:

■ A semiprivate room (two to four beds per room);

■ All your meals, including any special, medically-required diets;

■ Regular nursing services;

■ Special care units, such as intensive care, coronary care or a private hospital room if medically necessary;

■ Drugs, medical supplies and appliances furnished by the facility (casts, splints, wheelchair, etc.);

- Hospital lab tests, X-rays and radiation treatment billed by the hospital;

- Operating and recovery room costs;

- Rehabilitation services, such as physical therapy, occupational therapy and speech pathology provided while you are in the hospital or nursing facility.

Medicare Part A hospital insurance does <u>not</u> pay for:

- Personal convenience items such as television, radio or telephone;

- Private duty nurses;

- A private room, unless medically necessary;

- The first three pints of blood you receive, unless you make arrangements for their replacement.

■ ■ ■

J. How Much Does Medicare Hospital Insurance Pay?

1. Introduction

It's one thing to understand what sorts of bills Medicare will pay and quite another to determine how much of a particular bill will be covered. Unfortunately, before you can get a real feel for how much of your hospital bill Medicare Part A will pay in any given situation, you have to work your way through some Medicare lingo. These terms aren't really that hard to understand; it's more a question of keeping them straight. You may want to read the following material several times, paying particular attention to the examples, to be sure you have all the definitions straight.

2. "Benefit Period" or "Spell of Illness"

The first term for you to get acquainted with is "benefit period," also referred to as "spell of illness." It is called a benefit period because all the other rules about how much Part A coverage pays depend on how many days of coverage you claim during any one period of illness. A benefit period or spell of illness refers to the entire period of time you are treated in the hospital or nursing facility, or some combination of the two, until you have recovered from a particular illness or injury and its medical complications. The benefit period does not begin the first day you become sick or injured, but on the first day you enter the hospital as an inpatient. The same benefit period is considered to continue until you have been out of the hospital or skilled nursing facility for 60 consecutive days. In other words, if you are in and out of the hospital and/or nursing facility several times, without having stayed out completely for 60 consecutive days, all your hospital bills for that period of time will be figured as part of the same benefit period.

This "benefit period" business is important because there are significant limits to the amount of coverage you are provided during any one spell of illness. As you will see in the following section, this means that if it is possible to stretch your hospital or nursing facility stay into two benefit periods, it is often in your interest to do so. Quite simply, you will have more days of full Medicare coverage during two spells of illness than in just one. The use of home health care may assist you in staying out of the hospital or nursing facility for 60 days before you must return as an inpatient for further treatment. Of course, you should never jeopardize your health or recovery time simply to try to stretch your treatment into two benefit periods. That's being penny-wise and health foolish. Nevertheless, be sure to discuss the question of the timing of your hospitalization, and its effect on Medicare payments, with your doctor. A good doctor will consider the problem of Medicare coverage as a legitimate element of your overall treatment; anxiety and worry about how the hospital bills are being paid can have a significant effect on your recovery. Don't expect your doctor to make this issue the most important in your joint decision about when to be hospitalized, but the doctor should at least take it into account. If your doctor refuses even to consider the problem a part of the overall question of treatment, you probably should not allow the issue to interfere with more direct health care considerations. After your illness, though, you may want to consider getting a different doctor, one who is willing at least to consider the question of Medicare coverage as part of treating "the whole person" instead of just a particular condition.

EXAMPLE: Oscar Randle has had plebitis in his legs for several years. He's had a bad flare-up and has been in the hospital for a couple of weeks now, being treated with medication. His doctor finally decides to do a surgical procedure in which the major veins of the legs are opened up to help the flow of blood. "It'll make you feel like a new man, Oscar," the Doctor tells him. Oscar asks "One leg or two?" What Oscar means is, does the doctor operate on both legs at the same time or one and then the other? The doctor says he will only do one leg at a time, seeing how Oscar responds to one and leaving him with a leg to stand on, so to speak, while the other leg recovers. Since Oscar has already been in the hospital for a couple of weeks, he and his doctor plan the dates of surgery so he will be out of the hospital and convalescing at home, with the help of a home health care agency arranged by the doctor's office, for more than 60 days before he returns to have the second leg operated on. In that way, the period of time Oscar spends in the hospital after the second leg is operated on will be considered by Medicare to be part of a new "spell of illness," even though in fact it results from the same phlebitis condition which necessitated the first operation. It will save Oscar hundreds, perhaps well over a thousand, dollars in Medicare "co-insurance" payments (explained below). If there had not been a 60-day break between hospitalizations, Oscar would have been in the hospital a total of more than 60 days and would have had to pay an additional $76 a day co-insurance payment out of his pocket for every day after his 60th day in the hospital (up to his 90th day). Saving that money without creating any risk to Oscar's health will wind up helping Oscar back "on his feet" much sooner than if he had been facing a huge hospital bill when it was all over, don't you think?

110

3. How Much of Your Hospital Bill is Paid For?

Now that you are aware that Medicare Part A only pays certain amounts during any one benefit period, take a look at how much Part A does, and does not, pay for:

a. The Deductible Amount

For each benefit period, you must pay an initial amount of $304 before Medicare will pay anything. This is called the "hospital insurance deductible." The deductible is increased every January 1; $304 is the 1983 figure.

b. First 60 Days Hospitalized

For the first 60 days you are an inpatient in a hospital during any one benefit period, Part A hospital insurance pays all of the cost of covered services (remember, such things as TVs and phones are not covered; see Section I again). You pay only your $260 hospital insurance deductible. If you are in more than one hospital, you still pay only one $304 deductible per benefit period and Part A covers 100 percent of covered costs for each hospital during that first 60 days.*

c. 61 Through 90 Days

After your 60th day in the hospital during one spell of illness, and through your 90th day, you are personally responsible for a $76 per day "co-insurance" payment toward your covered hospital costs; Part A of Medicare pays the rest of covered costs. "Coinsurance" simply means the amount you have to pay out of your pocket for hospital costs.

d. Reserve Days

Reserve days are a kind of last resort coverage. They can partially cover your hospital bills if you are in the hospital more than 90 days in one benefit period, but the coverage is quite limited and can be used up quickly. It works like this: if you are in the hospital for more than 90 days in any one spell of illness, you can use up to 60 additional "reserve days" of coverage. During those days,

---

* WARNING: Current budget proposals would add a charge to the patient of 5 percent of the total covered hospital bill for the first 60 days hospitalization.

you are responsible for a "co-insurance" payment of $152 per day of your bill; Medicare pays the rest of covered costs. BUT, you have only a total of 60 reserve days in your life-time. They do not start over again in another benefit period. Whenever you use up a reserve day, it is gone for good.

It's entirely possible that, even though you are in the hospital for more than 90 days, you may want to save your reserve days for an even rainier day. For example, you may not want to use your reserve days because you have some supplemental private insurance which can help pay for those extra days you're in the hospital, or perhaps you have some extra money to pay for those extra days now and you think you might not have that insurance or extra money later on in life. (Various private insurance policies designed to sup-plement Medicare hospital coverage are discussed in full in Chapter 8.)

If you want to use your reserve days, you don't have to do anything; Medicare will automatically apply them to cover your hospital bills (minus the $152 a day co-insurance you have to pay, of course). But if you do not want to use those reserve days, or want to use some but not all of them, you have to notify the hospital administrator or billing office or the Medicare intermediary (see Section R, below) who handles Medicare hospital claims in your area, before the reserve days come up.

EXAMPLE: Annika Marx had a very serious case of diver-ticulitis, an intestinal disorder. She was hospitalized for two weeks, went home for a week, came back to the hospital for another ten days, was released again and then had a relapse and had to return to the hospital after only a few days at home. After two more weeks in the hospital, she and her doctor decided surgery was in order. Annika stayed in the hospital another week before the surgery could be per-formed, and then spent six weeks in the hospital recovering. Annika is home now, doing fine, with no signs that any more problems will show up. Unfortunately, her hospital bill does show up, causing her to feel almost as bad as she did the day after surgery. It looks like this:

———————————————■ ■ ■———————————————

Semiprivate room: 80 days at $240/day =	$19,200
Operating and recovery room	1,675
Intensive Care Unit, 7 days at $520/day	3,640
Laboratory (incl. X-ray)	980
Medication	465
Whole blood (6 pints, $32 pint)	192
Telephone	94
Television ($35 per week, 12 weeks)	420
	$26,666

It's a frightening number, isn't it? Fortunately, Medicare hospital insurance will pay for much of it. Take a look:

- First of all, Medicare will <u>not</u> pay for any of the telephone or television costs. Chalk that total of $514 up to Annika. (She could have bought a good TV for the $420 she paid to rent one, but of course, the hospital would never let it in.)

- Next, Medicare will <u>not</u> pay for the first three pints of blood Annika received (unless she replaces them). Chalk up another $96 to the amount for which Annika will be personally responsible.

- For the first 60 days, Medicare will pay for all covered costs, minus the $304 initial deductible. All of the operating and recovery room costs ($1,675), the intensive care unit costs ($3,640), and the second three pints of blood ($96) are paid in full by Medicare. That's $5,411 paid by them. And 53 days in a semi-private room in the first 60 days in the hospital were paid for ($12,720); the other seven days during the first 60 days were in intensive care. $900 of the $980 lab work was done in the first 60 days, and so was $420 of the $465 of medication. Medicare thus covers all of this total of $19,451, minus the $304 deductible, for a total during the first 60 days of $19,191. Annika had to pay only the $304 deductible.

- For the last 27 days in the hospital, Annika had to pay her co-insurance amount of $76 per day, for a total to her of $1,755. Medicare paid the rest.

Out of the $26,666 Annika had to pay $2,625. Medicare paid the rest of her more than $26,000 hospital bill. Remember, though, that Annika will still have to face her doctors' bills, which are only partially covered by Medicare Part B medical insurance, discussed in the following sections.

4. Limited Coverage for Psychiatric Hospitals

Medicare Part A hospital insurance will cover only a total of 190 days in a lifetime for inpatient care in a participating <u>psychiatric</u> hospital or in the psychiatric care unit of a general hospital. And another limit is applied to coverage for psychiatric care: if you were already an inpatient in a psychiatric hospital or in the psychiatric care unit of a general hospital at the time your Medicare coverage went into effect, Medicare counts back 150 days from the date your coverage begins and subtracts from your coverage the days you were an inpatient during that time. In other words, if you had spent 60 days in a psychiatric hospital during the five months before your 65th birthday, that 60 days would be subtracted from your lifetime total of 190 days coverage in a psychiatric hospital; it would leave you with only 130 days more coverage under Part A for psychiatric hospitalization. All other coverage rules described in the above sections apply to coverage for inpatient psychiatric care.

5. Coverage for Skilled Nursing Facility Bills

For each benefit period, Medicare will cover you for only a total of 100 days as an inpatient in a skilled nursing facility. For the first 20 days, Part A will pay for all your covered costs (again, not for TV, telephone, private room, etc.). For the next 80 days, you are personally responsible for $38.00 per day; Medicare pays for the rest of covered costs. There are no "reserve days" applicable to a stay in a skilled nursing facility; after 100 days in any one benefit period, you are on your own as far as Part A hospital insurance is concerned. Of course, as with hospital coverage, you can be covered for another 100 days if you later begin a new benefit period.

6. Coverage for Home Health Care

Medicare hospital insurance generally pays for the following services provided in your home by a participating home health care agency:

*Part-time skilled nursing care

*Physical therapy and speech therapy

If you are receiving part-time skilled nursing care, physical therapy or speech therapy, Medicare can also pay for:

- Occupational therapy

- Part-time home health aides

- Medical social services

- Medical supplies and equipment provided by the agency, such as hospital bed, walker, respiratory equipment, etc.

Medicare will not pay for:

- Full-time nursing care at home

- Drugs and biologicals administered at home

- Meals delivered to your home

- Housekeeping services

And how much of these home health care bills will Medicare pay for? Unlike hospital bills, Part A coverage pays the entire cost of your covered home health care, as long as the charges are "reasonable." You do not need to have been in the hospital before Medicare will cover home health care. There is no longer a limit on the number of visits to your home that Medicare will pay for. And you do not need to submit any bills to Medicare; the home health care agency will bill Medicare directly.

As you can see, the fact there is no limit to the number of home health care visits that Medicare Part A will pay for makes it a very valuable alternative to inpatient treatment in a hospital or nursing facility. If you are looking at a long period of convalescence, make sure you or your family and your doctor look into home health care as an alternative to a long seige in the hospital or nursing facility.

"Medicine is for the patient. Medicine is for the people. It is not for the profit."

> George Merck
> *(of the large pharmaceutical company),*
> *quoted in Time, Nov. 3, 1952.*

■■■

K. Who Is Eligible for Part B Medical Insurance?

The second half of Medicare coverage (Part B) is referred to as "medical insurance." It is intended to pay your doctors' bills for treatment by your doctor either in or out of the hospital, as well as part of the other medical expenses you incur when you're out of the hospital. The rules of eligibility for Part B medical insurance are simpler than for Part A: If you are age 65 or over and a citizen of the United States, or you are a resident of the United States who has been here lawfully for five consecutive years, you are eligible to enroll in Medicare Part B medical insurance, whether or not you are eligible for Part A hospital insurance.

L. How Do You Apply for Part B Medical Insurance?

Anyone who wants Part B medical insurance must "enroll" in the program. Everyone who enrolls must pay a monthly premium, currently set at $12.20. This premium is adjusted each year on July 1. You can expect it to continue to go up yearly since the adjustment is tied to the cost of living.

1. If you participate in Part A hospital insurance you will be enrolled automatically in Part B medical insurance. The monthly premium will be automatically deducted from your Social Security or Railroad Retirement check,* unless you inform your local Social Security office that you do not want to enroll in Part B medical insurance.

---

* If you are also receiving Medicaid, some states will pay this premium for you through Medicaid. See Chapter 7.

2.   If you are 65 or over but not eligible for Part A
hospital insurance, and you do want Part B medical insurance, you must enroll in Part B by filing a written application at your local Social Security office. IMPORTANT! Enrollment periods for Medicare Part B medical insurance are
limited.   There is an initial enrollment period of seven
months which begins three months before the month you first
become eligible for Medicare (usually the month you turn 65)
and which ends three months after the end of that month.
For example, if you first become eligible for Medicare in
July, your initial enrollment period starts April 1 and ends
October 31.

     If you don't enroll in Part B medical insurance during
your initial seven-month enrollment period, but later decide
you want to enroll, you can sign up during the general
enrollment period held January 1 through March 31 of every
year.   If you sign up during one of these general enrollment
periods, your coverage will not begin until July 1 of the
year you enroll.   Your monthly premium will also be higher
if you wait to enroll during one of the general enrollment
periods; your premium will be 10 percent higher than the
basic premium for each year you were eligible for coverage
but did not enroll.

M. What Kind of Coverage Does Part B Medical Insurance Provide?

     Basically, Part B medical insurance is meant to pay for
a portion of doctor bills, outpatient hospital charges,
laboratory work, some physical and speech therapy, and some
drugs and medical supplies. But the rules regarding what
is, and what is not, covered are quite strict and narrow.
And the amount of payment is limited. One thing is absolutely sure, however--you will not have all your medical
bills paid for by Medicare. In fact, estimates are that you
will be personally responsible for the payment of as much as
60 percent of your total medical bills, despite Medicare
coverage. For this reason, it will very likely be important
for you to consider additional medical insurance even though
you are "covered" by Medicare Part B medical insurance.
Private "medi-gap" insurance coverage is discussed in Chapter 8; if you cannot afford private insurance, you may be
eligible for Medicaid, a public program for low income
people which is explained in Chapter 7.

N. How Much of Your Medical Bills Does Part B Pay For?

Let's take a close look at how much Medicare Part B medical insurance actually pays for. As we said, when all your medical bills are added up, you'll see that Medicare often pays for only about 40 percent of the total. Medicare uses a lot of health industry and government double-talk to "explain" its rules, but when all the talk is boiled away, you are left with three major reasons why Part B medical insurance pays for so little. First of all, Medicare does not cover a number of major medical expenses, such as routine physical examinations, medicine, glasses, hearing aids, dentures, and a number of other costly medical services. Second, Medicare only covers what it decides are the "approved charges" or "reasonable charges" for a doctor's services. These amounts may seem reasonable to Medicare, but they are almost always considerably less than what the doctor has actually charged you; you are often personally responsible for the difference. Finally, even when Medicare decides that a particular bill is covered, and determines what the "reasonable" or "approved" charges are for the services performed, Part B medical insurance only pays 80 percent of those so-called reasonable charges.

Now that you know the worst, it's time to deal with the details. They're not hard to understand--just hard to swallow.

1. Deductible

Before Medicare pays anything under Part B medical insurance, you have to pay the first $75 of covered medical bills each year. This is called your deductible. Although Medicare is supposed to keep track of how much of your deductible you have paid in a given year, it's a good idea for you to keep track, too, so you can make sure you've been given accurate credit. Unfortunately, many people have found that the Medicare accounting practices of the private companies that administer the program are not all they should be. (More on these private companies later on in this chapter.)

2. Eighty Percent of "Approved Charges"

Herein lies the big rub. Part B medical insurance pays only 80 percent of what Medicare approves of as "reasonable" charges for a particular medical service or treatment.

(This amount is also referred to as the "approved charge.")
You have to pay the other 20 percent. And what is a "reasonable" charge, you ask? The answer, unfortunately, is
always much less than what the doctors charge you, and
expect you to pay, in the not-so-reasonable real world.
This means, in addition to the 20 percent of the approved
charges Medicare does not pay, you are often required to pay
the additional amount of any medical bill over the "approved" charges. How much more must you pay? The answer
depends on how much the difference is between what Medicare
thinks are "reasonable charges" and how much your doctor
actually charges. (A way out of this bind is the "assignment" method of paying your bills, in which the doctor
accepts Medicare's decision as to "reasonable charges" as
his or her full bill; "assignment" is discussed below and in
Section R(2)(a) of this chapter.)

Does all this about "reasonable charges" and actual charges seem confusing? It's not really. For virtually every kind of medical service, Medicare works out the "prevailing charge" for such service in your geographic area by taking a sampling of what doctors throughout your area charge for that service. Medicare compares this data to your doctor's customary charge for the same services and pays the lower of the two (unless your actual bill is even lower). The approved charges, unfortunately, are almost always quite a bit lower than your actual bills. This is partly because the statistics used to calculate the "reasonable charges" always lag behind the increases in real medical bills. In addition, it is Medicare's theory that if Medicare actually keeps up with doctors' bills, that would encourage doctors to continue raising their bills (knowing Medicare would pick up much of the tab). Whether Medicare is the culprit here or doctors' outlandish fees are to blame, there is no question who the victim is: the Medicare patient.

SUMMARY: Medicare Part B medical insurance generally pays only 80 percent of what it considers the "reasonable charge" for covered services. You are responsible for the remainder of your unreasonable but very real bill, in addition to your yearly deductible of $75.

IMPORTANT: GETTING YOUR DOCTOR TO ACCEPT "ASSIGNMENT:" One way you can try to get around the danger of being stuck with a big bill for the difference between 80 percent of Medicare's "approved charges" and the actual charges from your doctor is to make an arrangment for your doctor to accept an "assignment" from you of your Medicare claim. This assignment method of payment means that the doctor will accept whatever amount Medicare decides is the "reasonable charge" for your treatment as the full amount of your total bill for Medicare-covered services. Medicare pays 80 percent, you pay 20 percent. Doctors seem to be divided about 50-50; half will accept assignment, half won't. If you're looking for a doctor to treat you, the question of assignment of Medicare may be one of the things to check in advance. This assignment method of payment is explained more fully in Section R(2)(a) of this chapter.

O. What Services Does Part B Medical Insurance Cover?

1. Doctor Bills

Part B medical insurance covers medically necessary doctors' services, including surgery, whether the services are provided at the hospital, at the doctor's office or (if you can find such a doctor) at home. Part B also covers medical services provided by the doctor's office personnel or by hospital staff, who assist the doctor in providing care (such as nurses, surgical assistants, laboratory or X-ray technicians).

Under a special rule, Medicare medical insurance pays 100 percent of "reasonable charges" for services provided by pathologists or radiologists while you are an inpatient at a hospital if the pathologist or radiologist accepts an "assignment" of your Medicare benefits. If you are going to have X-rays or tissue-examination at the hospital, ask your doctor or hospital administrator if the radiologist and/or pathlogist will accept assignment of your Medicare payment. In addition to having 100 percent (instead of only 80 percent) of the bills paid, you are not required to meet your medical insurance deductible amount before Medicare will pay the radiologist or pathologist.

One more special rule--better get used to special rules because there are a lot of them--is that Medicare medical insurance puts a $250 per year limit on what it will pay for outpatient treatment by a doctor for mental illness.

2. Outpatient Hospital Care

Medicare medical insurance "covers" all charges (but of "approved charges" pays only 80 percent) for outpatient hospital treatment, such as emergency room or clinic charges, x-rays, injections which are not self-administered, and laboratory work and diagnostic tests, whether done at the hospital lab or at an independent laboratory facility (if that lab is approved by Medicare).

3. Outpatient Surgery

Medicare Part A covers the cost of surgery--operating and recovery room costs--if you are an inpatient at the hospital. But until very recently, if you had your surgery at an outpatient surgery clinic or at the doctor's office, Medicare Part A would not cover it at all and Part B would pay only 80 percent of approved charges, including the doctors bills. Now, though, the approved costs of many surgical prodcedures performed in walk-in surgical centers and doctors' offices can be paid 100 percent by Medicare Part B medical insurance. Both the doctors' bills and the cost of using the facility can be paid 100 percent (if the doctor accepts assignment of the Medicare payment as payment in full). This is a considerable improvement over the 80 percent of approved charges Medicare Part B would normally pay for doctors' bills if you were in the hospital. The reason? By offering to pay 100 percent of the doctors' bills, Medicare encourages doctors and patients alike to keep down Medicare costs by avoiding unnecessary hospitalization.

If you are considering minor surgery, ask your doctor if the surgery can be performed without you being hospitalized and ask your doctor's office to check with the Medicare carrier in your area to find out if the surgical procedure you will undergo can be covered by Part B medical insurance if performed without your being hospitalized.

4. Ambulance

Part B medical insurance covers the cost of an ambulance if the ambulance is medically necessary, meaning transportation by any other means might endanger your health, whether or not there is an emergency. Coverage only extends to a trip to or from a hospital or skilled nursing facility. Medicare will <u>not</u> pay for an ambulance trip to your doctor's office.

5. Administered Drugs

Drugs or other medicines which are administered to you at the hospital or doctor's office are covered by medical insurance; drugs you take by yourself at home, including self-administered injections, are not covered at all by Medicare, even though prescribed by your doctor.

6. Medical Equipment and Supplies

Splints, casts, prosthetic devices, body braces, heart pacemakers, corrective lenses after a cataract operation, and durable medical equipment such as oxygen equipment, wheelchairs and hospital beds (if prescribed by a doctor) are all covered by Part B medical insurance.

7. Oral Surgery

Surgery on your jaw or facial bones, or on the nerves or blood vessels associated with your jaw or face, can be covered by Part B medical insurance. Ridiculously, though, surgery on your teeth or gums related to injury or disease in your jaw or face may not be covered because Medicare does not cover "dental" costs. This is one of those crazy bureaucratic distinctions that often make no sense. Though normal dental care is not supposed to be covered by Medicare, damage to teeth or gums connected to an injury or disease is a medical as much as a dental problem. Repair of teeth and gums is essential to good eating, and good nutrition is the foundation of good health. Recently, the rules regarding work on the jaw or gums have been expanded somewhat. If the work is done by a dentist or oral surgeon, Medicare will cover it if physicians also provide the same kind of care and if Medicare would cover the care if a doctor had provided it. (You might take a look at Jake's situation in the book's Introduction for an example of how this rule works.)

8. Outpatient Physical Therapy and Speech Therapy

If it is prescribed by a doctor, Part B of Medicare will cover some of the cost of outpatient physical and speech therapy. But the way in which you receive the therapy will determine how much Medicare will pay.

■If you receive the therapy as part of treatment at your doctor's office, Part B medical insurance will pay the normal 80 percent of the "reasonable charges," less your deductible.

■If you receive physical therapy from an independent Medicare-certified therapist at his or her office or at your home, Part B medical insurance will only pay up to a $400 limit per year.

■If you receive physical therapy or speech pathology services as an outpatient from a hospital or skilled nursing facility, or from a home health agency, clinic, rehabilitation agency or public health agency (any of which must be Medicare-approved; physical therapy services must be prescribed by your doctor; speech pathology services can be established by a Medicare-approved speech pathologist), the organization which provides the services submits its claim directly to Medicare; they can bill you directly only for any part of your yearly deductible you have not yet paid and for the 20 percent of approved charges which Medicare does not pay, as well as for any charges Medicare does not cover at all.

■If you receive therapy while you are confined to your home, as part of a complete home health care program [see Home Health Care, Sections H(7) and Q)], Medicare will pay 100 percent of the costs with no dollar limit and no deductible.

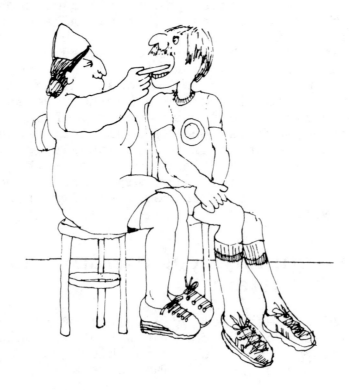

9. Chiropractors

Medicare medical insurance covers only one kind of treatment by a Medicare-certified chiropractor. The only treatment covered is "manual manipulation of the spine to correct a subluxation that can be demonstrated by X-ray." That means, generally, only manual manipulation of out-of-place vertebrae will be covered, and then only when you have been referred to the chiropractor by a physician. Apparently, Medicare somehow doesn't believe chiropractors can help any other part of the body. Medicare will not pay for any other diagnostic or therapeutic services provided by the chiropractor, including X-rays ordered by the chiropractor.

P. What Medical Treatment is NOT Covered by Medicare Part B?

When you look at the list of what Medicare medical insurance does not cover, it's easy to understand why people with Medicare wind up personally responsible for more than half of their medical bills. It also underlines the need for you to consider additional medical insurance, either through Medicaid or from one of the private "Medi-gap" plans, to protect yourself against medical bills Medicare does not cover. These additional kinds of coverage are discussed in detail in the next two chapters.

The following are categories of medical treatment and service which Medicare medical insurance does not cover at all:

1. Regular or Routine Physical Examinations

Even though it is unquestioned that preventive medicine, including routine physical check-ups, can significantly reduce the kinds and severity of illnesses, Medicare reflects the attitude of the traditional medical community in our country which refuses to put any real money or energy in the direction of public health education and disease prevention. There are several reasons for this. There is little or no tradition of preventive medicine in the United States, and no national, community-based public health policy or program to encourage preventive medicine. In addition, since most doctors receive little training in preventive medicine, they don't stress it in their contact with patients. And finally, since medicine is run almost purely as a business in the U.S., it emphasizes high-profit activities (treatment of disease) over low-profit activities (disease prevention programs). All of this is not to say that doctors are evil; it just happens to be the nature of business.

One result of this bias in American medicine is that Medicare does not cover regular physical examinations. This does not mean, though, that no physical examinations at all are covered by Medicare. Please follow this explanation carefully; if you do, you may be able to have fairly complete examinations on a somewhat regular basis and have them covered by Medicare medical insurance. Here's how it works: though regular or routine examinations are not covered, laboratory work, diagnostic testing and physical examination by your doctor are covered if they are part of diagnosis and treatment for a particular medical condition or complaint. In other words, if something is already wrong with you, Medicare will cover examinations to find out what it is, how bad it is and how the treatment is going. Now, there are no rules which say how bad your condition must be before a doctor can examine you; and it is pretty much up to the doctor to decide how broad an examination is necessary to find out what's wrong with you (though the examination must be reasonably connected to your complaint, or else it would not be "medically necessary," and thus not covered by Medicare). Are you getting the picture? To put it another way, if you and your doctor agree a physical examination and testing is necessary to find out what's wrong with you-- perhaps you've been tired a lot lately, or short of breath, or having trouble sleeping, or occasionally running a fever or having headaches, or dizziness, etc.--and the examination and testing is medically reasonable given your physical symptoms, then Medicare is likely--though not guaranteed--to cover it.

If you need to have a "check-up" or "physical" or other general testing done, it's not a bad idea to discuss the Medicare coverage question with your doctor ahead of time so he or she can explain in his or her notes, and then on the forms sent to Medicare, that your physical examination was to find out why you had certain problems or symptoms, and was not merely a routine or regular physical.

EXAMPLE: Maureen O'Rourke had been having trouble sleeping for a couple of months. She also seemed to get too many colds and was tired a lot. She decided it might be time to get a general physical examination since she hadn't had one for a couple of years. She called her doctor and asked to have a comprehensive physical examination scheduled. The doctor's secretary asked if there was any particular problem, and Maureen said, "No, not really; just the same things everyone my age complains of. I just thought it was time to have a check-up." Maureen was scheduled for an examination in three weeks.

When she came for the examination, the doctor asked Maureen if she had any particular problems. She told the doctor about her trouble sleeping, the colds and the tiredness, but she played it down. "Nothing out of the ordinary, doctor," she said, not wanting to sound like a hypochondriac. "I just thought it was time for a check-up." So, the doctor gave Maureen a full physical examination and sent her blood and urine samples to the laboratory for routine testing. Other than a slight low blood sugar, nothing out of the ordinary showed up. The doctor suggested some changes in Maureen's diet and sent her a nice, fat $380 bill. Maureen forwarded the bill to Medicare but they refused to pay any of it. The doctor had reported a routine physical check-up and Medicare doesn't cover routine physical examinations.

EXAMPLE: Maureen's neighbor, Mavis Dawson, seemed to be having pretty much the same problems as Maureen, but Mavis was a little wiser about handling her doctor's appointment. She called her doctor and asked the secretary for an appointment to have the doctor examine her, but told the secretary that she wanted to be examined for "some kind of virus or something" that Mavis just couldn't get rid of; it was making her tired, ruining her sleep and bringing on cold symptoms. The secretary made an appointment for two days later. Mavis told the doctor she felt like she must have some virus or something in her system which she couldn't shake and which was keeping her run-down and sick with cold-like symptoms. Could the doctor figure out what it was, please? We'll try, the doctor said, and proceeded to give Mavis the same examination, and send to the lab for the same tests, that Maureen had. The results were the same. "Take some vitamins, change your diet and check back with me in a couple of months, or sooner if you don't feel better," the doctor said.

Mavis submitted her $380 bill to Medicare and Medicare paid it's 80 percent share of the "reasonable charges" because the doctor's records indicated that Mavis had been examined and treated for an illness of which she complained.

Maureen had just asked for a check-up, and she paid for it. Mavis asked that her illness be treated and Medicare picked up its share of the tab. The moral: A rose by any other name does not always smell as sweet. Again, though, it must be emphasized that simply complaining of mild, unspecific symptoms and then asking for a broad general physical examination doesn't guarantee that Medicare will pay its share. It will depend on several things, including how broad the examination is in relation to your complaints, and how your doctor characterizes in his report what your symptoms were and why the tests and examinations were done.

And, realistically, luck may play a part. In borderline
areas such as these it can make a lot of difference who
reviews your Medicare application when it is submitted (see
the sections later in this chapter on how your claim is
processed). The key thing, though, in this kind of situation is the cooperation of your doctor. So remember to
discuss the question of Medicare payment with your doctor
before treatment begins.

2. Treatment That is Not "Medically Necessary"

Medicare will not pay its share of medical care which
it considers to be not "medically necessary." This includes
some elective and most cosmetic surgery,* and eliminates
virtually all alternative forms of medical care such as
acupuncture, acupressure, homeopathy and chiropractic (except
for the limited use of chiropractors discussed in the previous section). Alternative forms of medical care are not
usually provided by "physicians," you see, and therefore
according to the powerful traditional medical community,
which pulls the behind-the-scenes medical strings, these
services are defined as being not "medically necessary."

---

* "Cosmetic" surgery can be covered if it is needed because of accidental injury or to
improve the functioning of a malformed part of the body.

3. Vaccinations and Immunizations

Despite significant potential health benefits from some vaccinations and immunizations, these forms of preventive medicine are not covered by Medicare medical insurance. One exception exists in emergencies where, for example, they are required because of the risk of infection or because of exposure to a communicable disease. Another recent exception is made for the reasonable cost of pneumococcal vaccinations.

4. Drugs and Medicines at Home

This is one of the most costly areas of medical care not covered by Medicare. Though Part A hospital insurance does cover drugs administered to you while you are in the hospital, and Part B medical insurance covers drugs that cannot be self-administered which you receive while an outpatient being treated at a hospital or clinic or at the doctor's office, Medicare does <u>not</u> pay for any drugs--prescription or not--which you <u>can</u> administer or take yourself at home. Insulin, for example, is generally considered a drug which <u>can</u> be self-administered and thus is <u>not</u> covered by Medicare.

One way some people manage to get around some of the cost of such drugs is to ask the doctor who prescribes the drug, or your family doctor, if he or she has any "samples" of the drug which you can take. Pharmaceutical companies, in an effort to "push" their particular brand of drugs, send quantities of free drugs to doctors, and many doctors are willing to dispense those drugs to you free of charge instead of having you buy the drugs on your own, if they know you can't afford them. But many doctors forget what they have in the way of samples, and it may help if you ask your doctor if he or she has samples of the drug you need, explaining that it will be very hard on your pocketbook if you have to purchase them.

5. Eyesight and Hearing

Medicare medical insurance does not cover routine eye or hearing examinations, or eyeglasses or contact lenses (except after a cataract operation) or hearing aids.

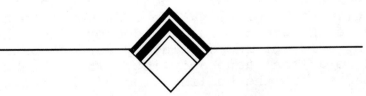

6. General Dental Work

As explained in the previous section on what Medicare medical insurance does cover, Medicare does <u>not</u> cover work on your teeth and gums if performed by a dentist or oral surgeon, unless the same work would be covered if performed by a physician. In other words, if it is considered "medical" rather than "dental," Medicare may cover it. But if the work to your teeth or gums is not the kind of work a doctor, as distinguished from a dentist or oral surgeon, would do, then Medicare will not cover it, even if the problem is unrelated to normal tooth decay or gum disease. This rule seems to be penny-wise and pound-foolish on the part of Medicare, since your teeth are obviously an important part of maintaining good eating habits and good nutrition. If your teeth and gums aren't taken care of, your general health is sure to suffer, in which case Medicare will wind up having to pay much larger medical bills on your behalf later on. But, then, we already know that government rules often tend to be shortsighted when it comes to spending money on human services.

7. Routine Foot Care

Unless the care is part of a disease involving more than just the exterior of your foot, Part B medical insurance will not cover it. In other words, Medicare will not cover removal of corns and most warts, treatment for flat feet or hygienic care. An exception to this is the removal of plantar warts, which Part B medical insurance does cover.

<u>EXAMPLE</u>: Willie Washington broke his wrist rollerskating with his five-year-old grandson. He had it X-rayed at the emergency room of the hospital. Willie's doctor came to the emergency room, checked the X-rays, set his wrist and put it into a cast. The doctor also gave Willie an injection for the pain and prescribed some pain pills. The doctor checked Willie's wrist again a couple of days later and told him that, normally, the cast would have to stay on for six to eight weeks. But the doctor added that he had been having a lot of success lately sending patients with fractures to a local acupuncturist. The acupuncture treatment seemed to cut the healing time of the fractures by

several weeks. Willie said he was willing to try. He went to the acupuncturist and when he returned to his doctor in four weeks, the doctor said the wrist had healed sufficiently to remove the cast. The doctor did suggest, however, that Willie not rollerskate for awhile.

Which of Willie's bills from all this will Medicare medical insurance cover? Medicare will cover the emergency room costs, including the X-rays and the cost of the cast. Medicare will also cover the doctor's bills for his services at the emergency room and for the two visits to the doctor's office. Remember, though, that Medicare only pays 80 percent of the "approved charges" for these covered services, and only after Willie has paid his $75 deductible for the year. Medicare medical insurance will cover the pain injection Willie got from the doctor at the hospital but it will not cover the cost of the pain pills Willie got from his pharmacy, despite the fact they were prescribed by his doctor. And even though the acupuncture treatment was recommended by Willie's doctor and produced excellent medical results, Medicare won't even consider paying it.

Q. Home Health Care Covered by Part B Medical Insurance

Under recent changes in Medicare regulations, the same home health care coverage is available under Part B medical insurance as is covered by Part A hospital insurance. There is no longer any requirement of prior hospitalization, there is no limit on the number of home health care visits that are covered, and there is no longer a deductible to be paid for home health care. The only basic requirements are that you be confined to your home because of an injury or illness, that your doctor determines you need part-time skilled nursing care or physical or speech therapy, and that the care be provided by a Medicare-approved home health care agency. Part B medical insurance, like Part A coverage, will pay for 100 percent of the reasonable charges of a participating home health care agency. See the more complete discussion of home health care under Part A hospital insurance in Section H(7) of this chapter. The coverage under Part B medical insurance is exactly the same.

R. How to Get Medicare to Pay Hospital and Doctor Bills

It's good to know that you have the right to receive medical coverage from Medicare, but it's even better when you actually receive a check. In this section, the procedures for getting your bills paid are explained, including a step-by-step examination of the process of appealing a decision by Medicare denying part or all of a medical payment you believe you should receive.

1. In-Patient Hospital Bills: Getting Them Paid in Full

Ordinarily, when you first check into a hospital or skilled nursing facility, or begin to receive visits from a home health care agency, you present your Medicare card to the proper admissions people and they take care of the rest. The "provider," as the hospital, skilled nursing facility or home health care agency is called in Medicare lingo, will send its bills directly to the Medicare "intermediary." The intermediary (more Medicare longhand) is a private company, either Blue Cross/Blue Shield or one of the other large insurance companies. This company will receive, review and pay your claim. Normally, the process is simple and you don't have to do a thing.

The hospital or other facility accepts as "payment in full" the amount the Medicare intermediary decides is a "reasonable charge" for the services provided you as an inpatient. Unlike doctors' bills, where you may be personally responsible for the difference between Medicare's reasonable charges and the actual amount of a doctor's bill, a hospital or nursing facility is not permitted to bill you for any inpatient charges over the amounts paid by Medicare. They can and will bill you, though, for any unpaid portion of your yearly deductible, for co-insurance, and for charges not covered at all by Medicare. The intermediary will send you a form called a Benefits Record. It will tell you what hospital services were paid for and how much of your deductible you are responsible for.

Initial approval of whether particular services are covered by Medicare is made by the Utilization Review Committee (URC) of the facility in which you are a patient or by the Professional Standards Review Organization (PSRO) in your area. Within a day of your admission to the facility, your claim for Medicare coverage will be reviewed by a URC or PSRO of doctors and other medical personnel who will decide whether your admission to the hospital or nursing facility, and the care you receive there, is "medically necessary." If your stay in the facility is a long one, these reviewing doctors may make periodic checks on your condition to determine whether your stay remains medically necessary and the care you are receiving is skilled medical care rather than merely "custodial."

The URC or PSRO makes its decision after looking at your medical records and, sometimes, consulting with your doctor. In making their decision, the review doctors have Medicare standards to refer to--for example, the Medicare assumption is that after release from a hospital after a heart attack, 10-14 days in a skilled nursing facility is medically necessary and not merely custodial care. However, these standards are not hard and fast rules and the reviewing doctors do not have to follow them if your particular condition requires different treatment. If you or your doctor feel that the URC or PSRO might question the medical necessity of your admission or of the treatment you are to receive, you may want to have your doctor contact the review committee or organization before your hospitalization or specific treatment begins. In that way, you can be sure that the reviewing doctors get a full explanation of your particular case; you may also be able to find out their decision before you commit yourself to that particular facility.

In most cases, the URC or PSRO will notify you of their decision within two days of your admission. If they approve your admission and treatment you don't have to do a thing. The hospital or facility will submit its bills directly to the Medicare intermediary and the intermediary will pay them, minus your deductible and any co-insurance amounts, directly to the provider. However, should the review committee decide that your admission to the facility is not medically necessary, or that your care has become custodial rather than medical, Medicare will stop coverage of your bills three days after you receive notice of the committee's decision. If you receive a negative decision from the URC or PSRO, your first step should be to ask them to reconsider their decision. Ask your doctor to speak personally with the committee to present more detailed information about your condition and to explain why your stay is medically necessary. If the reviewing doctors do not change their decision, you will have to assume personal responsibility for your bills from the date you are notified of the URC or PSRO's initial decision. Your only recourse will be to attempt to have this decision changed at a later date through the Medicare appeal procedures. These procedures are explained in detail in Section S(1) of this chapter.

■ ■ ■

2. Doctors' Bills: Getting Medicare to Pay Its Share

There are two different ways in which you can arrange to have Medicare pay its share of your doctors' bills. The difference between the two methods can mean a lot of money to you. Why? Under the "assignment method" your doctor will accept Medicare's "reasonable charge" as the full bill, but under the "payment-to-you" method, you will normally have to pay the difference between Medicare's "reasonable charges" and the actual amount of the doctors' bills.

IMPORTANT: Always check with your doctor before you receive treatment to find out if the doctor will accept assignment. If the doctor will not accept an assignment, as explained below, you may want to consider going to a doctor who will. Here's why.

a. Assignment Method

This is the cheapest method for the patient. Accepting an assignment means the doctor will accept as the full amount of the bill whatever Medicare decides is the "approved charge" for the treatment provided. Medicare pays the doctor directly for its 80 percent share of these reasonable or approved charges (subtracting any part of your deductible you have not met) and you are personally responsible only for the remaining 20 percent of the reasonable charges, plus any part of your deductible you have not already met for the year. You do not have to make up the difference between Medicare's approved charges and the amount the doctor actually charges for the treatment, even if the doctor charges non-Medicare patients far more than the amount Medicare sets as a reasonable charge.

In addition to this savings of out-of-pocket expenses, the assignment method has another advantage for you. The doctor's office handles all the initial paperwork. You simply sign an assignment form and the doctor's office sends its bill directly to Medicare. Medicare then sends its payment to the doctor's office, and sends a notice to you of how much it has paid the doctor, and how much you owe the doctor from your deductible and your 20 percent of the reasonable charges.

For the doctor, there are both advantages and disadvantages to the assignment method of payment. The disadvantage is clear: the doctor gets to collect only the amount of the approved charges as decided by Medicare instead of the higher charges he or she would normally bill. On the other hand, the doctor has an easier time collecting the money and is assured that at least 80 percent of the reasonable charges will be paid in full, in one lump sum. Unfortunately, about half of all doctors who accept Medicare patients will not accept the assignment method, but insist that you pay their higher fees under the payment-to-you method discussed below.

REMEMBER: Always check with a doctor before you begin treatment to find out if the doctor will accept a Medicare assignment. In some areas of the country, there are medical referral services which will supply you with the names of doctors in every medical specialty who accept Medicare assignments. There is sometimes a fee for this sort of referral service, but it may be well worth it if you wind up saving yourself the difference between Medicare's approved charges and the full amount a doctor might charge for treatment. Check with your local senior citizens center or with the local medical association to find these medical referral services.

EXAMPLE: Franco DiSantis was bothered by pain in his left hip; it was a pinching kind of pain that came and went, often shooting down his leg. It seemed to happen most if he had been sitting too long. Franco went to his regular doctor (an internist) who he knew accepted Medicare assignments. The doctor examined Franco but could not find the problem and referred him to an orthopedist. Franco asked his own doctor if the orthopedist accepted Medicare assignments. The doctor's secretary called the orthopedist's office to check. It turned out that this orthopedist did not accept Medicare assignment. Franco asked his doctor for a referral to someone else who did accept assignments. The doctor gave Franco the name of a different orthopedist and this doctor did accept Medicare assignments. Franco saw the orthopedist, who found that his sciatic nerve has been pinched. She prescribed an exercise program and warned Franco not to sit cross-legged with all his weight on the left side. Franco did the exercises and was careful how he sat, and the problem improved substantially.

Franco's internist charged $50 for Franco's original visit. The orthopedist charged $75. Both doctors sent their bills directly to the Medicare carrier because they had accepted assignment from Franco. Medicare decided that the approved charges for the two doctors would be $35 for the first doctor and $60 for the orthopedist. Since Franco's deductible had already been paid for the year, Medicare paid 80 percent of each approved charge: $28 to the first doctor, $48 to the orthopedist. Medicare sent these checks directly to the doctors. Because the doctors had accepted assignment, Franco only had to pay the 20 percent difference between what Medicare paid and the approved charges. If the doctors had not accepted Medicare assignment, Franco would have had to pay the difference between what Medicare paid and the full bill. In real dollars, Franco saved himself the difference between paying $19 ($7 to one doctor, $12 to the other) and having to pay $49 ($22 to the first doctor, $27 to the orthopedist). Good work, Franco.

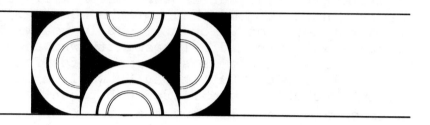

     After the Medicare carrier receives a medical insurance claim, it will send you a form called "Explanation of Medicare Benefits." This form shows you which medical bills Medicare covered and the amounts Medicare decided to approve for each service or treatment (see sample form on the next page).* These two figures are listed side by side in the middle of the form under the headings "Amount Billed" (meaning the amount of the doctor's actual bill for the particular service) and "Amount Approved" (meaning the amount Medicare determines is the reasonable charge for that service). These amounts are totalled at the bottom of the page, along with a statement of how much of your Medicare deductible has been subtracted by Medicare. Then the balance of the approved amount is set out. Medicare pays 80 percent of that approved amount balance. The total Medicare has actually sent to your doctors is at the very bottom of the form, next to "Total Medicare Payment." And now for the big question. How much do you owe? You owe to the doctor the amount shown in the box next to "Amount applied to annual deductible," plus 20 percent of the amount next to "Balance Payable at 80%."

     This will all seem simpler if you refer to the sample form on the next page which is filled out to show how much Franco had to pay in the example given above. The "Amount Approved" totalled $95 for the two doctors. Since Franco's deductible had already been met, the "Balance Payable at 80%" was still $95. Medicare paid its 80 percent, for a total of $76. Franco owed the remaining 20 percent, or $19. He was responsible for sending that $19 to the two doctors-- $7 to one, $12 to the other.

---

* This form varies somewhat from carrier to carrier, but all Explanation of Medicare Benefits forms contain the same information about covered charges, approved charges, deductible and amount actually paid by Medicare.

Explanation of Medicare Benefits

YOUR MEDICARE NUMBER
(HEALTH INSURANCE CLAIM NUMBER)

123-45-6789- A

ALWAYS USE THIS NUMBER WHEN WRITING ABOUT YOUR CLA

BENEFITS PAID TO ASSIGNEE

DATE: May 3, 1983

CN 0128-191-287
CK 0128-191-288
EX
RE 846

Hadley D. Maxwell, M.D.
4500 Doctorstown Blvd.
Thomasville, Md. 12345

Sharon Q. Russell, M.D.
178 Grover Place
Thomasville, Md. 12345

BENEFICIARY OR REPRESENTATIVE

Franco A. DiSantis
2311 Parkway Blvd.#311
Thomasville, Md. 12345

1. SERVICES WERE PROVIDED BY	FROM / TO	2. WHEN	3. AMOUNT BILLED	4. AMOUNT APPROVED	5. EXPLANATION OF ANY DIFFERENCE BETWEEN AMOUNTS BILLED AND APPROVED. MEDICARE DOES NOT PAY FOR:	SERVICE CODE (SEE RE...) PLACE
Maxwell		02-28-83	50.00	35.00	This Full Charge.	1
Russell		03-04-83	75.00	60.00	This Full Charge.	1

	TOTALS ▶	125.00	95.00	MEDICARE PAID ▼	REMARKS:
INPATIENT RADIOLOGY AND PATHOLOGY PHYSICIAN SERVICES AND CERTAIN LABORATORIES PAID IN FULL. ▶					Payment of 76.00 is being made.
AMOUNT PAYABLE AT 80% AFTER THE ANNUAL DEDUCTIBLE. ▶			95.00		
AMOUNT APPLIED TO ANNUAL DEDUCTIBLE. DEDUCTIBLE OF 75.00 IS MET FOR 1983 ▶					
BALANCE PAYABLE AT 80%. ▶			95.00	76.00	
	TOTAL MEDICARE PAYMENT ▶			76.00	

137

b. Payment-to-You and Reimbursement

The second method of obtaining Medicare payment of doctors' bills is almost always considerably more expensive to you. If your doctor will accept a Medicare assignment, you don't have to worry about it. Unfortunately, however, payment-to-you and reimbursement to the doctor is the method of payment insisted upon by about half of all doctors who accept Medicare patients in the first place. This direct payment-to-you method can best be explained step-by-step:

Step 1

Your doctor gives or sends you a bill for the full amount of the charges. Some doctors will agree to wait for payment until you have received your payment from Medicare, but others will demand some or all of it a soon as they treat you. Find out in advance whether or not your doctor will wait for payment until you are paid by Medicare.

Step 2

You fill out a Patient's Request for Medicare Payment (Form 1490S--see the blank form with instructions and the sample, filled-out form on the following pages). Your doctor's office probably has copies of this form for you.

■ ■ ■

If you cannot get the form at your doctor's office, your local Social Security office or Medicare carrier will have some. You must attach to the form itemized bills from the doctor; you can include bills from several doctors with one form. Make sure each itemized bill contains all of the following information:

- Date of each treatment, service or visit

- Place of each service (doctor's office, outpatient hospital or clinic, hospital or skilled nursing facility, patient's home, independent laboratory, (etc.)

- Description of each medical treatment, service or supply furnished

- Charge for each service, listed separately

- Doctor's or supplier's name and address; if more than one doctor's name is shown on the bill, circle the name of the particular doctor that treated you.

Make sure your Medicare number is written on each bill and your name appears exactly as it does on your Medicare card. Always keep copies of the forms and bills you send in; also, write down, on your own record, the date you sent in your Request for Payment.

NOTE: Sometimes your doctor's office will fill out a Medicare request form for you and send it directly to Medicare even though the doctor is not accepting an assignment. The form the doctor's office will use is the same one they would use if they were accepting an assignment, only they will indicate on the form they do not accept assignment. This form is called a Health Insurance Claim Form. If your doctor's office files this for you, you do <u>not</u> have to file a Patient's Request for Medicare Payment Form.

PATIENT'S REQUEST FOR MEDICARE PAYMENT

IMPORTANT— SEE OTHER SIDE FOR INSTRUCTIONS

PLEASE TYPE OR PRINT INFORMATION   MEDICAL INSURANCE BENEFITS SOCIAL SECURITY ACT

NOTICE: Anyone who misrepresents or falsifies essential information requested by this form may upon conviction be subject to fine and imprisonment under Federal Law. No Part B Medicare benefits may be paid unless this form is received as required by existing law and regulations (20 CFR 422.510).

1	Name of Beneficiary From Health Insurance Card (First) (Middle) (Last) Franco A. DiSantis	**SEND COMPLETED FORM TO:**

2	Claim Number From Health Insurance Card 1 | 2 | 3 | 4 | 5 | 6 | 7 | 8 | 9 | A ☒ Male ☐ Female

3	Patient's Mailing Address (City, State, Zip Code) Check here if this is a new address ➡ ☐ 2311 Parkway Blvd., Apt. 311 _(Street or P.O. Box—Include Apartment number)_ Thomasville, Maryland 12345 (City) (State) (Zip)	**3b**	Telephone Number (Include Area Code) (123) 456-7890

4	Describe The Illness or Injury for Which Patient Received Treatment Inflamed sciatic nerve on left side.

4b	Was illness or injury connected with employment? ☐ Yes ☒ No

If any medical expenses will be or could be paid by your private insurance organization, State Agency, (Medicaid), or the VA complete block 5 below.

5	Name and Address of other insurance, State Agency (Medicaid), or VA office none NOTE: If you DO NOT want payment information on this claim released put an (x) here ➡ ☐	Policy or Medical Assistance Number --

I authorize Any Holder of Medical or Other Information About Me to Release to the Social Security Administration and Health Care Financing Administration or Its Intermediaries or Carriers any Information Needed for This or a Related Medicare Claim. I Permit a copy of this Authorization to be Used in Place of the Original, and Request Payment of Medical Insurance Benefits to Me.

6	Signature of Patient (If patient is unable to sign, see Block 6 on other side.) *Franco A. DiSantis*	**6b**	Date Signed 3-8-83

IMPORTANT!

ATTACH ITEMIZED BILLS FROM YOUR DOCTOR(S)
OR SUPPLIER(S) TO THE BACK OF THIS FORM.

HCFA-1490S (6-80)   Department of Health and Human Services—Health Care Financing Administration

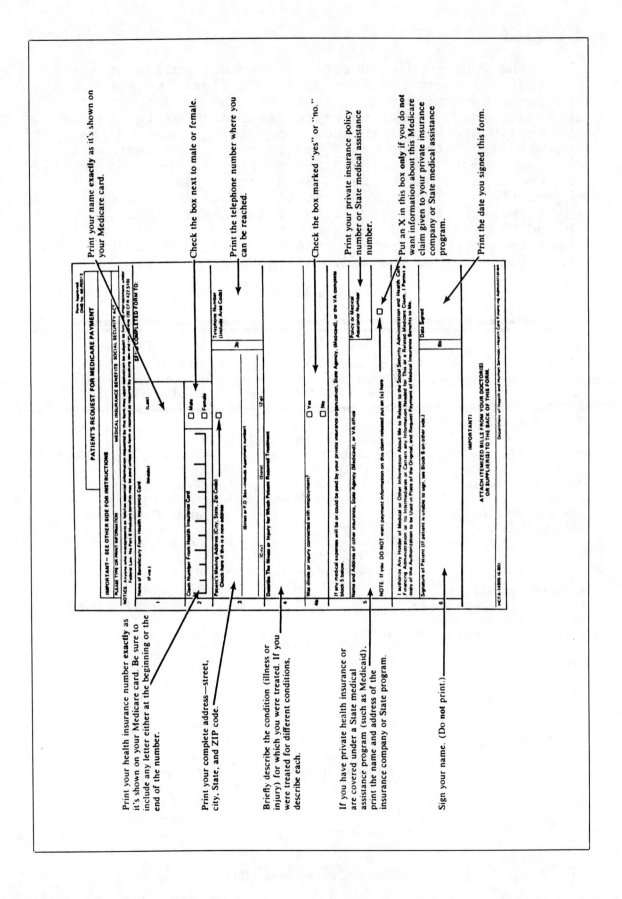

Print your name exactly as it's shown on your Medicare card.

Check the box next to male or female.

Print the telephone number where you can be reached.

Check the box marked "yes" or "no."

Print your private insurance policy number or State medical assistance number.

Put an X in this box only if you do not want information about this Medicare claim given to your private insurance company or State medical assistance program.

Print the date you signed this form.

Print your health insurance number exactly as it's shown on your Medicare card. Be sure to include any letter either at the beginning or the end of the number.

Print your complete address—street, city, State, and ZIP code.

Briefly describe the condition (illness or injury) for which you were treated. If you were treated for different conditions, describe each.

If you have private health insurance or are covered under a State medical assistance program (such as Medicaid), print the name and address of the insurance company or State program.

Sign your name. (Do not print.)

Step 3

Send your completed form and doctors' bills to the Medicare "carrier" for your area. Carriers are the private insurance companies which handle medical insurance claims for Medicare. Be sure to write "Medicare" on the outside of the envelope; these insurance companies get lots of mail and you will speed things up if you make it clear that your envelope should go to the department that processes Medicare claims. To find out where to send your claim, look on the Request form. The address may already be printed on it. If not, check the following list for the state where you received treatment. If the state has more than one carrier, check to see which carrier handles claims for the county where you received the medical treatment or services.

■ ■ ■

Alabama

Medicare
Blue Cross-Blue Shield of
Alabama
P.O. Box C-140
Birmingham, Alabama 35205

Alaska

Medicare
Aetna Life & Casualty
Crown Plaza
1500 S.W. First Avenue
Portland, Oregon 97201

Arizona

Medicare
Aetna Life & Casualty
Medicare Claim Administration
3010 West Fairmount Avenue
Phoenix, Arizona 85017

Arkansas

Medicare
Arkansas Blue Cross and Blue
Shield
P.O. Box 1418
Little Rock, Arkansas 72203

California

*Counties of: Los Angeles,
Orange, San Diego, Ventura,
Imperial, San Luis Obispo,
Santa Barbara*
Medicare
Transamerica Occidental Life
Insurance Co.
Box 54905
Terminal Annex
Los Angeles, California 90054

Rest of State:
Medicare
Blue Shield of California
P.O. Box 7968, Rincon Annex
San Francisco, California 94120

Colorado

Medicare
Blue Shield of Colorado
700 Broadway
Denver, Colorado 80273

Connecticut

Medicare
Connecticut General Life
Insurance Co.
100 Barnes Road, North
Wallingford, Connecticut 06492

Delaware

Medicare
Pennsylvania Blue Shield
P.O. Box 65
Camp Hill, Pennsylvania 17011

District of Columbia

Medicare
Pennsylvania Blue Shield
P.O. Box 100
Camp Hill, Pennsylvania 17011

Florida

Counties of: Dade, Monroe
Medicare
Group Health, Inc.
P.O. Box 341370
Miami, Florida 33134

Rest of State:
Medicare
Blue Shield of Florida, Inc.
P.O. Box 2525
Jacksonville, Florida 32231

Georgia

The Prudential Insurance Co. of
America
Medicare Part B
P.O. Box 95466
Executive Park Station
Atlanta, Georgia 30347

Hawaii

Medicare
Aetna Life & Casualty
P.O. Box 3947
Honolulu, Hawaii 96812

Idaho

Medicare
The Equitable Life Assurance
Society
P.O. Box 8048
Boise, Idaho 83707

Illinois

E.D.S. Federal Corp.
Medicare Claims
P.O. Box 66906
Chicago, Illinois 60666

Indiana

Medicare Part B
120 West Market Street
Indianapolis, Indiana 46204

Iowa

Medicare
Iowa Medical Service
636 Grand
Des Moines, Iowa 50307

Kansas

*Counties of: Johnson,
Wyandotte*
Medicare
Blue Shield of Kansas City
P.O. Box 169
Kansas City, Missouri 64141

Rest of State:
Medicare
Blue Shield of Kansas
P.O. Box 239
Topeka, Kansas 66601

Kentucky

Medicare
Metropolitan Life Insurance Co.
1218 Harrodsburg Road
Lexington, Kentucky 40504

Louisiana

Medicare
Pan-American Life Insurance
Co.
P.O. Box 60450
New Orleans, Louisiana 70160

Maine

Medicare
Blue Shield of Massachusetts-
Maine
P.O. Box 1010
Biddeford, Maine 04005

Maryland

*Counties of: Montgomery,
Prince Georges*
Medicare
Pennsylvania Blue Shield
P.O. Box 100
Camp Hill, Pennsylvania 17011
Rest of State:
Maryland Blue Shield, Inc.
700 East Joppa Road
Towson, Maryland 21204

Massachusetts

Medicare
Blue Shield of Massachusetts,
Inc.
55 Accord Park Drive
Rockland, Massachusetts 02371

Michigan

Medicare
Blue Shield of Michigan
P.O. Box 2201
Detroit, Michigan 48231

Minnesota

*Counties of: Anoka, Dakota,
Filmore, Goodhue, Hennepin,
Houston, Olmstead, Ramsey,
Wabasha, Washington, Winona*
Medicare
The Travelers Insurance
Company
8120 Penn Avenue, South
Bloomington, Minnesota 55431

Rest of State:
Medicare
Blue Shield of Minnesota
P.O. Box 43357
St. Paul, Minnesota 55164

Mississippi

Medicare
The Travelers Insurance Co.
P.O. Box 22545
Jackson, Mississippi 39205

Missouri

*Counties of: Andrew, Atchison,
Bates, Benton, Buchanan,
Caldwell, Carroll, Cass, Clay,
Clinton, Daviess, DeKalb,
Gentry, Grundy, Harrison,
Henry, Holt, Jackson, Johnson,
Lafayette, Livingston, Mercer,
Nodaway, Pettis, Platte, Ray,
St. Clair, Saline, Vernon, Worth*
Medicare
Blue Shield of Kansas City
P.O. Box 169
Kansas City, Missouri 64141

Rest of State:
Medicare
General American Life
Insurance Co.
P.O. Box 505
St. Louis, Missouri 63166

Montana

Medicare
Montana Physicians' Service
P.O. Box 4310
Helena, Montana 59601

Nebraska

Medicare
Mutual of Omaha Insurance
Co.
P.O. Box 456, Downtown
Station
Omaha, Nebraska 68101

Nevada

Medicare
Aetna Life & Casualty
P.O. Box 11260
Phoenix, Arizona 85017

New Hampshire
Medicare
New Hampshire-Vermont
Physician Service
Two Pillsbury Street
Concord, New Hampshire 03306

New Jersey
Medicare
The Prudential Insurance Co. of
America
P.O. Box 3000
Linwood, New Jersey 08221

New Mexico
Medicare
The Equitable Life Assurance
Society
P.O. Box 3070, Station D
Albuquerque, New Mexico
87110

New York
*Counties of: Bronx, Columbia,
Delaware, Dutchess, Greene,
Kings, Nassau, New York,
Orange, Putnam, Richmond,
Rockland, Suffolk, Sullivan,
Ulster, Westchester*
Medicare
Blue Cross-Blue Shield of
Greater New York
P.O. Box 458
Murray Hill Station
New York, New York 10016

County of: Queens
Medicare
Group Health, Inc.
P.O. Box A966,
Times Square Station
New York, New York 10036

Rest of State:
Medicare
Blue Shield of Western New
York
P.O. Box 600
Binghamton, New York 13902

North Carolina
The Prudential Insurance Co. of
America
Medicare B Division
P.O. Box 2126
High Point, North Carolina
27261

North Dakota
Medicare
Blue Shield of North Dakota
4510 13th Avenue, S.W.
Fargo, North Dakota 58121

Ohio
Medicare
Nationwide Mutual Insurance
Co.
P.O. Box 57
Columbus, Ohio 43216

Oklahoma
Medicare
Aetna Life & Casualty
Jamestown Office Park
3031 N.W. 64th Street
Oklahoma City, Oklahoma
73116

Oregon
Medicare
Aetna Life & Casualty
Crown Plaza
1500 S.W. First Avenue
Portland, Oregon 97201

Pennsylvania
Medicare
Pennsylvania Blue Shield
Box 65 Blue Shield Bldg.
Camp Hill, Pennsylvania 17011

Rhode Island
Medicare
Blue Shield of Rhode Island
444 Westminster Mall
Providence, Rhode Island 02901

South Carolina
Medicare
Blue Shield of South Carolina
Drawer F, Forest Acres Branch
Columbia, South Carolina
29260

South Dakota
Medicare
Blue Shield of North Dakota
4510 13th Avenue, S.W.
Fargo, North Dakota 58121

Tennessee
Medicare
The Equitable Life Assurance
Society
P.O. Box 1465
Nashville, Tennessee 37202

Texas
Medicare
Group Medical and Surgical
Service
P.O. Box 222147
Dallas, Texas 75222

Utah
Medicare
Blue Cross and Blue
Shield of Utah
P.O. Box 30270
2455 Parley's Way
Salt Lake City, Utah 84125

Vermont
Medicare
New Hampshire-Vermont
Physician Service
Two Pillsbury Street
Concord, New Hampshire 03306

Virginia
*Counties of: Arlington, Fairfax
Cities of: Alexandria, Falls
Church, Fairfax*
Medicare
Pennsylvania Blue Shield
P.O. Box 100
Camp Hill, Pennsylvania 17011

Rest of State:
Medicare
The Travelers Insurance Co.
P.O. Box 26463
Richmond, Virginia 23261

Washington

Medicare
Washington Physicians' Service
Mail to your local
Medical Service Bureau
*If you do not know which
bureau handles your claim, mail
to:*
Medicare Washington Physicians' Service
4th and Battery Bldg., 6th floor
2401 4th Avenue
Seattle, Washington 98121

West Virginia

Medicare
Nationwide Mutual Insurance Co.
P.O. Box 57
Columbus, Ohio 43216

Wisconsin

Medicare
Wisconsin Physicians' Service
Box 1787
Madison, Wisconsin 53701

Wyoming

Medicare
The Equitable Life Assurance Society
P.O. Box 628
Cheyenne, Wyoming 82001

American Samoa

Medicare
Aetna Life & Casualty
P.O. Box 3947
Honolulu, Hawaii 96812

Guam

Medicare
Aetna Life & Casualty
P.O. Box 3947
Honolulu, Hawaii 96812

Puerto Rico

Medicare
Seguros De Servicio De Salud
De Puerto Rico
G.P.O. Box 3628
San Juan, Puerto Rico 00936

Virgin Islands

Medicare
Seguros De Servicio De Salud
De Puerto Rico
G.P.O. Box 3628
San Juan, Puerto Rico 00936

■ ■ ■

Step 4

Several weeks* after you file your Patient's Request for Medicare Payment, you will receive from the Medicare carrier an "Explanation of Medicare Benefits" form, like the one Franco received (see Step 2). The same form is used whether or not your doctor has accepted a Medicare assignment. Either way, it supplies the same information about how much Medicare has paid. The only difference is in the amount you have to pay. When there is no assignment, you are personally responsible to the doctor for the difference between the total amount paid by Medicare (usually shown at the very bottom of the form) and the total amount of all the doctors' original bills. In Franco's situation, if his doctors had not accepted assignment, he would have been responsible not only for 20 percent of the approved charges (called "Amount Approved" on Franco's form), but also the difference between the approved charges and the actual doctors' bills. To be specific, Franco would have owed the doctors the difference between what Medicare actually paid,

---

* You should receive this form within thirty (30) days of the date you submitted your claim. If you don't receive it in that time, contact the carrier and inquire why the form has not been received.

$76, and the actual bills, $125. Or, put another way, Franco would have owed the two doctors $49 (as opposed to only $19 with the Medicare assignment).

Under the payment-to-you method, Medicare normally sends you its check for the amount it is paying. You are responsible for paying your doctors.

3. Getting Outpatient Hospital, Clinic and Lab Bills Paid

When it comes to outpatient care at a hospital, clinic or laboratory, Medicare medical insurance pays 80 percent of the approved charges minus your $75 yearly deductible. Usually, the hospital or other facility will prepare the forms for you and send them to the Medicare carrier for payment. The facility will then bill you directly for the remaining 20 percent of the reasonable charges, and for the unpaid portion of your deductible. Make sure you bring your Medicare card with you when you go to the facility; it will speed up the process. When Medicare pays its share to the facility, you will receive an Explanation of Medicare Benefits form just as you do when doctor bills are paid (see form at end of Section 2(a) of this chapter).

4. How Long Do You Have to Submit Your Medicare Claims?

You should submit all Medicare claims as soon as is reasonably possible. But legally, you have at least 15 months from the date you receive a particular medical service or treatment within which to submit your Patient's Request for Medicare Payment form. The following table explains exactly how these limits work:

For services you receive between:	Your claim must be submitted by
October 1, 1981 and September 31, 1982	December 31, 1983
October 1, 1982 and September 30, 1983	December 31, 1984
October 1, 1983 September 30, 1984	December 31, 1985

5. How to Get Help with Your Paperwork

If you are not sure what to put on one of the forms, or are not sure which bills to include with which forms, or you can't figure out how to read a form that Medicare has sent to you, there are several places to contact for assistance. First, try the Medicare carrier which is handling your claim. You can find their number in the telephone book under the United States Government listings, Department of Health and Human Services, Social Security Administration, Medicare. There is usually a separate listing for Medicare questions. If there is no separate listing for Medicare, call the local Social Security office and they can give you the Medicare number. Expect to have a hard time getting through on the phone, though. Since the intermediaries and carriers for Medicare don't consider people with Medicare claims to be "paying customers," they don't provide them with very good services. You may get a busy signal for hours on end at a Medicare information number. Keep trying, or write to them with your question.

It may be easier to get help with forms and have simple questions answered at your local Social Security office. Go

147

early in the day, as the wait for assistance tends to be a long one. And remember that Medicare questions are not always answered with an eye toward giving you the broadest possible coverage. However, if you have a simple question, such as what information to include on which form, or a question about something Medicare sent you in the mail, the information you get from Social Security will probably be accurate and up-to-date.

If your question about Medicare is more sophisticated, such as what kind of "strategy" to use in getting a certain bill covered, or how to get certain borderline medical treatment covered by Medicare in the first place, you are probably better off to seek assistance at your local senior citizens center. Many centers have classes and counseling sessions dealing specifically with Medicare problems. Even if no classes or counseling sessions are regularly scheduled, there is often a staff member or volunteer who is knowledgeable about Medicare and is willing to help you figure out the best way to collect your benefits. And if there is no one at the center who can help you with your particular problem or question, they will be able to refer you to someone who can help. Since so many older Americans have Medicare, the senior centers are used to handling Medicare questions and problems. Best of all, their services are free and their attitude positive.

■■■

S. What Can You Do if Your Medicare Claim is Denied?

Unfortunately, not every Medicare request for payment runs a smooth course. Sometimes the Medicare intermediary or carrier will deny coverage entirely for what you believe is a covered medical service. On other occasions, Medicare will cover some but not all of what you think should be covered, or will cover only 80 percent of approved charges when you think the charges should be paid under a rule that pays 100 percent. In any of these cases, you may appeal the decision of the intermediary or carrier through specific Medicare procedures. The procedures themselves are not complicated. The separate procedures for Part A and Part B coverage are explained step-by-step in the following sections. The most important element of these appeals, and sometimes the most difficult to arrange, is the cooperation of your doctor. As you will see, the decision on an appeal often depends on what the doctor says in his or her report about the medical condition and its treatment, and on how much assistance you can get from your doctor in providing whatever clarification or additional information is needed during the course of your appeal.

It is unfortunate but true that many doctors view their responsiblity to the patient as ending with the completion of the technical treatment of the ailment, such as the prescription of drugs or reading of test results. This sort of doctor is not particularly concerned with how you pay the bill, as long as you pay it. If you are lucky enough to have a doctor who will give some attention to your needs relative to Medicare coverage, you will find the Medicare appeal process much easier (and probably won't find yourself having to deal with any appeals at all). But if your doctor refuses to spend the small amount of time it takes to listen to your problem and help you with the paperwork or write the brief letter it would take to solve a problem, you are sure to have a frustrating time. Indeed, it may be so annoying that you may even consider changing doctors. Many progressive health care people believe that if a doctor will not treat the "whole person," including a patient's pocketbook, then he or she is not a "whole doctor." Or, as a wise country doctor once said, "Good doctors don't treat diseases, they treat people."

1. Appealing Denial of Your Hospital Bill Claim

Generally, there are three reasons why a Part A hospital insurance claim might be denied:

- It is determined the services provided you in the hospital were not "medically necessary;"

- The services could have been provided without you being an inpatient;

- Your stay at the hospital or nursing facility was, or became, "custodial" rather than for legitimate medical treatment.

Who decides these questions?

How to Appeal
Denial of Your Hospital Bill Claim

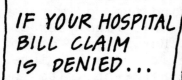 IF YOUR HOSPITAL BILL CLAIM IS DENIED...

GET YOUR DOCTOR'S ASSISTANCE. (THIS WILL MAKE THINGS MUCH EASIER.)

SUBMIT A FULL BILL TO MEDICARE

REQUEST RECONSIDERATION FROM THE HOSPITAL'S "UTILIZATION REVIEW COMMITTEE"

 CHECK "THE "WAIVER OF LIABILITY RULE" (SEE STEP 5)
o YOU MAY BE HOME FREE UNDER THIS RULE.

 REQUEST RECONSIDERATION BY THE INTERMEDIARY
o DO THIS IN WRITING
o EXPECT A WRITTEN REPONSE

DON'T FORGET TO KEEP COPIES OF EVERYTHING!

FILE A REQUEST FOR A HEARING
o WITHIN 60 DAYS OF DENIAL

 HEARING
o THESE FOLLOW THE SAME RULES AS SOCIAL SECURITY (SEE CHAPTER 5)

 APPEAL TO THE APPEALS COUNCIL

 FILE A LAWSUIT

Step 1. The First Review

Your admission to a hospital or nursing facility is initially reviewed by the Utilization Review Committee of the facility at which you are a patient or by your area's Professional Standards Review Organization, as explained in Section R(1) of this chapter.

■

Step 2. Reconsideration by the Utilization Review Committee

If your admission to a hospital or skilled nursing facility, or some medical service you receive while an inpatient, is initially denied Medicare coverage by the Utilitzation Review Committee or Professional Standards Review Organization, your first step should be to ask them for reconsideration of their decision. Ask your doctor to contact URC or PSRO and provide them with any additional information which might support your claim. A personal appearance by your doctor in front of the Committee or Organization, or at least some personal or telephone contact with its members, can be very important in convincing these reviewing doctors to change their decision and rule that your admission and treatment is medically necessary.

■

Step 3. Submit Your Bills to Medicare

Even if the URC or PSRO will not change its decision, you should insist that the hospital or facility submit your bills to Medicare. Since the Utilization Review Committee does not have the final say whether Medicare will or will not pay for the hospitalization, the billing department of the facility must forward your bills to the Medicare inter- mediary if you request it. Unfortunately, during the period when the intermediary--Blue Cross/Blue Shield or one of the other large insurance companies that handles hospitalization claims for Medicare--is reviewing your claim and deciding on its own whether or not to pay for it (a process that could take weeks or months) you are personally responsible to the hospital or skilled nursing facility for all of your bills. If the intermediary later decides your inpatient treatment is covered, it will pay the hospital or facility directly. If you have already paid some or all of your bill, the Medicare intermediary will then reimburse you.

■■■

Step 4. Reconsideration of the Intermediary's Denial of Your Claim

Whether the hospital or nursing facility review committee approves or denies Medicare coverage of your admission and treatment, the intermediary makes its own independent decision on Medicare coverage. In most instances, the intermediary will follow the decision of the URC or PSRO, since they are all using the same Medicare regulations and thus usually reach the same conclusions. But whether or not the facility review committee denies your claim, if the intermediary approves the claim, Medicare will pay. If the intermediary denies the claim, however, Medicare will not pay.

If this happens, the next step is to request reconsideration by the intermediary. This request must be in writing and must be filed within 60 days of the date you receive notice of the denial of all or part of your claim. A form called "Request for Reconsideration" is available from the intermediary or from your local Social Security office. If you receive notice of denial of your claim, call the number given on the notice of denial and ask that the intermediary send you a reconsideration form. This reconsideration doesn't really amount to much, however, unless you can present new information which the intermediary did not consider on its initial review. Again, the involvement of your doctor can be very important. Have your doctor write a detailed explanation of why your inpatient treatment was medically necessary or why certain services should be covered. Also, be sure the hospital sends the intermediary any medical records, laboratory reports, etc., which the intermediary did not have at the time of the initial decision. The hospital or nursing facility administrator's office is required to forward such information if you so request.

REMINDER: Always keep copies of all correspondence and other papers concerning your Medicare coverage. Also, keep notes on all conversations you have either with your doctor's office, the hospital or the Medicare intermediary. Write down the dates of conversations and the name of the person with whom you talked. Also, make sure you keep track of the dates you mailed any correspondence or information to the intermediary. You never know when something might get lost in the mail or in the shuffle of papers in a big office, or when someone may forget a conversation they had with you. Keep track.

■ ■ ■

Step 5. Eligibility for "Waiver-of-Liability" Rule

There is a minor safety valve in the Medicare payment procedure that may protect you even though the intermediary decides your inpatient bills are not covered by Medicare. If the intermediary determines the services provided you were not medically necessary or that your care was "custodial" only, it then decides whether the "provider" (the hospital or nursing facility) and/or you, the patient, knew or should have known the services would not be covered by Medicare.

If neither you nor the provider knew or should have known that the services would not be covered--because, for example, a new Medicare regulation went into effect or because some technicality prevents coverage--Medicare will pay the bills. This is known as the "waiver-of-liability" rule.

If the provider should have known there would be no coverage, but you, the patient, did not know, the provider would be stuck with the bill. In this situation, Medicare won't pay, but you won't have to, either. Unless the hospital or nursing facility, through the Utilization Review Committee, informed you in writing that your stay in the facility and the services provided would not be covered by Medicare, it is presumed you did not know you would not be covered. In other words, if the hospital or nursing facility never told you in writing that your bills would not be paid by Medicare, you can be pretty sure you won't be personally responsible for payment.

What should you do if you were informed by your doctor, or by the Utilization Review Committee of the hospital or nursing facility, or both, that your inpatient status was medically necessary, but the Medicare intermediary denies coverage? Explain to the intermediary, in writing, why you believed your inpatient status was covered by Medicare and make sure to mention the failure of the hospital or nursing facility to inform you in writing you were not covered, if this is what happened. And again, involvement by your doctor may be crucial; have your physician write to the intermediary and explain that you were informed that the inpatient care was medically necessary and would be covered. If you received any information about a particular Medicare rule from a hospital, provider or Social Security itself, explain this as well. If you were honestly led to believe your inpatient care would be covered by Medicare, you must insist you were unaware of the fact you would not be covered. The waiver-of-liability rule exists to protect you in such situations; if your case fits the rule, do not hesitate to demand the rule be applied. That's what it's there for.

■

Step 6. Request a Hearing

If the Medicare intermediary decides your bills are not covered by Medicare hospital insurance and you are not excused from paying the bills by the "waiver-of-liability" rule, the next step after reconsideration is to file a written request for a "hearing." Within 60 days of the date you receive written notice of the reconsideration decision, you must file a written request for a hearing. Forms are available at your local Social Security office. Note, though, you are entitled to a hearing only if the amount you are contesting is $100 or more.

The hearing on your appeal will be held in front of a Social Security Administration administrative law judge. The hearing is conducted much like other Social Security appeals hearings. For a full discussion on how these hearings work, see Chapter 5, Section E. In a Medicare hearing, perhaps the single most important element is your doctor's "testimony." Although your doctor can appear personally at a hearing and testify in front of the judge, most doctors will simply write out an explanation of why your medical condition required inpatient care and submit that written statement to the judge instead of appearing in person. The doctor can either give you such a written statement and you can forward it to the judge, or the doctor can send it directly to the judge.

Though it may take months to get a hearing, it is definitely worth the time and effort if the amount of money you are contesting is considerable. A fairly high percentage of cases are won on appeal. If you are organized and prepared and follow the instructions outlined in Chapter 5, you may well win your right to coverage through the appeal process.

■

Step 7. Appeal to the Appeals Council

If you disagree with the decision of the administrative law judge after a hearing, your next step is to file an appeal with the Social Security Administration Appeals Council in Washington, D.C. Again, refer to Chapter 5, Section E for a brief description of this process. It's only a brief discussion because the Appeals Council review is not much to talk about. Initially, they receive no new information that is not already in your file, and only rarely grant an actual hearing. If they do grant a review, they may permit you to submit new evidence. Why bother filing the appeal then? Because in order to move on to the final appeal step, you must go through the motions of filing an appeal with the Appeals Council.

■

Step 8. File a Lawsuit

As with most other Social Security Administration decisions, Medicare hospital insurance decisions can be appealed to the federal courts by filing a lawsuit. Such a lawsuit can only be filed, however, if the amount of money you are contesting is $1,000 (one thousand dollars) or more. If it is, consider finding legal help and filing a lawsuit as discussed in Chapter 5, Section E.

2. Appealing Denial of Your Medical Insurance Claim

It is very likely that during the course of one or more of your Medicare medical insurance claims, you will disagree with the carrier's decision about how much is an "approved charge" or about whether a particular treatment or service is covered by Medicare. Unfortunately, your right to appeal these Medicare Part B decisions is more severely limited than is your right to appeal Part A hospital insurance decisions. The success rate of medical insurance appeals is likewise lower.

How to Appeal
Denial of a Medicare Bill Claim

IF YOUR MEDICARE CARRIER DOESN'T PAY A MEDICAL BILL

GET YOUR DOCTOR'S ASSISTANCE

REQUEST RECONSIDERATION BY THE CARRIER

o FILE A FORM WITHIN 60 DAYS OF THEIR DENIAL

REQUEST A HEARING FROM THE CARRIER

o WITHIN 60 DAYS

o IF THE AMOUNT IS $100. OR MORE.

GET A LIMITED HEARING CONDUCTED BY THE CARRIER'S OFFICER

THIS DECISION IS FINAL

a. Reconsideration by the Carrier

   Decisions concerning payment of Medicare medical insurance claims are made by the local Medicare "carrier," either
Blue Cross, Blue Shield or one of the other large insurance
companies. And appeals of the carrier's decisions are first
heard and decided by--you guessed it--the carrier. If you
think this sounds like asking the fox to guard the chickens,
you're right. But it's a common practice in government
programs, and it has survived challenge in court, so it
seems it's the Medicare medical insurance appeal system
we're stuck with.

   Within 6 months of the date you receive an Explanation
of Medicare Benefits notice, you must file a written request
for review of the carrier's decision. This request can be
made in a simple letter to the carrier (the address will be
in your Explanation of Medicare Benefits notice) in which
you explain why you believe that there has been an error.
Include with your request your full name, Medicare claim
number and any information or copies of records the carrier
may not have had at the time of its decision.

   The review consists only of a check of the documents in
your file for errors or miscalculations and a consideration
of any new materials submitted after the original decision
was made. You do not have an opportunity to appear in
person at this stage of the appeal process. Though sometimes clerical errors and errors of omission--failing to
include a particular bill, for example--are corrected at
this stage of the appeal process, not too many other kinds
of coverage decisions get changed here. Disputes about
whether a particular service should have been covered, or
about special circumstances which should have made the "approved charges" for your treatment higher than what the
carrier decided, will probably have to wait for the next
level of appeal to have a serious chance to be reversed.

b. Medicare Appeal Hearing

   If the amount you are disputing is $100 or more, you
may appeal the decision of the carrier within 6 months from
receipt of the notice of the carrier's decision after review. If your complaint involves less than $100, you're out
of luck. You may file a request for a hearing either with
the carrier or at your local Social Security office.

   Although your Medicare Part B appeal will get you a
hearing, it is a very limited one. In Part B medical insurance hearings, you may present evidence and explain in
person why your coverage should be different, or why a
particular treatment or service you received should be given

a higher "approved charge" than normally given for that type of service. You do not have any official subpoena power (to compel witnesses to appear in your behalf), but you may bring witnesses to testify on your behalf. Your most important evidence, as in many Medicare disputes, may be a letter from your doctor explaining in detail why the treatment provided should be covered by Medicare medical insurance, or why the particular treatment or service provided should be given a higher approved charge--because of something unusual about your case or about the treatment or service provided--than the amount allowed by the carrier.

The hearing officers who listen to your appeal and make the decision are appointed by the carrier. Strange, eh? Though human nature tells us they will not consistently make decisions which run against the interests of the people who hired them, they are more impartial than one might first imagine. Medicare makes periodic reviews of the rate of reversals of decisions on appeal, and will not permit across-the-board denials. Also, the hearing officers are professionals in the field of health care administration and their professional "impartiality" works to balance their inclination to want to please the "boss." The result is that if you have clearly been wronged in a Medicare decision, you stand a good chance of having that decision reversed at the hearing. If it is only a question of shading an interpretation of a rule one way or the other, however, or of deciding if "reasonable" charges should be more reasonable, you will probably find that in most instances you will come up empty.

You will receive a written notice of the decision of the hearing officer. And that's it. Finished. Kaput. There are no further appeals after the hearing in front of the carrier's chosen hearing officer. You do not have any right to appeal the decision of the hearing officer to the Social Security Administration Appeals Council or to file a lawsuit in court. That's the law. You are in the hands of the carrier.

Medicaid:
Filling Some of the
Holes in Medicare

CHAPTER 7

Highlights

You may be eligible for Medicaid assistance in paying your medical bills even though you are also eligible for Medicare, you have private health insurance and/or you own your own home [see Section (C) & (I)].

If your spouse is in a nursing facility or other institution for a prolonged stay, your income and separate assets need not be counted in determining his/her Medicaid eligibility [see Section (D)].

Medicaid may be able to pay for some medical bills for up to three months <u>before</u> you actually filed an application [see Section (E)].

Medicaid can pay for Medicare deductibles and co-insurance amounts, and, in some states, for medical costs Medicare does not cover at all, such as prescription drugs, eyeglasses, preventive examinations, etc. [see Section (F)].

Some states require prior approval before you can be covered by Medicaid for certain medical services [see Section (G)].

"How old would you be if you didn't know how old you was?"
Satchel Paige, *quoted in Garson Kanin,*
It Takes Time to Be Young

■ ■ ■

A. Introduction

Let's repeat the sobering fact about Medicare that we noted at the beginning of the previous chapter. When all types of medical expenses for older Americans are added up, Medicare winds up paying for only about 40 percent. So the question becomes, other than staying healthy, what can you do about the other 60 percent? The answer can often be found in two different approaches, depending on your financial circumstances. On the one hand, if you are particularly financially needy--that is, have a low income and few assets--you may qualify for the Medicaid program in your state. On the other hand, if you have substantial income or assets and are thus not eligible for Medicaid, another option is to find and pay for private health insurance to supplement your Medicare coverage. Medicaid is discussed in this chapter, while the private health insurance alternative is covered in the next.

■ ■ ■

B. Medicaid: What Is It?

Medicaid is a program established by the federal government and administered by the individual states which provides medical assistance in the form of payments of medical costs for financially needy people. For low income seniors, Medicaid operates <u>in addition to Medicare</u> to cover some of the medical costs Medicare does not pay for. The basic difference between the two programs is simple: Medicare is available to most everyone age 65 or over, regardless of financial need, while Medicaid is available only to those who are financially needy. "Need" is defined by the Medicaid program in the state in which a person lives. There are currently more than 25 million people who receive some form of Medicaid assistance; about one-fourth of them are also on Medicare. [Refer back to the chart in Chapter 6, Section C, for a side-by-side comparison of Medicare and Medicaid.]

Federal guidelines exist for Medicaid, but these guidelines are fairly broad and each state is permitted to make its own rules regarding eligibility, coverage and benefits. Therefore, it's impossible to tell you here exactly what the rules are for your state's Medicaid program. What the following sections do explain are the basic eligibility and coverage rules of Medicaid which are common to most states so that you can be aware of the benefits which might be available to you. You must check with the local social services or welfare agency in your area to find out the specific details of Medicaid in your state.

IMPORTANT: All questions about Medicaid go to your local (state or county) social services, health department or welfare office, not to the Social Security office.

C. Who Is Eligible for Medicaid?

The rules regarding Medicaid eligibility vary widely from state to state, but generally there are just two different approaches to who is eligible.

1. "Categorically Needy"

To qualify as "categorically needy," your income and assets must be at or below specific, predetermined dollar amounts. The standards for income and assets vary among the states. Some of the states use the same eligibility rules that are used for the federal Supplemental Security Income

(SSI) program (see Chapter 9) to determine Medicaid eligibility, while other state have their own, stricter or easier standards.

a. SSI Rules

In some states, you automatically receive Medicaid if you are eligible for SSI benefits. The SSI eligibility rules are discussed in detail in Chapter 9, but generally you can be eligible even if you own your home, regardless of value, own an automobile worth no more than $4,500 current market value, and have cash and other liquid assets of no more than $1,500 ($2,500 for a couple), as long as you have a very low current income.

b. Stricter Rules

Some states require even lower levels of income and assets than SSI standards, including dollar limits on the value of your home and lower limits on the value of your automobile and personal property, in order to qualify for Medicaid.

2. "Medically Needy"

Although they are not required to do so by federal Medicaid rules, some states provide Medicaid coverage for certain people who would not be eligible for it under SSI (or stricter) rules. A state that provides Medicaid to the "medically needy" typically covers people whose medical expenses, when subtracted from their income and assets, would bring their available income and assets down to the eligibility levels for that state. In other words, if your savings are a thousand dollars more than what is allowed by the categorically needy rules in your state, but you have medical bills of more than a thousand dollars that are not paid for by Medicare, you can be considered "medically needy" and thus eligible for Medicaid. This process of subtracting actual medical bills from income and assets is called "spending down," in Medicaid slang. This is because medical bills would force you to spend your extra money down to the point that you would meet eligibility levels.

By now you should understand the broad difference between "medically needy" and "categorically needy." If you're unsure, re-read the last few pages.

The following states provide Medicaid to the "medically needy" as well as to the "categorically needy."

Arkansas
California
Connecticut
District of Columbia
Guam
Hawaii
Illinois
Kansas
Kentucky
Louisiana
Maine
Maryland

Massachusetts
Michigan
Minnesota
Montana
Nebraska
New Hampshire
New York
North Carolina
North Dakota
Oklahoma
Pennsylvania
Puerto Rico

Rhode Island
Tennessee
Utah
Vermont
Virgin Islands
Virginia
Washington
West Virginia
Wisconsin

IMPORTANT LIMITATION ON SERVICES: Even though these states provide some Medicaid coverage to those who are only "medically needy," budget-cutting has led many of them to send their medically needy Medicaid recipients to county or other local health clinics rather than permitting them to go to private doctors, clinics or hospitals. These county health providers are generally understaffed, overworked and impersonal. And the wait for services many be many hours long.

D. Whose Money Is Counted in Determining Medicaid Eligibility?

Generally, Medicaid will not consider the income or assets of your children or any other relative in deciding your eligibility. This is true even if you are living in the same household as your children or other relatives. An exception to this, however, comes when you are receiving regular financial support from a relative; in that case, the support you actually receive would be counted as part of your income/assets, though the rest of that relative's income and assets would not be counted "against" you.

Your husband or wife's income and assets are a different story, though. All of your spouse's income and assets are "deemed" to be available to you if you are living together (though not if you are divorced or separated and living apart, except to the extent that your separated spouse is actually contributing to your support). This rule, unfortunately, has had the effect of keeping many older couples from marrying; they fear if they are married a serious illness could bankrupt not only themselves but also their loved one before they would become eligible for Medicaid assistance.*

A special situation exists if your husband or wife is in a nursing facility or other institution for a stay of more than one month. If the spouse who remains home is not eligible for Medicaid, then his or her assets and income are not counted in deciding whether the spouse in the nursing facility or other institution is eligible for Medicaid.

■ ■ ■

E. How to Apply for Medicaid

In order to qualify for Medicaid, you must file a written application to the state agency which handles Medicaid in your state, usually the Department of Social Services, Health Department or Welfare Department. (In some states you can apply at your local Social Security office if you are also applying for SSI benefits. See Chapter 9.) If you or your spouse are hospitalized, ask to see a medical social worker in the hospital. He or she will help you fill out the applications.

You will be interviewed and assisted in filling out your application by a Medicaid eligibility worker. There may be lots of forms to fill out and you may have to return to the office for several different interviews. Don't get discouraged. Medicaid is part of a huge bureaucracy that puts everyone through the wringer before the application process is completed. Delays, repeated forms and interviews do not mean you are being suspected of "cheating" or that you are not going to be eligible. To keep costs down, the state tries to make it difficult for people to get through the qualification process so that some people will give up and fail to claim benefits to which they are entitled. Remember, in Medicaid application, patience is not only a virtue, it's pretty close to an absolute necessity. Don't give up.

---

* The other side of this coin, though, is that if couples are not married, one cannot take advantage of the benefits payable to the "spouse" of the other through Social Security, SSI or private pensions.

Normally, you will receive a decision on your Medicaid eligibility within a couple of weeks; the law states a decision must be made within 45 days. If you do not hear from Medicaid within a month of your application, don't be shy; call up the social worker who interviewed you and ask what the story is on your application. Sometimes it takes a little polite pushing to get a decision out of an overworked social services agency.

If you are found to be eligible, Medicaid can even cover you for a limited period before your application was submitted, if you have already incurred medical bills. This retroactive eligibility can go back to the beginning of the third month prior to the date you filed your application. Make sure your Medicaid eligibility worker understands you want your Medicaid coverage to apply to the period before your application if you had medical bills during that time.

How long does Medicaid coverage last? That depends on your financial position and your medical costs. Medicaid eligibility is reviewed periodically, usually every six months and at least once a year. If your financial situation has not improved sufficiently in that period of time to put you over the eligibility limits for your state's Medicaid program, you will be continued on Medicaid until the next review period. But if you were eligible for Medicaid because of extraordinary medical costs (in a state which gives Medicaid to the "medically needy"), and those medical costs are not continuing, you may be dropped from Medicaid. Of course, if new medical costs arise, you may apply again for Medicaid coverage.

F. What Services Does Medicaid Pay For?

Medicaid covers the same kinds of services that Medicare covers and, in most states, also covers an additional list of medical services Medicare does not. In addition, Medicaid can pay much of the amounts Medicare does not pay in hospital and doctor bills. Specifically, this means:

▪Medicaid can pay the inpatient hospital insurance deductible that Medicare does not pay [see Chapter 6, Section J(3)(a)].

■Medicaid can pay the Medicare medical insurance deductible [see Chapter 6, Section N(1)].

■Medicaid can pay the 20 percent of the "reasonable charges" that Medicare medical insurance does not pay of doctor bills and other outpatient care.

■Medicaid can, in some instances, pay for the monthly premium charged for Medicare Part B medical insurance.

"Mandatory" Coverage

Whether or not you are covered by Medicare, Medicaid covers the following "mandatory" medical services (this is true in every state):

■Inpatient hospital or skilled nursing facility care

■Outpatient hospital or clinic services

■Independent laboratory and X-ray services

■Physicians' services

■Home health care services

■Transportation (ambulance, if necessary) to and from the place you receive medical services

"Optional" Coverage

In many states, Medicaid will also cover some of the following "optional" medical services:

■State-licensed practitioner's care (chiropractor, optometrist, podiatrist, acupuncturist, etc.)

■Eye glasses

■Dental care

■Prosthetic devices

■Prescribed drugs

■Physical, speech and occupational therapy

■Private-duty nursing

■Diagnostic, preventive, screening and rehabilitative services

■Inpatient psychiatric care for those 65 and over

SHE SAYS SHE'S PREPARED TO BE PATIENT, BUT SHE'S NOT LEAVING THIS OFFICE UNTIL SHE GETS SOME DEFINITE ANSWERS.

Remember, though, the kind and amount of optional services covered vary widely from state to state. You must check with your state's social services or social welfare office to find out whether a particular medical service is covered by Medicaid in your state. If you have any doubt about whether a specific medical service is covered by Medicaid, don't take a simple yes or no answer over the telephone. Go down to the office which handles Medicaid in your area and discuss the matter with a Medicaid coverage worker.

G. Requirements for Medicaid Coverage of a Medical Service

As with Medicare, the fact that a particular medical service or treatment is generally covered does not necessarily mean it will be covered in every instance. There are some limits to whether a covered medical service will be paid for in any given case:

■The care or service must be prescribed by a doctor and provided by a doctor or facility that "participates" in Medicaid. This means the doctor or facility accepts Medicaid payment (or Medicare plus Medicaid) as payment in full and is approved by Medicaid to accept Medicaid patients. The number of such hospitals and clinics in a given area may be quite small. REMINDER: Services for the "medically needy" in some states can be covered by Medicaid only if provided by county health clinics.

■Inpatient services must be approved as "medically necessary" by the Utilization Review Committee of the facility. For a full discussion of this Utilization Review process, see Chapter 6, Section (R)(1);

■Medicaid coverage for certain special medical services must get prior approval by a Medicaid "consultant" before you obtain the services. The rules vary from state to state, requiring prior approval for such services as elective surgery, nursing facility care, some dental care, durable medical equipment, and, in some states, any non-emergency inpatient hospital care. If you have any question that a particular medical service you need requires prior Medicaid approval, be sure to check with a Medicaid worker at your local social service or welfare office before beginning the treatment or receiving the service. They will then refer your request to the Medicaid consultant for prior approval, if necessary.

H. Will You Have to Pay Anything for Medicaid?

1. No Payments to Medical Providers

Hospitals, doctors and other providers of medical care that accept Medicaid patients must accept Medicaid's payment of reasonable charges for the services provided as payment in full. If you are eligible for both Medicare and Medicaid, and you are treated by a medical facility or doctor that accepts Medicaid patients, the Medicare decision about what the reasonable charges are will be the amount the doctor must accept from Medicare and Medicaid payments combined; you cannot be billed for any extra amounts for the covered services.

IMPORTANT: Before you obtain care from a particular doctor or medical facility, make sure they are aware you are covered by Medicaid and they "accept" Medicaid patients, meaning they accept Medicaid payment as payment in full.

2. Fees to States that Administer Medicaid

Federal law does permit states to charge some small fees to those people who qualify for Medicaid as "medically needy" (see Section C, above). If you qualify as "categorically needy," however, states can only charge you a fee if you receive one of the "optional" covered services (see Section F in this chapter for a list of "optional" and "mandatory" services). The rules regarding the amounts and types of fees that can be charged to the "medically needy" and to the "categorically needy" for optional services vary from state to state, but will probably take one of the following forms:

■Enrollment fee: Some states charge a small, one-time only fee when you first enroll in Medicaid. However, this fee cannot be charged to "categorically needy" Medicaid qualifiers.

■Monthly premium: States are permitted to charge a small monthly fee to "medically needy" Medicaid participants, whether or not they actually use Medicaid that month. The amounts vary with your income and assets, but usually come to no more than two or three dollars.

■Co-payments: State Medicaid programs are permitted to charge a co-payment (like the 20 percent of your bills Medicare medical insurance makes you pay) which is a fixed amount for each Medicaid covered service you receive. If you do not use a Medicaid service, you have no co-payment to pay. Except for "optional" services, the co-payment can only be charged to the "medically needy."

NOTE: At this point, these categories may seem a little confusing. If so, read the chapter again, slowly, to get an understanding of what "medically needy" and "categorically needy" mean, and what is meant by "mandatory" services and "optional" services. Then you can check with a Medicaid worker at the social service or welfare office where you apply for Medicaid. The Medicaid worker can tell you whether you are in one category or another, whether the particular medical treatment or service you are seeking is covered by Medicaid in your state, and whether you will have to pay anything to the state in order for Medicaid to cover that service or treatment.

I. Can You Have Private Health Insurance and Still Receive Medicaid?

You are permitted to have any amount of private health insurance and still qualify for Medicaid. The amount of your private health insurance premiums is deducted from the calculation of your income when Medicaid determines if you are under the allowable income levels to qualify for Medicaid in your state.

If you do have private health insurance, however, and the same medical service is covered by both your private insurance and by Medicaid, Medicaid will pay only the amount not paid by your insurance. If you receive a payment directly from your insurance company after Medicaid has already paid the bill, Medicaid will require you to return that insurance money to Medicaid.

J. What to Bring When You Apply for Medicaid

Since eligibility for Medicaid depends on your financial need, many of the papers and documents you need to show to the Medicaid eligibility worker have to do with your income and assets. Although the following list does not include everything a Medicaid eligibility worker might require from you, if you have everything on this list when you go to the social service, health department or welfare office, you should at least be able to get the application process started.

■Pay stubs, income tax returns or other evidence of your current income, if you have any;

■Papers showing all your financial assets, such as bank books, insurance policies, stock certificates, etc.;

- Rent receipts, lease agreements or cancelled rent checks if you are a renter, mortgage payment books and the latest tax bill or assessment on the property if you own your own home (or own any other real estate);

- Automobile registration papers, if you own a car;

- Your Social Security card or number;

- If you live with your spouse, bring information about his/her income and separate assets;

- Medical bills from the previous three months, as well as medical records or reports which confirm the medical condition which will require treatment in the near future; if you don't have copies of these bills, records or reports, bring the names and addresses of the doctors, hospitals or other medical providers which are treating you.

Even if you do not have all these papers available, go to your local social services, health department or welfare department office and file your application for Medicaid as soon as you think you may qualify for assistance because of present or upcoming medical costs. The Medicaid eligibility workers can help you get whatever papers and records are necessary.

K. Reminder: Don't Take No for an Answer

The rules regarding Medicaid coverage are complicated and subject to many different interpretations. If you think you should be eligible for Medicaid, or be covered for a particular service, but on your first try with a Medicaid worker you are denied eligibility or coverage, don't give up. Some Medicaid workers are more sympathetic than others; some might understand you better than others; some know the rules, and the loopholes in the rules, better than others, and some are more willing than others to take a chance on your behalf. If the first worker you talk to denies your claim and you are not satisfied with the reasons they give you, return and speak with someone else. If none of the workers you speak to will approve your claim, politely but firmly ask to see a supervisor. It is unfortunate, but sometimes you have to push hard to get the services you qualify for.

L. What to Do if You Are Denied Medicaid Coverage

If your efforts at convincing Medicaid eligibility workers fail to get you onto Medicaid, or if you are notified that a particular medical service will not be covered for you by Medicaid, or your Medicaid coverage is ending, you have a right to a hearing to determine if the Medicaid decision is correct. This is called a "fair hearing," although sometimes the hearings don't seem as "fair" as you would like. If you are denied Medicaid coverage of any kind for which you believe you are eligible, immediately inquire, at the office where you applied, about the procedure in your state for getting a "fair hearing." In some states, if you request a hearing in writing within 10 days after the notice that existing coverage is going to end, your coverage can stay in effect until after the "fair hearing" officer makes a decision.

A fair hearing is much like a Social Security appeal hearing described in full in Chapter 5, Section E. The rules vary from state to state, but in every state you are permitted to present evidence in the form of witnesses to testify for you or letters or documents indicating your income, assets or medical expenses. If your medical condition and treatment, as opposed to your income and assets, is the question at the hearing, then a letter from your doctor explaining your condition and treatment would be most important. You are permitted to have a friend, relative, social worker, lawyer or other representative appear with you to help at the hearing. The hearing itself is usually held at or near the welfare or social service office. It will not be too formal and you will be given an opportunity to explain your position in your own words to the hearing officer. This person is not a judge, but usually a lawyer or Medicaid eligibility specialist.

Though the odds of getting a reversal of a Medicaid denial are not in your favor at a fair hearing, such reversals do happen frequently and it's definitely worth the effort if you feel you've been wronged. If the amount of Medicaid coverage in question is significant, give it a try. Even if the fair hearing officer decides against you, usually within 90 days of the hearing, there may be procedures in your state for further appeal. Check with your local social service or welfare office for the procedures in your state for further appeal after a fair hearing.

"Medi-Gap"— Private Health Insurance

■CHAPTER 8■

HIGHLIGHTS

The federal government now provides certification for all medi-gap policies which meet certain minimum standards; make sure that any medi-gap policy you consider is government certified [see Section (C)(2)].

Make sure that the policy you get pays on a "service" basis, which means the amounts are tied to the actual charges for the services you receive, instead of an "indemnity" policy which only pays a fixed amount for any treatment, no matter how much the actual bill is [see Section (C)(3)].

Comparison shop before you buy any medi-gap insurance policy, using the charts provided [see Section (C)(4)].

Beware of traps for the unwary buyer, including "elimination periods," pre-existing illness exclusions, multiple policies, high-pressure salesmanship, etc. [see Section (D)(1) & (E)].

Consider "major medical" insurance policies and Health Maintenance Organizations (HMOs) before buying a medi-gap policy [see Section (F) & (G)].

> *"The Indian Summer of life should be a little sunny and a little sad, like the season, and infinite in wealth and depth of tone — but never hustled."*
> Henry Adams,
> *The Education of Henry Adams*

■■■

A. Introduction

If you are not eligible for Medicaid coverage to help you pay the many hospital and medical bills that Medicare doesn't pay, how can you avoid getting financially wiped out by a serious illness or injury? The answer for about one-half of all Americans 65 or over is to buy some kind of private health insurance to supplement Medicare. This type of policy is commonly called medi-gap insurance.

The term "medi-gap" derives from the notion that such policies are tailored for people who have Medicare and are designed, at least in part, to cover the "gaps" in (the amounts not paid by) Medicare. Unfortunately, like every-thing else in the insurance business, most medi-gap coverage isn't nearly as complete as its advertising would lead to you to believe. Most medi-gap policies do cover the initial Medicare deductibles and 20 percent co-insurance payments. (Remember, the deductibles are the amounts you must pay before Medicare will pay anything; the co-insurance is the 20 percent of the approved charges which Medicare does not pay under medical insurance and the amount you must pay per day for a hospital stay of more than 60 days.)

EXAMPLE: If you are hospitalized for five days and run up a $2,000 hospital bill plus another $800 of doctor bills, Medicare would normally pay your full $2,000 hospital bills minus the $304 hospital insurance deductible. Without pri-vate medi-gap insurance or Medicaid, you would be personally responsible for paying that $304 deductible. With most medi-gap policies, however, the insurance company would pay the $304. If the doctor bill was $800, Medicare might decide $600 was the "approved" charge for the doctor's service and Medicare medical insurance would then pay 80 percent of that $600, minus your $75 medical insurance deductible. Medicare would thus pay 80 percent of $525 ($600 - $75), which equals $420. You would be personally responsible for the $75 deductible, the unpaid 20 percent of reasonable charges ($105), and, if your doctor had not accepted assignment of your Medicare claim, the remaining $200 difference between Medicare's reasonable charges of

$600 and the actual bill of $800. Most medi-gap insurance policies would pay the $75 deductible and the unpaid 20 percent of reasonable charges ($105).

If you are paying close attention, you will have noticed that nothing in the above example explained what happened to the unpaid $200 difference between the reasonable charges and the doctor's actual bill. What do most medi-gap insurance policies do about that difference if your doctor does not accept assignment? The answer, unfortunately, is often nothing at all. Virtually no medi-gap policies cover this entire unpaid balance; they may work out "reasonable charges" of their own as the basis of their payment, but none picks up the entire balance of actual doctor's bills and many policies pay nothing toward this unpaid balance. So, even with medi-gap insurance, it may be very important for you to find doctors who will accept assignment of your Medicare medical insurance claim [for a refresher on how "assignment" works, see Chapter 6, Section R(2)]. Likewise, medi-gap policies usually do <u>not</u> cover services which are not covered by Medicare. For example, most medi-gap policies do not cover self-administered prescription drugs, one of the most significant medical costs for older persons. ("Major medical" policies, on the other hand, often do cover drugs. "Major medical" insurance is discussed in Section F of this chapter.)

There are too many individual health insurance policies for us to examine them all here. But what we can do is give you a guide to the types of medi-gap health insurance which supplement Medicare. This information can help give you a sense of what to look for and what to avoid. Additionally, the alternatives of "major medical" health insurance policies and Health Maintenance Organizations (HMOs) are discussed in the latter part of the chapter.

B. Protection Between Age 55 and 65

A number of people have health insurance through their work, but risk losing that health coverage if they take an "early" retirement before age 65. (And remember, unless disabled for 24 months or more, there is no Medicare for persons under age 65.) There are several things to consider here. Many health insurance group policies permit you to continue on the group policy, or transfer to a personal policy with similar coverage for reduced premiums, after you leave your employment. Usually, though, you must transfer your coverage within a short time after you leave your job. Well before you quit or retire, you should check with the health insurance or personnel office where you work to see about continued coverage.

Major medical policies, discussed in more detail later in this chapter, are also a possibility during the years between retirement and Medicare coverage. Though they charge significant premiums, they do protect you against huge medical bills and often they can be switched to a medi-gap policy with the same company when you do become eligible for Medicare. Finally, Health Maintenance Organizations, which are also discussed more fully later in this chapter, are sometimes a less expensive and more comprehensive alternative to private insurance during the years before you are eligible for Medicare.

■ ■ ■

C. Comparison Shopping for Medi-Gap Policies

The best way for you to make sure you get the best Medicare supplementary coverage for your money is to compare a number of different policies and then decide which policy--or no policy--bests fits your needs and income.

1. Using an Insurance Agent

One of the advantages of using an insurance agent in selecting a medi-gap policy is the agent should be familiar with the various provisions of several policies and can be helpful in finding a policy that fits your needs. The major disadvantage is the insurance agent is trying to make a buck, and often makes more money on certain policies, or from certain companies, than from other policies or companies. Thus they don't always make you aware of all the policies available to you and sometimes even steer you in a direction more profitable to them than to you. Also, one agent may not be aware of some policies available from companies he or she doesn't do business with, or of policies which are available through senior organizations or other groups. So, even if you do use an insurance agent, keep your own ears and eyes open for policies which might fit your needs better than the policies offered by your agent. Any honest insurance agent should be willing to find out the details of a policy you have located yourself; if the agent cannot or will not check on such a policy, it's probably time to find a new agent. Likewise, if an insurance agent is unwilling to sit down with you and compare the coverage and costs of different policies, side by side, then you ought to do some comparison shopping for a new insurance agent.

Insurance agents must be licensed to do business in your state. If an insurance agent seems a little shady to you, or pushes only one policy at you a little too hard, you might want to check to make sure the agent is licensed. Ask if the "agent" is an insurance agent or just the representative of a particular insurance company. If the agent cannot show you proof of an agent's license, don't buy any policy from him or her. And remember, a business card is <u>not</u> a license. If you have any doubts about a particular insurance agent, check with the Insurance Department of your state government; they know who is and who is not licensed as an insurance agent in your state.

2. Getting a Government Certified Policy

As of July 1, 1982, a federal law provides minimum standards for medi-gap policies. These standards include such things as minimum coverage, limits on exceptions to policy coverage, disclosure of renewal provisions, as well as provisions dealing with truth in advertising and standardization of terms. In addition, certified policies must prove they pay out total benefits to all their policy holders equal to or greater than 75 percent of all the premiums they take in on group policies and 60 percent of premiums they take in on individual policies. (This does <u>not</u> mean your personal benefits must meet these figures, however.)

Though compliance with these standards is voluntary--
meaning it is perfectly legal to sell insurance which does
not meet these standards--only those policies that do con-
form to the standards will be given a certificate by the
Department of Health and Human Services. Policies that have
received such certification, or which have received similar
certification from your state's Insurance Department will
bear a certification seal or emblem. One way to protect
yourself is always to insist on seeing the certification
emblem for any policy you are shown. If you have any doubt
about whether a given policy is really certified, check with
your state's Department of Insurance or with your state or
local consumer protection agency or local district attorney's consumer fraud division.

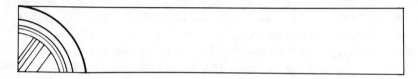

3. "Service" Instead of "Indemnity" Policies

One of the main things to consider when shopping for a
medi-gap policy is to find one that pays on a "service"
rather than on an "indemnity" basis. A service benefits
policy pays all, or a certain fixed percentage of, the
actual charge left unpaid by Medicare. An indemnity policy,
on the other hand, is not tied to the amounts you receive
from Medicare. Indemnity policies pay only a fixed amount
for each day in the hospital or for each specific medical
service you receive. Service policies tend to cover more
of the bills unpaid by Medicare and will increase their
coverage automatically as medical costs rise. Indemnity
policies have fixed amounts which may lag way behind actual
medical costs.

EXAMPLE: A service policy may pay all of the Medicare
medical insurance deductible and the unpaid 20 percent of
Medicare's approved charges for a doctor's surgery charge.
An indemnity policy, on the other hand, may offer $500, for
example, as a fixed amount for surgery to repair a broken
leg. If your doctor charged you $800 for your surgery,
though, and Medicare declared the approved charges to be
$600, Medicare would pay 80 percent of that, or $480. Since
the indemnity policy only covers up to $500 for surgery on a
broken leg, the indemnity policy might only wind up paying
you $20 (the difference between what Medicare paid and the
$500 limit). A service policy, on the other hand, would pay
the entire $120 difference between the 80 percent Medicare
paid and the entire approved amount of $600.

4. Filling as Many Medicare Gaps as Possible

It may sound obvious to say find a policy that fills as many of the significant gaps in Medicare coverage as possible. Unfortunately, too many people are sold on just one good aspect of a policy and overlook the fact it leaves many other gaps unfilled. At the very least, a medi-gap policy should cover the Medicare hospital <u>and</u> medical insurance deductibles and the medical insurance co-payment (the 20 percent of approved charges Medicare doesn't pay for). You should also look for a policy that covers at least part of the hospital insurance co-insurance for hospital stays of over 60 days [see Chapter 6, Section J(3)]. Also, make sure the policy does not have too short a limit on the total number of inpatient hospital days which are covered.

Of medical costs to older persons which usually remain unreimbursed, after the deductible and co-payments are covered, nursing facility care and prescription drugs account for about 50 percent. So, try to find a policy that covers at least part of these costs. Medical "appliances"-- eye glasses, hearing aids, dentures--is another area in which to seek coverage.

Probably no one policy is going to cover (at a reasonable price) everything you want covered. But try to see to it that the greatest gaps in Medicare coverage are filled, and then compare the prices offered and the extra coverage included in various policies before making a decision. In comparing prices and how they make up the gaps in Medicare, you may want to use the charts on the following pages. These charts list the kind and amount of coverage Medicare provides in different situations, and have a private insurance checklist for you to fill in next to the Medicare coverage so you can compare policies side by side. Use these charts, too, if you are considering changing from a policy you already have to a new policy.

MEDICARE—HOSPITAL INSURANCE BENEFITS (PART A) / PRIVATE INSURANCE CHECKLIST

SERVICE	BENEFIT	MEDICARE PAYS	YOU PAY**	YOUR CURRENT INSURANCE PAYS	PROPOSED POLICY #1 PAYS	PROPOSED POLICY #2 PAYS	PROPOSED POLICY #3 PAYS
HOSPITALIZATION .... Semiprivate room and board, general nursing and miscellaneous hospital services and supplies. Includes meals, special care units, drugs, lab tests, diagnostic X-rays, medical supplies, operating and recovery room, anesthesia and rehabilitation services.	First 60 days	All but $304	$304				
	61st to 90th day	All but $76 a day	$76 a day				
	91st to 150th day*	All but $152 a day	$152 a day				
	Beyond 150 days	Nothing	All costs				
	A Benefit Period begins on the first day you receive services as an in-patient in a hospital and ends after you have been out of the hospital or skilled nursing facility for 60 days in a row.						
POSTHOSPITAL SKILLED NURSING FACILITY CARE ... In a facility approved by Medicare. You must have been in a hospital for at least 3 days and enter the facility within a short time, generally 14 days after hospital discharge.	First 20 days	100% of approved amount	Nothing				
	Additional 80 days	All but $38 a day	$38 a day				
	Beyond 100 days	Nothing	All costs				
	MEDICARE AND PRIVATE INSURANCE WILL NOT PAY FOR MOST NURSING HOME CARE. YOU PAY FOR CUSTODIAL CARE AND MOST CARE IN A NURSING HOME.						
POSTHOSPITAL HOME HEALTH CARE	No limit	100% of approved amount	Nothing				
BLOOD	Blood	All but first 3 pints	For first 3 pints				

* 60 Lifetime Reserve Days may be used only once; days used are not renewable.

MEDICARE—MEDICAL INSURANCE BENEFITS (PART B) / PRIVATE INSURANCE CHECKLIST

SERVICE	BENEFIT	MEDICARE PAYS	YOU PAY	YOUR CURRENT INSURANCE PAYS	PROPOSED POLICY #1 PAYS	PROPOSED POLICY #2 PAYS	PROPOSED POLICY #3 PAYS
MEDICAL EXPENSE Physician's services, inpatient and outpatient medical services and supplies, physical and speech therapy, ambulance, etc.	Medicare pays for medical services in or out of the hospital. Some insurance policies pay less (or nothing) for hospital outpatient medical services or services in a doctor's office	80% of approved amount (after $75 deductible)	$75 deductible* plus 20% of balance of approved amount (plus any charge above approved amount)**				
HOME HEALTH CARE	Up to 100 visits	100% of approved amount (after $75 deductible)	*Subject to deductible				
OUTPATIENT HOSPITAL TREATMENT	Unlimited as medically necessary	80% of approved amount (after $75 deductible)	* Subject to deductible plus 20% of balance of approved amount				
BLOOD	Blood	80% of approved amount (after first 3 pints)	For first 3 pints plus 20% of balance of approved amount				

*Once you have had $75 of expense for covered services in a calendar year, the Part B deductible does not apply to any further covered services you receive in that year.

**YOU PAY FOR charges higher than the amount approved by Medicare unless the doctor or supplier agrees to accept Medicare's approved amount as the total charge for services rendered.

180

D. Types of Medicare Supplement Insurance Coverage

There are several types, and combinations of types, of coverage available in Medicare supplement insurance policies (medi-gap policies). The major types of coverage are outlined below.

1. Hospitalization (In-Patient) Insurance

"Service" type coverage pays your initial deductible and usually your co-insurance amount ($76 per day) for a stay of between 61 and 90 days. Most service-type policies also cover some of your co-insurance amount ($152 per day) for a stay of more than 90 days (your "reserve days"). Some policies even pay for a percentage of your hospitalization costs after all your Medicare reserve days are used up, though these policies are unusual and even they have a maximum number of days of coverage. Service type coverage is generally better than "indemnity" coverage, described below.

"Indemnity" type coverage pays a specific, fixed amount for each day in the hospital, up to a limit on the total number of days covered. The payments are not tied to the amounts you are actually charged nor to the amounts Medicare pays. Since the payments are fixed at a certain amount, they do not rise with inflation or special needs. Avoid indemnity policies if possible.

CAUTION!: Some policies have what is called an "elimination period." The elimination period is a period of several days minimum stay in the hospital before any coverage will begin. This eliminates coverage for relatively short stays in which you would have to pay all of your deductible.

2. Medical Insurance

U.C.R. type policies pay based on the Usual, Customary, and Reasonable (U.C.R.) charges for a given medical service in your geographic area. The insurance company starts with what your doctor usually charges for the service, compares it with the customary range of fees charged by doctors in the same geographic area, and takes into account whether a higher fee is reasonable given any special medical circumstances. This process is something like the way Medicare figures its approved "reasonable" charges, but the U.C.R. rates are usually a good bit higher than Medicare's approved charges. The insurance company pays the difference between the U.C.R. rate and the amount Medicare actually pays (in other words, the difference between the U.C.R. rate and 80 percent of Medicare's approved charges).

EXAMPLE: Let's say your doctor charges $150 for a service and does not accept assignment. Medicare decides the approved charges are only $100. Medicare will thus pay only 80 percent of $100, or $80. If the insurance company determines the U.C.R. rate is $130, they will then pay the difference between the U.C.R. rate of $130 and the Medicare payment of $80. The insurance company would thus pay you $50. This would leave you personally responsible for $20.

Many doctors who will not take an assignment of your Medicare claim alone, will take an assignment of Medicare plus a U.C.R. policy as payment in full. Referring back to the example above, this would mean Medicare would pay $80, the insurance company would pay $50 and the doctor would accept that $130 total as payment in full. You would not be responsible for the remaining $20 of the bill.

U.C.R. policies have the advantage of being flexible in that they increase payments as inflation pushes up medical costs. Some of the U.C.R. policies pay the yearly Medicare medical insurance deductible, some do not. Make sure to check to see if the U.C.R. policy you are considering pays this deductible.

Co-payment type policies pay only the co-payment of 20 percent of approved charges that Medicare does not pay and some also pay the medical insurance deductible. In the example above, a co-insurance policy would pay the $20 difference between Medicare's 80 percent payment and the balance of the $100 approved charge. But if your doctor had not accepted an assignment, you would still be personally responsible for the $50 difference between the doctor's actual bill of $150 and the Medicare reasonable charge of $100. If the doctor did accept an assignment of your Medicare claim plus your co-payment insurance policy, your bill would be paid in full by the combination of Medicare and private insurance payments. But doctors, understandably, are less likely to accept assignment if you have this co-payment type policy than they are if you have a U.C.R. type policy.

Indemnity type policies pay a fixed amount for each specific medical service or treatment you receive, minus what Medicare pays. These policies generally pay the least and give the poorest protection.

E. Things to Watch Out for in Choosing a Medi-Gap Policy

1. Pre-Existing Illness Exclusion

Many policies contain a provision which excludes any coverage for a certain period of time at the beginning of your policy period for any illness or medical conditions for which you received treatment within a given period prior to the effective date of the policy. For example, a policy with a six-month exclusion period for a pre-existing illness would not cover you for any medical treatment you received for any medical condition for the first six months after your policy begins if you received any medical treatment for that condition within the six months before the policy went into effect. If you have a serious medical condition which may require costly medical treatment at any time, and you have been treated for that condition within the past six months, you must be very careful about buying a policy with such an exclusion.

There are a number of policies with no pre-existing illness exclusions, and many policies have three-month exclusion periods. But in no case should you consider buying a policy that excludes coverage for a condition existing more than six months before the effective policy date, nor one that extends the non-coverage period to more than six

months after the effective date of the policy. And don't be
fooled by a policy that advertises "No medical examination
required!" If they have a long pre-existing condition exclusion, they don't need to examine you; they just don't pay
you.

2. Mail-Order Policies

Beware of policies you receive unsolicited in the
mails; their flashy promises often far outstrip their coverage. If you do become aware of a policy through the mails,
and the provisions of that policy seem good to you after
comparing it with other policies, make sure you check the
reputation of the company offering the policy with your
state's insurance department or commission, or your state or
local consumer protection agency.

3. Seniors' Associations

There are a number of organizations of seniors or
retired persons which offer medi-gap insurance policies.
Some offer excellent policies, with a good range of cover-
ages and premiums. Organizations may be able to provide
good policies because insurance companies will compete for
the large business they provide.* On the other hand, there
are some organizations for seniors or retired persons which
are not much more than fronts for insurance companies.
These organizations may appear to exist for the benefit of
older Americans; they offer a number of programs or services
for seniors, most of which you will discover on closer
examination are nearly worthless. In fact, these organizations exist to sell poor quality or over-priced insurance
under the "umbrella" of protecting senior citizens. The
best way to tell whether the policies offered by a particular organization are good or bad is to compare their specific coverage provisions with those of other policies offered
by different insurance companies.

REMEMBER: The fact that an insurance policy comes to
you through a reputable organization doesn't make it a
better policy. It is the terms of the policy, not the good
intentions of the organization, that determine your coverage. The insurance company, not the seniors' organization,
pays--or doesn't pay--your claims.

---

* One such organization is the National Council of Senior Citizens, with main offices at 925
15th St., N.W., Washington, D.C. 20005. This is not a plug for any particular policy they
are offering--the terms of different policies offered change too fast to recommend any one
policy or policies here--but the NCSC has a good record over the years in providing medi-gap
policies. However, as with ANY policy you consider, compare the specific provisions and
costs; don't just accept the good name or reputation of a company or organization offering
the policy.

4. Multiple Policies

As a general rule, you should only need one policy to supplement your Medicare coverage. With more than one policy there will inevitably be duplicate coverage and it is unlikely that very many people can afford to pay for the same thing twice these days. And even if you pay for coverage twice, you can be sure when you make a claim you will be paid only once. If an insurance agent tries to convince you you have to buy two policies, or tries to get you to buy a second policy on top of the one you've already got, it may be time to look for a new insurance agent instead of a new policy.

5. Replacement Policies

Be extremely careful if you are considering replacing your existing policy with a new one. Even if your new policy would ultimately provide better coverage, it may have a pre-existing condition exclusion [see (1) above] that would deny you coverage for up to six months after you switched policies. So, if you have been treated in the previous six months for any serious medical condition that might require further treatment in the near future, don't cancel a basically good policy for one that is only slightly better.

Always ask yourself why an insurance company or agent may want to sell you a new policy. The answer is usually that they make their money that way. Of course, there are times when a new policy would significantly improve your coverage. If so, and if the pre-existing condition exclusion would not make you run any serious risk of non-coverage, great! Go ahead and switch. Just make sure you compare the policies carefully before you do so, including the question of pre-existing condition exclusion.

6. "Nursing Home" Coverage

Do not be misled into thinking that a medi-gap policy will cover you or a loved one for a stay in what is sometimes called a nursing home, rest home, board-and-care home or the like. Some medi-gap policies do provide some limited coverage for skilled nursing care in a skilled nursing facility but if the home is not a skilled nursing facility, approved as such by Medicare, or if you or your family member is not receiving skilled nursing care [as opposed to "custodial care"--see Chapter 6, Section H(1)], no medi-gap policy will cover the costs. A stay in a skilled nursing facility is usually covered only after a previous stay in a hospital for treatment of a specific medical condition. A stay in a nursing home or the like because a person needs assistance in feeding, dressing or getting around is <u>not</u> covered by medi-gap policies.

7. Maximum Benefits Limits

Even though a policy may look like it has wonderfully broad coverage, it may have a limit on the total number of days of hospital coverage, or on the total amount of dollars that can be paid in one year, which puts a serious limitation on all its coverage. Most policies have some maximum coverage limits. Make sure the policy you have doesn't have limits so low the other coverage provisions become meaningless.

8. Your Right to Renew

If a policy permits the insurance company to cancel you on an individual basis, which they might do if your claims are too high or you are involved in a dispute about payment, don't buy it. Most policies have a provision that says you cannot be cancelled unless the company cancels <u>all</u> policies of that type throughout your state. You should have an automatic right to renew your policy each year.

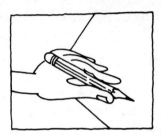

9. Beware of Short-Time Enrollment Periods

Just about everyone has heard or seen advertisements for insurance that say: "Limited offer! One month only! Buy now, the greatest offer in years! Once the offer is over, you'll never get another chance at an opportunity like this again! Once-in-a-lifetime offer!" Stuff and nonsense. Bunkum. If it's a reputable company with a legitimate policy to offer you, the same or similar terms will be available to you at any time (though there are sometimes legitimate time limits placed on enrollment because of <u>your</u> age). These advertising slogans are just another way insurance companies have of pressuring you into buying something without carefully considering and comparing the terms of the policy. Don't be rushed into anything. Like most things in life, if it's really good, it will still be there tomorrow.

10. Ten-Day Review Period

Most policies permit you to look over your policy and carefully examine its terms for 10 days before you are obligated to keep it. If you decide you don't want the policy, for any reason, you can return it within 10 days to the company or to the insurance agent you bought it from and get a refund of all the money you have paid up to that point.

■ ■ ■

11. Policy Delivered Within Thirty Days

Any policy should be delivered to you within 30 days from the date you sent in your application and your first premium payment. If you don't receive the policy within 30 days, contact your insurance agent or the company. If you have not received your policy by 60 days after submission of your application and premium payment, unless you have received a satisfactory explanation in writing from the company, you should report the matter to your state's Department of Insurance or Consumer Protection Agency.

12. Never Pay Cash

Always make your policy premium payment by check or money order (keeping a receipt) made out to the insurance company, not to the agent.

F. Alternative Insurance: Major Medical Policies

Another option, instead of a medi-gap policy, for additional coverage beyond Medicare is the "major medical" health insurance policy. Major medical policies provide substantial coverage for "catastrophic" or long-term illnesses, the kind of illnesses that can wipe out even a financially secure family. These policies provide good coverage for long-term hospitalization, covering you after your Medicare coverage has run out, and for a number of services not covered at all by Medicare (such as self-administered prescription drugs). On the other hand, major medical premiums are usually quite a bit higher than for medi-gap policies. And major medicals have their own deductibles, often very high. Finally, these policies probably will not cover Medicare's co-insurance for most routine medical services and treatments.

If you are financially able to handle the yearly hospital or medical deductible and medical insurance co-payment for most routine medical costs--assuming you are in relatively good health--a major medical policy might provide greater protection for your money than a medi-gap policy. You sacrifice smaller, short-term coverage for larger long-term protection. As with any insurance shopping, compare different major medical policies, and then compare them with the best medi-gap policies before you decide to buy.

One problem with major medical policies is many (but not all) will not insure you for the first time if you are already 65 or older. If you are reaching age 65 and you think you may want to have a major medical policy, it may be a good idea to become insured before your 65th birthday. Once you have a major medical policy, you will be able to renew it after you turn 65, even though someone already 65 could not begin coverage under that same policy.

"With years a richer life begins,
  The spirit mellows:
Ripe age gives tone to violins,
  Wine, and good fellows."

John Townsend Trowbridge, *Three Worlds*

■■■

G. Health Maintenance Organizations (HMO's)

One growing alternative to the traditional insurance company policy is the Health Maintenance Organization, which provides both the medical services and the insurance coverage. There is an increasing number of such organizations around the country, though they are still not available in many areas.* Basically, HMOs provide a prepayment plan under which you pay a monthly fee that covers virtually all of your medical needs. They also provide the doctors and facilities for treatment in the organization's own hospitals and clinics. These organizations often have arrangements with Medicare to receive your payments directly from Medicare; your monthly prepayment is all you pay.

The advantages of HMOs are significant: your prepayment usually covers treatment for most any medical problem; you don't have to worry about non-covered medical costs depleting all your savings; you don't have to go from place

---

* There are large HMOs which have their own complete hospitals, such as the Kaiser-Permanente Medical Plan which operates in California, Washington, D.C., Texas, Colorado, Ohio, Oregon and Hawaii and the Health Insurance Plan of New York (HIP) which has facilities in New York and New Jersey. There are also smaller HMOs and group practices that operate their own clinics and have arrangements with local hospitals to use their facilities for inpatient care. To find an HMO or group practice in your area, you can write to the trade associations of HMOs and group practices, the Group Health Association of America, Washington, D.C.

to place searching for a particular doctor or clinic to treat a specific medical problem; and you don't have to submit complicated claim forms. On the other hand, large HMOs often have the disadvantage of being "impersonal;" you may see different doctors who are not familiar with your overall health picture and with your particular need; you may have to take a more active role in bringing things to the doctor's attention. And some larger HMOs are criticized for long waiting times and the usual bureaucratic snafus associated with any big organization.

If an HMO is available in your area, first inquire about its cost for a Medicare recipient, then find out about its range of services. When you have a clear picture of the "numbers" of the HMO compared with various insurance policies, try to find out about the intangibles. Ask people who belong to the HMO what they like and dislike about it; ask about waiting time, about whether you can easily see the same doctor, and about the helpfulness of personnel. Only when you have answered these questions to your satisfaction should you make a decision about an HMO.

Supplemental Security Income— A Little Back-Up Help

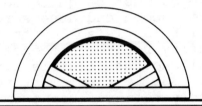

CHAPTER 9

HIGHLIGHTS

If you are 65 or over, or disabled, and have limited income and assets, you may be able to receive monthly payments from SSI even though you own your own home and car [see Section B].

Even though you have some earnings, you may be able to qualify for a substantial SSI payment because much of your income is not "counted" when determining SSI payments [see Section B].

In many states, the relatively low federal SSI payment is supplemented by state payments which can raise the total to close to $500 a month for an individual, $800 for a couple [see Section C].

"Man arrives as a novice at each stage of his life."
Chamfort, *Caracteres et anecdotes*

∎∎∎

A. Introduction

Supplemental Security Income (SSI) is neither a Social Security nor an "entitlement" program.* SSI is a joint federal-state program intended to guarantee a minimum level of income to financially hard-pressed older, blind and disabled persons. About 4 million people receive some SSI benefits. SSI is available based on financial need; no consideration is given to how long you have worked, or how much you have paid into the Social Security system. Not surprisingly, then, you must be quite needy to qualify. Indeed, the level of income and assets required to qualify as "needy" under SSI rules is so low that many people who receive Social Security retirement benefits as their only source of income will not be eligible for SSI. And those who are eligible for SSI to supplement their Social Security benefits will probably receive just a small amount from the SSI program. Nevertheless, if after reviewing the rules explained in this chapter you think you are at all close to meeting the "need" requirements for SSI eligibility, it will be worth your while to apply for it.

Why bother to apply for SSI if the amount you receive would be small, assuming you qualify at all? Well, aside from the obvious fact that every little bit of money helps, SSI eligibility might also mean you could be eligible for significant non-cash benefits, such as Medicaid (see Chapter 7) and food stamps, as well as free rehabilitation and home care programs, should you need them. So, to repeat the important point, even if you think your monthly cash benefit from SSI would be very small, apply anyway. There's no harm in asking--even a little money helps--and you may be surprised at how useful some of the non-cash benefits can be.

B. Who is Eligible for SSI Benefits?

There are three basic requirements you must meet to establish that you are eligible to receive SSI cash benefits:

---

* One often confusing fact is although SSI is a separate program from Social Security, it is administered by the Social Security Administration. In most cases, application for SSI benefits is made at the local Social Security office.

192

■You must be either 65 or over, blind or disabled;

■Your monthly income must be less than a certain minimum amount established by the state in which you live;

■Your assets, not counting your home and car, must not be worth more than $1,500 ($2,250 for a couple), though there are certain items excepted from this amount.

The rules for each of these requirements are more complicated than they first appear. As you will see as you read along, though, they are complicated in ways that almost always make it easier for you to qualify than you might first imagine. What does this mean? Simply that, generally speaking, you are permitted to have more income and assets than the initial figures indicate. Press on and you may find that, despite these low figures, you are eligible for SSI benefits.

Here are the more specific rules:

1. Qualifying as Blind or Disabled

SSI uses the same rules as does the Social Security disability program for deciding when a person is legally blind or disabled. Basically, this means you are considered legally blind if your vision is no better than 20/200, or your field of vision is limited to 20 degrees or less, even with corrective lenses. You are considered disabled if you have a physical or mental impairment which prevents you from doing any substantial work and which is expected to last at least twelve months, or to result in death. For a more complete explanation of these rules, see Chapter III, Social Security Disability.

2. Maximum Income to Qualify for SSI

Take these income rules slowly because they are a bit complicated. In the first place, there are really two SSI payments: one is the federal SSI payment; the second is a state SSI payment which some state's pay over and above the federal benefit and which some states pay alone if you qualify for it without qualifying for the federal payment.

Not all income is "counted" when deciding whether you qualify for SSI. In fact, more than half of your earned income (wages and self-employment income) is not counted towards SSI limits. Further, even though you may have "counted" income over the allowable maximum for federal SSI payments, you may still qualify for your state's supplemental payment, depending on the maximum allowable in your state. Why is this? Well, some states have simply set a higher limit than the federal SSI program does. The limit on "counted" income to qualify for the federal SSI payment is $284.30 per month ($426.40 per month for a couple). In some states, however, you would qualify for the state's SSI supplement payment even if your "counted" income is more than $400 a month. You will have to check the income levels for your state's supplement, if it has one, by contacting your local Social Security office.

a. What Is "Counted" Income?

If all this is beginning to sound a mite confusing, it can be simplified a little by understanding what is meant by "counted" income. In general, subject to the exclusions explained below, any income you earn in wages or self-employment, and any money you receive from investments, pensions, annuities, royalties, gifts, rents or interest on savings is "counted" against the SSI limits. Social Security benefits are also considered "counted" income. In addition, any regular provision of food or housing you receive from friends or relatives may be considered "counted" income by SSI. (Such arrangements are sometimes considered in figuring the amount of your SSI benefits rather than in disqualifying you from receiving a check in the first place.)

b. What Is Not Considered "Counted" Income?

The following are the amounts of money and support which are not counted in determining whether you are over the limit to receive SSI benefits. This means you can receive these amounts without suffering any impact of your SSI eligibility or payment amount.

■The first $20 per month you receive from any source (except other public assistance based on need);

■The first $65 per month of your earned income (wages or self-employment);

■One-half of all your earned income over $65 a month;

■Irregular or infrequent earned income (such as from a one-time only job) if such income is not more than $10 a month;

■Irregular or infrequent unearned income (such as a gift or dividend on an investment) up to $20 per month;

194

■Food stamps or housing assistance from a federal housing program run by a state or local government agency;

■Some work-related expenses for blind or disabled persons which are paid for through public assistance.

Because these rules regarding how much is "counted" as income are fairly complicated, and because of the different income amount limits in various states, let us give you one general suggestion. If you are living on a small fixed income and have relatively small assets (see the following section), you should definitely apply for SSI benefits. Do this even though you really don't think you'd qualify. The local Social Security or social welfare office workers may treat certain income differently than you do and you may be pleasantly surprised to learn you are eligible for some SSI help. To see how SSI benefits are calculated, check the following example.

EXAMPLE: Carmela Siqueiros receives Social Security survivors' benefits of $210 a month. She also receives a small $20 per month retirement pension from her years of working as a seamstress in the garment industry. In addition, she takes on a few private jobs doing fine reweaving work. Over the past month, she earned $110 on several of these jobs. Her only other recent income came from a quarterly dividend check of $25 she receives from a small stock investment she and her deceased husband made many years before. How would SSI determine her income levels to see if Carmela qualified for benefits?

Carmela receives a total of $230 a month from her Social Security and pension benefits. Her other unearned income is the $25 dividend check. Infrequent income like a dividend check would not be counted if it were $20 a month or less, but since the dividend check is for $25, it is counted income. So the $25 would be added to the $230 to make a total of $255 in unearned income. Since the first $20 of income from any source is not counted, the $255 total would be reduced to $235 countable unearned income.

Carmela's earned income is $110 for the month. Since the first $65 a month of earned income is not counted, her earned income amount would be reduced to $45; and since one-half of all earned income over $65 a month is not counted, half of this $45 ($22.50) would not be counted for SSI purposes. This leaves Carmela with $22.50 countable earned income for the month.

What is Carmela's official total, then? She has $235 countable unearned income for the month and $22.50 countable earned income for a total of $257.50 countable income. Since this amount is under the federal SSI limit of $284.30 per month, Carmela would be eligible for federal SSI benefits as well as for state supplement benefits in her state, if her state offers a supplement.

3. Maximum Assets and Resources to Qualify for SSI

In addition to the limits on your income, SSI rules limit the amount of assets and other resources you may have and still qualify. The general limit is $1,500 in resources for an individual, $2,250 for a married couple living together. But as you will see from the explanations below, there are many resources which are not counted in determining your total resources, so actually you are allowed to have much higher resources than the above limits would first indicate. The term "resources" is used by SSI to mean money in the bank, investments of any kind, real estate, personal property and household goods. Fortunately, though, the following are several important categories of assets which are not counted as "resources:"

■ Your home and the land it sits on, regardless of value. <u>WARNING</u>: A vacation or second home, however, is counted;

■ Your automobile, up to a current market value of $4,500; if your car is used in your work, or getting to and from a job, or getting to and from regular medical treatment, or specially equipped for the transportation of a handicapped person, the value of your car is not counted, no matter how much it is worth;

■ Your personal property and household goods up to a total current or "equity" value of $2,000. Equity value does not mean what the articles cost new, but only what you could sell them for now, less the amounts you still owe on them. Personal property refers to clothing, jewelry (your wedding and engagement rings are not counted); household goods means furniture, appliances, tools and the like.

∎Property essential to self support--such as tools, machines, etc. used in your trade--are not counted;

∎Life insurance policies with a total face value of $1,500 or less per person, burial policies, or term life insurance policies with no cash surrender value.

IMPORTANT: Even if your countable assets appear to be over the limits, it is still possible for you to qualify for some SSI benefits. You may begin to receive SSI payments if you agree to dispose of--either sell or spend--enough of your property to bring you under the limits within a certain time period (six months for real estate, three months for personal property and liquid assets). However, make sure the sale or transfer is a real one. Simply transferring "title" on the property to someone else while you keep control or use of it is not enough; neither is "selling" something for a token sum.

EXAMPLE: Rose and Peter Wong are living on Peter's Social Security retirement benefits and on Rose's pension from her years as a teacher. They have qualified under the SSI income limits, but they are worried they have too many "resources" to qualify. Rose and Peter have been careful over the years and have managed to accumulate the following assets: their own home and a car that is paid for, a savings account with about $1,500, and some stocks worth another $500 or $600. Their personal property and household goods of any particular value are their kitchen appliances, worth about $300 current market value, their TV, worth about $100 if they tried to sell it, Rose's stereo set, worth about $150, Peter's carpentry tools, worth about $400 or $500, and Rose's jewelry, which, aside from her gold wedding band, is worth about $200 (that sapphire pin Peter gave her for their 25th wedding anniversary). When the SSI folks add all this up, will the Wongs still qualify for SSI?

Despite the fact Rose and Peter's house is now worth $80,000 in the crazy real estate market, it is not counted as an asset. Their 1979 station wagon still runs like a top, but since its current value is not over $4,500, it is not counted as a resource. Their personal property and household goods add up to about $1,200, but none of it will be counted against them because this is below the permissible amounts for personal property. Their total counted assets, then, would be their savings and stocks worth about $2,000. Since the SSI limit on resources is $2,250 for a couple, Rose and Peter would qualify for some SSI benefits. For how much the benefit would be, see the following sections.

By the way, what if Rose and Peter had been over the limit by a few hundred dollars? Would they be out of luck? The answer is SSI might permit them to dispose of some assets worth a few hundred dollars within a three-month period and still receive SSI. They would have to prove, however, they really had spent the money or sold an asset and used the money in order to qualify.

C. How Much Are Your SSI Benefit Payments?

Because the supplement payments vary from state to state, the amount of your SSI check will vary depending on where you live, as well as on the amount of your income and assets. The basic federal SSI payment for the second half of 1983 is $304.30 a month for an individual, $456.40 for a couple.* State supplements to this amount can increase payments for an individual to close to $500 a month, and to more than $800 a month for a couple.

These maximum benefit amounts, though, are reduced by any income you make over allowable countable limits:

■Your benefit check will be reduced by one dollar for every two dollars you earn in current wages or self-employment over $65 a month.

■Your payment will be reduced dollar for dollar by the amount of unearned income you receive over $20 a month; such "unearned" income includes your Social Security benefits, pensions, annuities, interest on savings, dividends, or any money from investments or property you own.

■Your SSI payment will be reduced by one-third if you live in a friend or relative's home and receive support "in kind" (food or clothing) from that person or family.

---

* This figure will go up on January 1, 1984 in a cost-of-living increase tied to the Consumer Price Index. A cost-of-living increase is scheduled for every January.

The following examples, taken from figures worked out by the Social Security Administration, show how SSI payments are calculated for a person age 65 or over.

EXAMPLE #1: Carl Johnson lives alone in a home he owns. His only income is his Social Security retirement check of $170.30 per month. Here's how his SSI payment would be figured. Carl's current unearned income is his $170.30 Social Security check. From that, $20 is excluded, making his total countable unearned income $150.30. Since he has no countable earned income, his total countable income would be the same--$150.30.

The basic SSI benefit for a single person is $304.30 a month. (Remember, though, that in some states the basic amount could be much higher because of the state supplement.) From this basic SSI benefit, Carl's total countable income of $150.30 is subtracted, leaving $154. That would be his monthly SSI payment. His total monthly income, then, would be his Social Security check of $170.30 plus his SSI benefit of $154, for a total of $324.30.

EXAMPLE #2: Now let's assume Carl marries Beverly and together they collect a combined monthly Social Security check of $255.50. Carl and Beverly's SSI payment would be figured like this:

Twenty dollars would be exempted from the $255.50 Social Security check, for a total countable income of $235.50 a month. That $235.50 would be subtracted from the basic SSI benefit for a couple of $456.40, leaving a monthly SSI payment of $220.90. When added to their Social Security check of $255.50, Carl and Beverly's total monthly income would be $476.40.

EXAMPLE #3: If either Carl or Beverly took a part-time job which paid $100 a month, this earned income would change their SSI payment. Their SSI check would be figured like this:

Carl and Beverly's countable unearned income is still the same $235.50 a month (their Social Security check minus $20). But now they have an _earned_ income of $100 a month. The first $65 of this $100 is not counted under SSI rules. Of the remaining $35 of earned income, only one-half of it, or $17.50, is considered counted income. In other words, only $17.50 is added to the $235.50 of counted unearned income, making a total countable income of $253.00 a month.

The basic SSI benefit for a couple, you remember, is $456.40 per month. The $253 countable income would be subtracted from this $456.40, leaving a monthly SSI payment to Carl and Beverly of $203.40. Their monthly income would thus be their Social Security check of $255.50, plus their part-time income of $100, plus their SSI check of $203.40, for a total of $558.90.

EXAMPLE #4: Finally, let's leave Carl and Beverly and have a look at Adam Chinasky's situation. Adam lives in his daughter and son-in-law's house and his only income is his Social Security retirement check of $170.30 a month. But his daughter and son-in-law provide food and a few other things for Adam, as well as giving him a place to live. In return, Adam helps take care of the garden, raises vegetables for the family, does all the repairs around the house his accountant son-in-law has no talent for, and helps take care of his two grandchildren. Adam's SSI benefits would be figured like this:

The basic SSI benefit of $304.30 for an individual would be reduced by one-third because Adam receives food and lodging from his daughter and son-in-law. This would leave a basic SSI amount of $202.87. Adam's income is his Social Security check of $170.30; twenty dollars of that amount is not counted, leaving a total countable income of $150.30. This countable income is subtracted from his basic SSI amount of $202.87, leaving a monthly SSI payment to Adam of $52.57. Adam's total monthly cash income would thus be his Social Security check of $170.30 plus his $52.57 SSI check, for a total of $222.87.

REMEMBER: Even if your monthly federal SSI payment would be very small, in many states you might receive a supplement well above the federal payment. And eligibility for SSI benefits, no matter how small your monthly cash benefits are, could make you eligible for Medicaid coverage, food stamps, hot meal programs, in-home care and other social services. Remember, too, that the examples above are just that--only examples--and even if you believe you might not qualify for SSI, it's worth the effort to apply and find out for sure.

"The old age of an eagle is better than the youth of a sparrow."
Greek proverb

■ ■ ■

D. How to Apply for SSI Benefits

Your application for SSI benefits should be made at your local Social Security office. You may file your claim for SSI benefits at the same time you file for retirement, disability, dependents' or survivors' benefits. However, a separate form is required for SSI. Be sure to ask the Social Security office worker for an SSI application as well as the forms for Social Security benefits.

1. What to Bring With You

When applying for SSI benefits, you should bring with you to the Social Security office as many of the following papers as possible. (As with Social Security claims, always remember to keep for your own records a copy of any paper you file with the Social Security Administration.)

■Your Social Security card or number;

■Proof of your age (if you are already receiving a Social Security check, you do not have to prove your age again);

■If you own real estate other than your own home, bring the latest tax bill or assessment on the property;

■Papers showing all your financial assets, such as bank books, insurance policies, stock certificates;

■If you own a car, bring your registration papers;

■Pay stubs or other evidence of your current earned income, if you have any;

■If you are applying based on disability or blindness, bring medical records and reports which confirm your condition; if you don't have copies of these records or reports, bring the names and addresses of the doctors, hospitals and clinics that have provided treatment to you;

■If you live with your spouse, bring information about his/her income and assets.

Even if you don't have all these papers available, go down to your local Social Security office and file your application for SSI as soon as you think you may qualify for assistance. The workers at the Social Security office can help you get whatever papers and records are necessary.

2. How Long Does It Take to Get a Benefit Check?

It may take from four to eight weeks after you have completed the necessary paperwork before you receive your first regular monthly SSI check. And if your claim is based on a disability that has not already been established for Social Security disability payments, it may take up to three months. When you do get your money, however, it can cover the entire period from the time you file your claim until the time you receive your first check. It is also possible to get some money while your claim is being processed. If you appear to meet all the eligibility requirements for SSI and you need immediate cash assistance to meet a financial emergency, the Social Security office can issue you an emergency advance payment. The amount of this emergency payment will be deducted from your first regular SSI check.

If you claim SSI benefits based on a disability, and you have already qualified for Social Security disability payments, you may be approved for and begin receiving SSI benefits immediately, without any further medical review. If you must prove your disability for the first time, the process will be the same as for Social Security disability (see Chapter 3), with the state disability office making the final determination. If you are financially eligible, and appear to meet the disability requirements, you can receive SSI payments for up to three months while your claim is being reviewed by the disability office.

E. Periodic Review of Your SSI Eligibility

SSI rules require that your eligibility to receive payments be reviewed periodically. This "redetermination" checks to make sure you are still eligible and the amount of your payment is correct. These reviews take place at least once every three years (in most cases the review is made yearly). You will be notified by the Social Security office that a redetermination of your eligibility is needed. Remember, it's just a periodic review and does not mean anything is wrong. You will have to produce the same kinds of information you did for the original application: your income, assets, living arrangements and, if claiming on a disability, up-dated medical information. Often, most of this redetermination process can be handled by mail or phone, though you may have to make a trip to the Social Security office for an interview.

F. Reporting Changes in Your Status

You are legally responsible for reporting to SSI any changes in your financial status or living arrangements which may affect either your eligibility or the amount you receive. Forms for reporting such changes are available at your local Social Security office. And remember, if your monthly income goes <u>down</u> for any reason, report that, too. You may be able to get higher SSI benefits.

   <u>WARNING</u>: Whether in the periodic review or otherwise, if you fail to report a change in your financial or living situation which would affect your SSI payment, you could be required to pay back money you received over the amount you should have received because of the change in your situation.

G. Your Right to Appeal Denial of Your Claim

   If your claim for SSI eligibility is denied, or if it is ended after once having received SSI payments, or if the amount you receive is less than you believe is correct under SSI rules, you have a right to appeal the decision. The right to appeal, the procedures and time limits involved, are virtually the same as in Social Security appeals. These appeal processes are explained in detail in Chapter 5.

Government Employment, Railroad Worker and Veterans Benefits

CHAPTER 10

HIGHLIGHTS

If you leave federal employment, you can leave your retirement fund money with the government to guarantee a pension or you can take it out at any time you want it before you reach retirement age [see Section (B)].

Give consideration to several factors before deciding whether to take a reduced civil service pension to provide for a pension for your surviving spouse [see Section (D)].

The rules regarding when you are considered "disabled" for purposes of civil service disability benefits are much easier to qualify for than for Social Security disability benefits [see Section (F)].

Some people who have worked for both the railroad and for jobs outside the railroad may be eligible to collect <u>both</u> Railroad Retirement and Social Security retirement benefits [see Section (J)].

■ ■ ■

■■■

Even though your service-connected health problems were not originally serious, or did not show up until years after you left the military, you may be eligible for Veterans Administration disability benefits and medical treatment [see Section (P)].

If you are a veteran age 65 or over with a low income, you may be eligible for a veteran's pension even though you have savings, assets or own your own home [see Section (Q)].

Veterans and dependents or survivors of disabled veterans, or of veterans who received a veterans' pension, may be eligible for free or low-cost medical treatment at Veterans Administration hospitals [see Section (R)].

"To be seventy years young is sometimes far more cheerful and hopeful than to be forty years old."

O.W. Holmes, *Letter to Julia Ward Howe* *(on her 70th birthday).*

■■■

A. Government and Public Employment Pensions: Introduction

It is estimated that in the early 1980's over 15 percent of the total work force in this country is employed by one or another local, state or federal government agency, department or public institution. And while the wages and salaries of these government jobs may not be as high as some of those offered in the private sector, the comprehensive pension systems covering public employees, coupled with the opportunity to retire at a reasonably early age, contributes to making government employment attractive to many people. How widespread are government pension plans? Over 6,000 state and local public employment pension plans cover more than 10 million workers. And the Federal Civil Service Retirement system, plus a number of smaller federal pension programs, cover another three million federal government workers.

Though the rules and regulations of these many pension plans vary considerably, most public pension plans have a number of general characteristics in common. And many of these can be fairly viewed as more advantageous to the worker, certainly providing more options, than programs offered by most private companies. Generally, public pensions provide for full granting of future retirement rights after only five years of service, permit retirement--with some restrictions--as early as age 55, and adjust benefit amounts yearly to keep pace with inflation.

The basic rules of Federal Civil Service Retirement are discussed below. It is not possible here, of course, to discuss the rules of 6,000 different state and local pension plans, but understanding how the federal system works will go a long way toward your ability to understand how your state or local plans, almost all of which have great similarities to the federal system, work. If you are covered by a state or local government pension plan, the details of that plan can be made available to you through the personnel department or retirement plan office of the government agency or public institution where you work, or through the pension office of your public employees' union, if you belong to one. On request, the pension office will also provide you with a statement of all earnings credited to your pension account and an estimate of how much your retirement benefits would be if you retired at the various possible retirement ages.

B. When Are You Eligible for Federal Civil Service Retirement Benefits?

Virtually everyone who works for the federal government--from the letter carrier who puts mail in your mailbox to the space scientist who puts rockets on the moon--is covered by the Civil Service Retirement System. If you work for the federal government in almost any capacity, you participate--employee contributions are automatically deducted from your pay. And to qualify for a Civil Service Retirement pension (in legalese this means to have your pension rights "vested"), you only need to have worked for the federal government for a total of five years.* The amount of your benefit, of course, will depend on how long you work and on how much you earn. Once you have worked the required five years, you are eligible for retirement bene-

---

* In computing the number of years you have worked for the federal government, years of military service can be counted. But you must have at least five years of civilian employment to qualify for a retirement pension.

fits at age 62, whether or not you still work for the government at the time you reach that age, and whether or not you receive a private pension as well. You may also choose to retire at age 60 if you have worked 20 years for the government. To do this, it's not necessary for the work to have been for the same branch or agency of the government. If you have 30 years of employment with the federal government, you may retire at age 55.

If you leave employment with the federal government before claiming a retirement pension, you will be eligible for retirement benefits only if you leave your retirement fund contributions (the accumulated deductions from your pay) in the Civil Service Retirement fund after you leave your federal job. If you leave federal employment, you have the choice either to collect all your retirement fund pay deductions in a lump sum when you end work for the federal government, or to let the money stay in the retirement fund and then collect a pension from that fund when you reach retirement age. Obviously, it's tough to let that cash sit there when you leave your job. But, if you are still working after you leave your federal job, you may very well be wise to take in your belt a notch or two and let the money stay in the retirement fund so you can enjoy the generous federal retirement pension when you retire. As part of making this decision, you will want to figure out how much you would receive at retirement (the rules are explained below) if you left the money in the fund. IMPORTANT! If you leave the money in the retirement system but later decide you want the money, you can collect it in a lump sum at any time before you reach an age at which you are eligible to receive a pension (actually, within 31 days of being eligible).

EXAMPLE Kazuo Tanaka worked for the federal government as an agricultural inspector from 1955 through 1962. When he left his job with the Department of Agriculture, he had contributed a couple of thousand dollars to the retirement fund. But since Kazuo didn't know what the future would bring, and since he got another good job and didn't immediately need the money, he left his contributions in the Civil Service Retirement fund. Kazuo's new job was with a large food processing company where he worked until 1982, when he decided that with twenty years of service and a nice company pension, he would retire at age 62. Since Kazuo's federal Civil Service pension would not be very much (having worked only seven years at a fairly low paying job), he decided to take his money out of the Civil Service Retirement fund before he turned 62 and use it to put a downpayment on that nice boat he had been eyeing for a while. Kazuo called the money his Civil Service Sailing Fund; he named the boat "The Aggie," after the federal department which had made it all possible. Remember, under the rules, to get his money out of the Civil Service retirement plan in a lump sum, Kazuo had to ask for it at least 31 days before he would be eligible to receive a pension at age 62.

There are some special retirement pension rules concerning anyone laid off because of a federal agency-wide reduction in personnel or other reasons not connected to misconduct or delinquency on the part of the worker. If you have worked twenty years or more for the government and are then laid off, you may be eligible for one of these reduced "optional" or "discontinued service" pensions. If you have been laid off in this sort of situation, check with the personnel office at your agency (or former agency) to see if you qualify.

■ ■ ■

C. How Are Civil Service Retirement Benefits Computed?

There are two factors used to figure the amount of your federal retirement pension:

■ The number of years you are employed by the federal government; and

■ Your "high-three" year average wage or salary.

The "high-three" average pay is the highest average pay you earned during <u>any</u> three consecutive years of federal employment. To compute this high-three average, you start with the three consecutive years in which you earned the most pay and compute the average yearly pay for those three years.

Once your high-three average is computed, your pension benefits can be figured by adding:

(a) 1.5 percent of your high-three average pay, multiplied by your first five years of service; plus

(b) 1.75 percent of your high-three average pay, multiplied by your years of employment more than five and up to ten; plus

(c) 2 percent of your high-three average pay, multiplied by the number of years of service over 10.

<u>EXAMPLE</u>: John Castaneda put in 25 years delivering mail for the post office; he ended his career as a postal inspector. John's highest three consecutive years of pay were $18,000, $20,000 and $22,000. His high-three average pay was thus $20,000. After his 25 years, John's retirement pension would be figured like this:

■ 1.5 percent of $20,000 is $300; that $300 is multiplied by the first five years of service, for a total of the first five years of service of $1,500; plus

■ 1.75 percent of $20,000 is $350; that $350 is multiplied by the second five years of service, for a total for the second five years of $1,750; plus

■ 2 percent of $20,000 is $400; that $400 is multiplied by the remaining 15 years of service, for a total for the last 15 years of service of $6,000.

Together, the three parts of John's pension would add up to a yearly benefit of $9,250.

IMPORTANT NOTE: One of the best features of Civil Service Retirement benefits is they are increased usually every year to keep pace with the rising cost-of-living. As with Social Security benefits, but unlike most private pensions, Civil Service Retirement benefits receive cost-of-living (COL) increases tied to the rise in the Consumer Price Index, a yearly indicator of the cost of goods and services throughout the whole economy. This cost-of-living increase hovered around 10 percent per year during the late 1970s and early 1980s, but the 1982 increase dropped to 7.4 percent. These cost-of-living increases will be lower or higher in the future, depending on the economy and on Congressional action.

D. Providing for Your Surviving Spouse

As with many private pensions, the federal worker has a choice at retirement to take the maximum retirement benefits or to accept reduced benefits so that if his or her spouse survives the worker's death, some benefits will continue to go to the surviving spouse. To put it a slightly different way, if you are willing to accept a somewhat reduced pension at retirement, you can guarantee your spouse will continue to receive some of your pension after you die. How much will your pension be reduced if you choose to provide this "survivor annuity" for your spouse? Your pension will be reduced by 2.5 percent of the first $3,600 per year ($90 off

of the first $3,600), plus 10 percent of any amount over
$3,600. Your surviving spouse's annuity would be 55 percent
of what your pension would have been without these deductions. It is also possible to choose to have only a portion
of your pension reduced for the survivor annuity; in other
words, if your pension is $5,000 per year, you can take
$3,000 of it as a full pension and have the remaining $2,000
reduced (by 2.5 percent) as part of a survivor annuity.
The amount your surviving spouse actually receives would be
55 percent of the $2,000, rather than 55 percent of your
full $5,000 pension.

IMPORTANT REMINDER: If your spouse is or will be
entitled to Social Security retirement benefits, any public
employment pension money he or she receives will be considered "earned" income when Social Security determines if
his or her benefits must be reduced because of outside
income over the yearly limits (see Chaper 2, Section E).

The decision about whether or not to take a reduced
pension is not easy. The decision is an individual one,
different for each couple. But here are a few things you
may want to consider in arriving at your decision:

- If your spouse is considerably younger and likely to
  outlive you by many years, taking a reduced pension
  now could guarantee a pension for your spouse for
  many years to come.

- If your spouse is considerably older than you, or in
  poor health, and is not likely to survive you by many
  years, if at all, then the advantage of taking a reduced pension now is diminished.

- If your spouse has or will have a substantial retirement pension of his or her own, there is less need to
  reduce your pension in order to protect your spouse.

- If your spouse is working now and earning a salary
  that will enable you to afford to live on your reduced
  pension, it may make sense for you to take that reduced
  pension if your spouse will not have a retirement
  pension of his or her own.

EXAMPLE: Returning to John's pension of $9,250 a year,
how much of that would he get if he took a reduced pension
in order to provide for Dolores, his wife? The first $3,600
would be reduced by 2.5 percent; that would mean John would
receive $3,510 of that first $3,600. The remaining $5,650
would be reduced by 10 percent, leaving $5,085. John's
total pension would be $8,595 a year instead of $9,250, a
reduction of $655 a year. For that reduction, Dolores would

be entitled to receive a surviving spouse's pension of 55 percent of the original $9,250, which works out to a pension for Dolores of $5,087.50 a year if John dies.

E. What Happens to Survivors of a Federal Worker Who Dies Before Retirement?

If a federal worker dies while still employed by the government, the surviving spouse and children can receive survivors' benefits if the worker had been employed by the government for at least 18 months. For the surviving spouse to collect benefits, either the marriage must have been at least a year old at the time of the worker's death, or the surviving spouse must be the parent of the worker's child. Unlike Social Security benefits for survivors, Civil Service Retirement pays the surviving spouse regardless of the spouse's age. In addition, if the surviving spouse works for the federal government too, he or she will be entitled to collect <u>both</u> survivor's benefits and his or her own retirement pension. The unmarried children of a deceased federal worker will receive benefits until each is 18 years old.

The amount of a survivor's benefits is figured by taking 55 percent of the lesser of:

- 40 percent of the worker's high-three average pay (see Section C for the explanation of "high-three"); <u>or</u>

- The regular pension the worker would have received if the worker had continued working until age 60.

F. Civil Service Disability Benefits

If you have worked for the federal government for five years or more, you may be eligible for broad Civil Service benefits in the event you become disabled before you reach retirement age. The rules concerning Civil Service disability protection are much more protective of workers than are Social Security disability rules. Under Civil Service, you are considered disabled, if, because of disease or injury, you are unable to perform useful and efficient service in the Civil Service grade or class of position you held at the time of your disability. Thus, even though you may be able to perform some gainful work, you are considered disabled if you are unable to perform work at the Civil Service job level you had reached at the time you became disabled.

If you receive disability benefits, you will be required to take periodic physical examinations, at government expense, to determine whether or not the disability continues. However, if it is determined your disability is permanent, or if you reach age 60 without recovering from the disability, you will receive permanent disability retirement benefits. These benefits consist of at least the lesser of:

(a) 40 percent of your high-three average pay (defined in Section C, above); or

(b) The regular pension you would have received if you had worked until age 60 (if you did not work that long).

You are permitted to earn a considerable amount of other income while receiving Civil Service disability benefits. However, if you are under age 60, and for two years in a row you earn more than 80 percent of the present salary of the job you held before going on disability, you will be considered recovered from the disability and your benefits will end. When you do recover from a disability, you may be eligible for up to one full additional year of disability benefits in order to give you time to find a new job.

G. How to Apply for Civil Service Benefits

Decisions about Civil Service benefit claims are made by the Bureau of Retirement, Insurance, and Occupational Health (BRIOH), a part of the Civil Service Commission. Applications for retirement benefits are made on BRIOH forms; you will receive a written notice from BRIOH explaining the amount of your retirement benefits or the reasons benefits have been denied. If you disagree with BRIOH's decision, you may file a written appeal to the Civil Service Commission Appeals Review Board. The Review Board may permit you to present further evidence. Occasionally they will allow you to appear in person to state your claim. If you feel a personal appearance would add to your chances of success on the appeal, make a written request to the Board that you be permitted to appear in person.

Appeals of Civil Service disability claims are slightly different. Your claim is decided in writing, by BRIOH. You may ask that the decision be reconsidered by BRIOH within fifteen days of the time you receive notice of their decision. Your request for reconsideration must be in writing. If your claim is again denied, you have another fifteen days within which to file a written appeal with the Federal Employee Appeals Authority. The Appeals Authority will permit you to appear in person, and present evidence, if you file a written request for a hearing. The Appeals Authority's written decision may itself be appealed to the Civil Service Commission Review Board. And all decisions of the Civil Service Review Board, whether on retirement, survivors' or disability claims, may be appealed to the federal courts.

H. Railroad Retirement System: Introduction

Approximately half-a-million workers are covered by the Railroad Retirement System. The Railroad Retirement System provides coverage for just about any one whose work is directly connected to the operation of the railroads: members of railway labor unions, workers at most railroad terminals, REA express workers, et. al. Not covered, however, are people who work for local or city rail and rapid transit systems.

In general, the coverage of the Railroad Retirement system is quite similar to Social Security system coverage, except that the level of benefits paid by the Railroad Retirement system tends to run slightly higher than Social Security benefits. The Railroad Retirement system provides retirement disability and survivors' benefits under rules approximately the same as for Social Security. Railroad Retirement also provides a supplemental retirement annuity under some circumstances and, perhaps most important, permits some retirees to collect both Railroad Retirement and Social Security benefits.

I. Retirement Benefits Under the Railroad Retirement System

You must have a minimum of 10 years employment on jobs covered by the Railroad Retirement system to be eligible for retirement benefits. If you do, you may claim retirement at age 65. You may also claim early retirement at any time between age 62 and 65. However, early retirement means permanently reduced benefits of 1/180th of your total for each month you are under age 65 when you retire. If you have 30 years employment in covered railroad jobs, though, you may retire at any time after age 60 without any reduction in benefits.

EXAMPLE: Walter Littlefeather has worked for 28 years on the Santa Fe lines all over the Southwest. He's 62 now and he'd dearly love to retire; it seems the railroad doesn't get the respect it once did, and Walter just doesn't get the same kick out of it he used to. If he waited until age 65 to retire, Walter would get a pension of $780 a month. How much of that would he lose if he retires at age 62? Walter would lose 1/180th of $780, which is $4.33, for each month under age 65. If he retired during the month of his 62nd birthday, he would be three years, or thirty-six months, under age 65. Multiplying thirty-six months times $4.33 equals $155.88. That $155.88 would be subtracted from his basic pension of $780, to leave Walter with a pension at age 62 of $624.12 a month.

Notice, though--and let's hope Walter notices too--since he will have thirty years employment with the railroad by the time he reaches age 64, he could retire then, if he wanted, without losing any monthly benefits. He would not have to wait until age 65 to collect his full $780 a month.

NOTE: If you work less than ten years in a job covered by the Railroad Retirement System, the years will be credited to your regular Social Security retirement account, just as if you had been working for an employer covered by the Social Security system.

> *"To me every hour of the light and dark is a miracle,*
> *Every cubic inch of space is a miracle."*
> Whitman, *Miracles*

J. Dual Benefits: Railroad Retirement and Social Security

One of the advantages for workers in the Railroad Retirement system is that it permits some workers to collect both Railroad and Social Security retirement benefits, if qualified for both. Why is it that Railroad workers have been afforded this double coverage? As railroad employment began to decline about thirty years ago, and as the remaining employees were forced into more and more seasonal lay-offs, it became necessary for railroad workers to work in more than one industry to survive. And, if they split their work time between two pension programs, but were forced to choose between the two on retirement, they would effectively be deprived of credit for a large part of their work. So, to encourage workers to stay in the declining railroad industry, and to fairly compensate them through pension coverage if they did, Congress passed a law permitting railroad workers to collect both Social Security and Railroad Retirement pensions, if they had earned them. The dual benefits system is now being phased out, however; budget cuts have also eroded Railroad Retirement benefits, reducing them by about 20 percent as of October 1, 1981.

The rules about who can collect dual Social Security and Railroad Retirement benefits work like this:

■The "old rule" still hanging on is that if you worked 10 years or more in the railroad industry, you are eligible for Railroad Retirement pension benefits, and if you worked enough years in other jobs covered by Social Security, you can collect Social Security benefits as well.

■If you are receiving dual benefits from both Railroad Retirement and Social Security before January 1, 1975, you will continue to receive them, but you will not receive any further cost-of-living increases.

■If you were qualified to receive both retirement benefits by January 1, 1975, but you had not yet retired, you will receive both benefits when you retire if you had 25 years of service in the railroad industry or if you have a "current connection" to the railroad industry at the time of retirement. Current connection means you have had 12 months of service in the railroad industry within the 30 months immediately prior to your retirement.

If you do not have either 25 years of service in the railroad industry or a current connection to the industry, you can qualify for dual benefits only if you were already qualified to receive Social Security retirement benefits prior to your leaving the railroad, if this was prior to January 1, 1975. This does not mean you actually had to have started receiving Social Security retirement by that time, only that you were eligible to receive it.

K. Disability Benefits Under Railroad Retirement

Disability benefits are available for both present and former railroad employees. Present employees are eligible for "occupational disability" benefits if they have 20 or more years employment with the railroad, or are over age 60, regardless of how many years they have worked for the railroad. An occupational disability is one that prevents you from performing your job with the railroad; it does not necessarily prevent you from working at some other kind of work, however.

"Total and permanent" disability benefits are available for both present and former railroad employees. This form of disability is closer to the disability defined by the Social Security disability program in that it requires you to be unable to perform any kind of substantial gainful employment. Benefits for total and permanent disability are available to anyone who worked for the railroad for at least 10 years, or who is over age 60 when he or she becomes disabled. You need not be working for the railroad at the time you become disabled in order to claim these total and permanent disability benefits.

If you have worked enough years in jobs covered by Social Security to qualify for Social Security disability benefits, you should apply for both types of disability. Though the requirements for Social Security disability are stricter than for railroad occupational disability, if you qualify and have more years of credit under Social Security than under the Railroad Retirement system, your disability benefits may be higher from Social Security. Apply for both and see.

218

L. Survivors' and Dependents' Benefits Under Railroad Retirement

1. Survivors

Under certain conditions, the surviving spouse and young children of a worker who dies while employed in the railroad industry may collect survivors' benefits if the worker had been employed in the industry for at least 10 years. A surviving spouse and children are eligible for survivors' benefits if:

■ The spouse is age 60 or older;

■ The spouse is age 50 through 59 and disabled;

■ The spouse is any age and caring for the unmarried child(ren) under age 18 of the deceased worker;

NOTE: Benefits to a surviving spouse will end if the spouse remarries.

■ The children are unmarried and under age 18;

■ The children are disabled before age 22.

The parent of a deceased worker may also be eligible for survivors' benefits if the parent is aged 60 or over and was dependent on the worker for support at the time of the worker's death.

NOTE: LUMP-SUM DEATH BENEFIT: At the death of a railroad worker with 10 years of service, survivors are entitled to a one-time payment of what is called a lump-sum death benefit. This payment is intended to help pay the cost of funeral or burial expenses. The amount of the payment is usually the same as the Social Security death benefit, currently $255.

2. Dependents

Certain dependents of a railroad worker who is receiving either railroad retirement or disability benefits will be eligible for dependents' benefits:

■A spouse age 65 or over;

■A spouse who is caring for a worker's eligible child;

■An unmarried child under age 18:

■An unmarried child who is disabled before 22.

M. Railroad Retirement Supplemental Annuities

For long-time railroad workers, the Railroad Retirement system has what could be called a bonus pension. If you have 25 years of service with the railroad and stay on a railroad job until retirement at age 65 (or at age 60 or older if you have 30 years service), you are eligible for this Supplemental Annuity. You receive an extra monthly amount based on your years of service; the extra amounts range from about $25 to $50 per month. Note, however, if you also receive a private railroad pension paid by an employer, this Supplemental Annuity--not your whole retirement pension--will be reduced by the amount of your private pension.

N. How to File a Railroad Retirement Claim

Application for any Railroad Retirement system benefit is made to a local office of the Railroad Retirement board. There are local offices in all major cities; you can find the address and phone number of your local office by looking in the telephone directory under United States Government, Railroad Retirement Board. They have all the forms necessary for each type of claim and will tell you what papers are needed with your application. The Bureau of Retirement Claims will rule on your application and notify you in writing of its decision. If you want to appeal the decision, you must file a written notice of the reasons for your appeal within one year of the Bureau's decision. You will be granted a hearing* before a Railroad Retirement referee (sort of like a judge, but less formal). The referee will notify you in writing of the appeal decision.

If you want to further appeal the decision of the referee, you can file a notice of appeal with the Railroad Retirement Board itself within four months of the referee's decision. The Railroad Retirement Board's appeals division will review your file and the referee's decision, but you will probably not be given another hearing. The Board will notify you in writing of its decision. If you are still dissatisfied with the action on your claim, you may file a lawsuit in federal court challenging the Board's decision.

---

* This "hearing" is essentially the same as the hearing provided by the Social Security Administration for Social Security appeals. See Chapter 5 for a description of how these hearings work.

O. Veterans' Benefits: Introduction

In addition to the pensions and benefits to which a worker may be entitled because of both public and private employment, many older Americans may also be eligible for certain benefits based on their military service. Since military service is often just a distant memory for many seniors, too many neglect the valuable Veterans Administration (VA) benefits--including disability benefits, pensions and free medical treatment--to which they may be entitled. The following outline of some of these benefits may remind you that you are entitled to take advantage of certain programs because of those fondly, or not so fondly, remembered years in the service.

The Veterans Administration operates a number of programs providing financial, medical and other assistance to veterans. Help with housing, job-training and counseling may all be available through various VA programs. But for older veterans, there are three major benefit programs of particular value: disability compensation, veterans' pensions and, perhaps most significant, free or low-cost medical care through VA hospitals and medical facilities. While complete details of VA procedures are not presented here, a description of the general eligibility requirements for these three programs is offered to bring to your attention benefits of which you might not be aware.

■ ■ ■

P. Disability Compensation: "Service-Connected Disability"

Compensation is available for veterans who were wounded, injured or became ill while on active duty in the armed forces. The illness or injury must be "service-connected," meaning that it must have occurred while you were on active duty. But if the condition arose or injury occurred during time of war or "national emergency,"* you may be compensated even though the injury or illness was not the direct result of performing military duties. Technically, if your condition arose while you were on active duty not during time of war or national emergency, your disability must have been the direct result of the performance of military duties. In reality, though, all this requirement

---

* Periods of war or "national emergency" include: World War I, April 6, 1917 to November 11, 1918; World War II, December 7, 1941 to December 31, 1946; Korean War, June 27, 1950 to June 27, 1955; and the Viet Nam War, August 4, 1964 to May 8, 1975. Note that the periods of time considered part of the Second World War and the Korean War are longer than the timespans normally attributed to those conflicts.

does is rule out injuries sustained while on leave, for example, or while AWOL or committing some militarily punishable offense. Virtually everything else is considered part of your military duties.

The amount of your disability compensation depends on the seriousness of your disability. When you apply for disability compensation, your medical records are examined and usually you have a VA medical examination. Your disability is "rated" based on the extent to which it interferes with the "average" person's ability to earn a living. This rating is expressed in percent of disability; zero percent to 100 percent disabled, in increments of 10 percent. Unfortunately, this rating system does not normally take into account the real effect of your disability on the work you do; rather, it applies arbitrary percentages (20 or 30 percent for the loss of a finger or toe, for example) to the non-existent "average" person's ability to earn a living. Obviously, the loss of a finger affects a piano player or plumber much more than it affects an insurance salesman; nonetheless, the VA usually applies its fixed "schedule" of disabilities to common injuries and diseases. If your disability is not easily classified, though, you may be able to convince the VA that the effect of your condition on the work you normally do deserves an "extra-schedular" high rating.

Most service-connected disabilities appear either during service or within a relatively short time--a year or two--after discharge from the service. What, then, is the significance of disability compensation rules for older Americans? Either you have been receiving disability compensation for a long time, or you haven't. Right? Well, not necessarily. Although most service-connected disabilities do show up during or soon after military service, there are some conditions that either did not appear at all, or appeared but were not too "disabling," until many years after you got out of the service. Additionally, many disabilities rated low when they first appear will grow progressively worse in later years. In either case, the older veteran who believes he has a legitimate claim should apply for disability benefits or for an upgrading of an already existing disability rating even if he isn't sure to what extent the disability is service-connected.

"Age in a virtuous person, of either sex, carries in it an authority which makes it preferable to all the pleasures of youth."
Richard Steele, *The Spectator*, No. 153

■ ■ ■

EXAMPLE #1: Claudio Soliste had his knee bashed by a falling crate of potatoes while serving as a cook at a basic training camp during World War II. The knee seemed to heal up pretty well in a couple of months and although he always had a little stiffness in the knee when he woke up in the morning, Claudio had no serious trouble with the knee during the war or the years immediately thereafter. However, as he got into his fifties and sixties, Claudio's knee got steadily worse; it ached, became stiffer and more painful, and finally would "lock" on him so that at times he could barely walk. His doctor told him he had developed a serious arthritic condition in the knee, most probably as a result of the wartime injury.

EXAMPLE #2: Ernie Driscoll was stationed in Japan during the Korean War. He was an M.P., patrolling the GI's who frequented waterfront bars near the base where he was stationed. At some point while in Asia--perhaps while in Japan, but maybe while on leave in Malaysia or Singapore--Ernie picked up an infection which moved into his lungs and which the army doctors could not figure out. It bothered Ernie off and on for a couple of months, enough to get him transferred to less strenuous duty, but not enough to get him a medical discharge. Over the years, Ernie continued to have minor respiratory difficulty when he exerted himself, but never to a point where he became seriously ill. Ernie applied for a service-connected disability and was given only a 10 percent disability rating. However, as he got older, Ernie experienced more and more breathing difficulties; finally, even mild exercise or exertion made Ernie's breathing very painful and dangerously difficult. His doctor said the earlier respiratory ailment had left his lungs scarred and clogged and that poorer circulation with age was making the condition worse.

Would Claudio and Ernie have any claim for service-connected disability benefits? Absolutely. Claudio's arthritic knee was certainly a direct result of his wartime injury and though he did not claim a disability when he got out of the service, he was entitled to do so as soon as the knee interfered with his normal activities. Ernie, on the other hand, had already applied for a disability and had it approved, but only for a 10 percent rating. That rating, however, was based on the state of his respiratory condition at the time he applied. Since the condition has become worse, he could apply for an upgrading of his disability rating which could result in much higher benefits. Remember, though, if Claudio gets his disability rating, or if Ernie gets his rating upgraded, the benefits based on the new rating will be effective only from the date of the new application; it is not retroactive to the time of the original injury or condition, or to the original claim for disability.

Q. Pension Benefits for Financially Needy Veterans

A monthly cash pension benefit is available to a financially needy veteran with some "wartime" military service if age 65 or over, or if any age and totally disabled. For purposes of this pension, the disability does not have to be service-connected, but it does have to be "permanent and total." In order to qualify for this pension, at least 90 days of your active duty must have been during a period of war (see the dates for official periods of war in the footnote to Section P). Though this service must have been during a period of war, there is no requirement that you served in or near actual combat.

The pension is based on need. In order to be eligible for any veterans' pension amount, you must be financially needy as determined primarily by your current income. Your savings or other assets are not generally considered. Even if you have a substantial nest-egg, you may be eligible for a veterans' pension if you have little or no current income. The amount of your pension will depend on how much income and how many dependents you have. The basic monthly pension for 1982 was $413 per month for an eligible individual, and $541 per month for a veteran with one dependent. Remember, though, these amounts are reduced if you have current income, including any Social Security benefits.

The surviving spouse or children (regardless of age) of a veteran who was receiving a veterans pension will be able to continue collecting a portion of that pension after the veteran's death. Eligibility for this continuing pension depends on the need of the spouse or children. And even if a deceased veteran's grown children do not qualify for survivors' pension benefits because of their income, they may qualify at a later time if they become needy. Thus, for example, if a World War I veteran qualified for a pension, his children may become eligible for survivors' benefits some twenty, thirty or fifty years after his death. If your deceased parent was a veteran who at one time collected a veteran's pension, no matter how long ago, it may be worth your time to apply for survivors' benefits if you are currently without substantial income.

R. Medical Treatment for Veterans

One of the most important benefits available to veterans is free or low-cost medical care. The VA operates more than 150 hospitals throughout the country. In addition, there are a great number of outpatient clinics providing health care for veterans. And unlike many public facilities, the level of care available in most VA hospitals is first-rate; in fact, specialized care may be available to you at no charge through a VA hospital while the same care might be unavailable or beyond your means in the world of private medicine. Basically, a veteran is eligible for medical care in a VA facility if unable to afford the care elsewhere. And dependents and survivors of veterans who have service connected disabilities, or who receive veterans' pensions, are entitled to care in VA facilities if they are unable to afford private care.

Even if you qualify for treatment at a VA medical facility, however, you may not be able to get the care when you need it, or you may only be provided the treatment at a facility far from your home. The reason for these limits, even for eligible patients, is while there are close to 100,000 beds in VA hospitals, there are a lot more than 100,000 veterans and dependents in need of medical care. So the VA has established a priority system for deciding who gets medical treatment, particularly in-patient hospitalization. The sequence of priorities for admission to a VA hospital, or for special medical treatment of any kind for which there is a limited availability, is as follows:

1. First priority is for emergencies and for those patients who have already begun treatment at a particular facility;

2. Second priority goes to the treatment of service-connected conditions;

3. The next level of priority is for those patients who are receiving, or who are eligible to receive, VA disability compensation and who need treatment for non-service connected conditions;

4. The remaining hospital beds are usually filled by those veterans and their dependents/survivors who are age 65, receiving a VA pension and who are unable to afford the care elsewhere.

S. Application for Veterans' Benefits

In addition to the benefits described above, your local VA office can give you information on a number of other programs available to assist veterans. Applications for all the programs and benefits can be made through a local VA office. Requests for medical treatment or admission to a VA medical facility can also usually be handled at the admitting office of the medical facility itself. The veteran's discharge papers, medical records concerning disability, and wage or tax records indicating current income are the most important documents to get together before making application for veterans' benefits. And like other federal benefits programs, decisions of the Veterans Administration concerning benefit eligibility are appealable through the formal, written appeals process established by the VA. The details of such appeals procedures are available at your local VA office.

Private Pensions: Small Consolation

CHAPTER 11

HIGHLIGHTS

When figuring out how much your pension will be,
and deciding when to retire, beware of the "integration" of your pension plan with Social Security
benefits; it could reduce your company pension to
almost nothing [see Section (D)(3)].

If you are working part-time, or are facing lay-
offs, be aware of how the totals 500 hours per
year and 1000 hours per year affect your pension
rights [see Section (G) and (H)].

The federal government provides some protection
for your pension rights if your company or pension
fund goes broke, but that protection is very
limited [see Section (I)].

There are important choices to be made concerning
the way in which you are paid your pension; these
choices can have important consequences for your
spouse [see Section (L)].

A. Introduction

Pension plans became popular during the Second World War at a time when there were more jobs than workers. Employers used fringe benefits, such as pensions, as a way of attracting and keeping workers without violating the wartime wage freeze rules. Since the early 1950s, unions and employers have both recognized pension plans as crucial elements in labor negotiations. But until the mid-1970s, "having" a pension plan and collecting a pension benefit check were two different animals. Many people were promised a pension as part of the terms of their employment, and many workers contributed to pension funds through payroll deductions, but relatively few actually received much in the way of benefits at retirement. The reasons for this failure to collect on promised pensions were several: people changed jobs and had to leave their pension rights behind; workers were not-so-mysteriously "let go" just before they reached retirement age; and pension plans, or whole companies, went out of business.

Since the passage of the Employee Retirement Income Security Act of 1974, commonly called ERISA, at least some of the worst sorts of disappearing pension acts have been halted. ERISA sets minimum standards for pension plans, guaranteeing that pension rights cannot be unfairly denied or taken from a worker. ERISA also provides some protection for workers in the event certain types of pension plans cannot pay all the benefits to which workers are entitled. But while ERISA does provide the protection of federal law for certain pension rights, its scope is limited. It is particularly important at the outset to realize that ERISA does not guarantee anyone a pension. Indeed, only about half of the country's total private work force (about 40 million people) are employed by companies which have some kind of pension plan; ERISA does nothing to protect the uncovered half of the work force.

ERISA also does nothing to limit the impact on workers of the growing trend in pension plans to "integrate" their benefits with Social Security benefits. Integration with Social Security means, simply, the amount of your monthly pension benefits is reduced by a percentage of your monthly Social Security retirement check. For most low-to-middle income workers, this means their actual pension check will be very small, or even nonexistent. The way this "integration" scheme works will be explained in more detail in Section D of this chapter.

Inflation is an old enemy of your right to receive a decent retirement pension. The figures an employer shows you as your potential pension benefit may seem decent at the time you are hired, and may even pay a reasonable amount when you first retire. But because virtually no private pension plans are indexed to the rising cost of living, an amount sufficient at the time you retire will seem smaller and smaller as inflation cuts into the value of your pension dollar. In other words, the cost of living will go up but your pension check won't. Unfortunately, ERISA has no provision requiring pension plans to respond to inflation's bite into your retirement benefits.

Though ERISA is a very limited step in protecting private pension rights, and fails to deal with several major problems, it is a step in the right direction, and if you are lucky enough to have earned a pension, you'll want to know how ERISA works. And, of course, you'll also want to have an understanding of how the rules of your particular pension plan operate. The following sections will explain the terms and rules of the various major types of pension plans and the ways in which ERISA protects your rights to pension benefits. But remember, there is nothing in ERISA or any other state or federal law that says a private employer must have a pension plan, and if it does have one, there is no requirement it must pay you any minimum amount of money.

B. Pension: Terms Defined

As you read this chapter, you'll discover the world of pensions has pretty well abandoned the English language in favor of "pensionese." Here are some helpful definitions. As you read through this chapter, refer back to these definitions as necessary.

■Participate: This seems like a normal enough word, but it has a specific meaning with regard to pensions. You "participate" in a pension plan when your time on the job begins to count toward qualifying for retirement benefits and you and your employer begin making contributions to the pension fund on your behalf. ERISA requires that a pension plan must permit you to participate if you are at least 25 years old and have worked at least one year for the company.

■Defined-benefit plan: This is the most common type of pension plan in which you receive a fixed amount as a monthly retirement benefit. The amount is based on either your number of years with the employer or on your average wages combined with the number of years you worked.

■ Defined-Contribution plan: This is the other major type of pension plan. Here there is no fixed amount set for your benefits, but there is a fixed amount the employer contributes to the pension fund on your behalf, based on how much and how long you work. Your pension benefit depends on how much money has accumulated in your account over the years you have worked.

■ Accrual: As you work, you accumulate (accrue) months and years of credit toward your pension. The amount of your retirement pension will be determined, at least in part, by how long you have worked. After you have begun to participate in a pension plan, you will "accrue" credits (usually counted in months or years) toward your pension. All "accrue" really means is to add up or accumulate benefit credits.

■ Vesting: A pension plan is no good if you don't have a right to get the pension when you retire, right? Well, "vesting" simply means getting a legal right to collect your pension when you retire. When your right to a pension is vested, it cannot be taken away from you because you change jobs, quit work, get fired or cuss out your boss. A vested right to a pension guarantees you will receive some benefit amount, though how much you receive will still depend on how long you work and on the other rules of the pension plan. There are many different rules about how and when benefits vest under various pensions. These rules are discussed in Section H.

■ Break-in-Service: A "break-in-service" is an interruption in the time you work for a particular company. The break--the time you are not actually working for the company--could be for any reason, including health, lay-offs, or simply working for someone else. It is considered a break-in-service if you later return to work for the original employer. Breaks-in-service affect your benefit rights in different ways as explained in Section G.

■ Pay-out options: The "pay-out" refers to the way in which your pension benefit payment is actually made to you. Pay-out options are the different ways your money can be divided up and sent to you. Many plans give you several choices of pay-out options which vary as to when you retire, whether you elect an option that includes survivors' benefits, etc.

Now that you have a little better feeling for this strange pension language, take a plunge into the other sections of this chapter to see how your pension works and how ERISA makes sure you receive what you are entitled to.

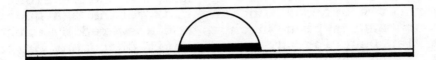

C. How to Get Information About Your Pension Plan

One of the good things enactment of ERISA did was to ensure that you can find out how your pension works and what your benefits are. ERISA requires that all employees be provided with a "Summary Plan Description," describing how the plan works and what the benefit choices are; an employee must be provided a Summary Plan Description within 90 days after qualifying as a "participant" in the plan. The description explains rules regarding participation, benefit accrual, vesting, pay-out options, retirement ages and claim procedures. You can get an up-dated Summary Plan Description at any time at the personnel or pension plan administrator's office where you work, or at the pension office of your union, if you belong to one which administers a pension plan.

Before you start swimming through all the information in this chapter about how different pension plans work, it would be a good idea for you to get from your company's pension office a description of your own plan. Then you will be able to compare the description of your plan with the explanations in the chapter of how your type of plan is supposed to work. It will make the explanations in the chapter clearer to you and will keep you from wasting your time reading, and trying to figure out, all the rules for pension plans that have nothing to do with your own.

In addition to the general plan description, you are entitled to a statement of your personal benefit account. Once a year, you may make a written request for a benefit statement which will explain how many benefits you have accrued and what benefits have vested (or when they will vest). Remember, though, you may have to make a written request for this statement; though many companies provide the statement routinely, ERISA does not require the company provide it unless you make a request. You are also entitled to a copy of your benefit statement if you leave your job (or have a break-in-service).

ERISA also requires each pension plan to make a yearly

report to the federal government about the investments of the money in the plan fund. A copy of the latest annual report must be made available for you to inspect, or for you to receive a copy at minimal expense, at the pension plan administrator's office. And any time you have a question about your pension plan which is not answered by either the Summary Plan Description, your benefit statement or the summary of the annual report, make a written request for the information you want to the plan administrator. If the administrator's office does not give you a satisfactory answer, then direct your questions to the local area office of the federal government's Labor-Management Services Administration. You'll find their number in the telephone book under United States Government, Department of Labor.

D. Pensions: What Are They Exactly?

A pension is an agreement between you and your employer (or you, your union and your employer) under which each contributes a certain amount of money during the years you work for that employer (or group of employers). These contributions create a money fund out of which you are paid a certain amount of money when you retire, usually at age 65. But it's important to understand at the onset that pensions, like beauty, come in many shapes and sizes. In the first place, most all pension plans can be divided into two basic categories: "defined-benefit" and "defined-contribution" plans. These basic types have a number of variations, the most common of which are explained below. But no matter what type of plan your company has, it's very important to realize the benefit you actually receive may be much lower than figures presented by the plan first indicate if the plan is "integrated" with Social Security benefits. This devilish "integration" of pensions is explained at the end of this section.

1. Defined-Benefit Plans

These are the most common pension plans. Under a defined-benefit plan, you receive a definite, pre-determined amount of money upon retirement or disability. The fixed amount is based on your years of service with the employer; most often, the amount of your monthly benefit is a fixed amount of money for each year of service. For example, a plan may pay $10 per month for each year of service. This means if you worked 20 years for the company, your pension would be $200 per month.

Payments under a defined-benefit plan may also be calculated on a percentage of your salary over the years. The benefit is figured by taking your average salary over all the years you worked, multiplying that average by the fixed percentage established by the pension plan, and then multiplying that total by the number of years you worked for the company. For example, if your average salary over 20 years was $10,000 per year, and the pension plan credits one percent of yearly salary, your pension would be one percent of $10,000, which is $100, multiplied by your 20 years of service, for a yearly pension of $2,000.

2. Defined-Contribution Plans

These plans do not guarantee any particular pension amount upon retirement. Instead, they guarantee only that the employer will pay into the pension fund a certain amount every month (or every year) for each employee. The amount paid in is usually a fixed percentage of the employee's wages or salary, but sometimes the amount is a fraction of the company's profits (profit-sharing), with the size of each employee's profit-share depending on the amount of wage or salary. However your money gets into a pension fund, once there it is invested in various supposedly safe, long-term growth investments (stocks, bonds, real estate, etc.) along with the money that has been added into the fund on behalf of all the other employees. Upon retirement, each employee is paid a lump-sum pension, or is paid a yearly annuity, the amount of which is determined by the amount contributed to the fund on behalf of the individual employee over the years, plus whatever earnings that money has accumulated as part of the investments of the pension fund as a whole.

EXAMPLE: Earline Harris worked for We're Wired, Inc., an electronics company that had a defined-contribution pension plan. She had 20 years of accrued benefits when she retired. The plan called for the company to pay into the pension fund six percent a year of an employee's salary. Over the 20 years Earline was covered, her average salary was $10,000 a year. The company, therefore, had to contribute six percent of $10,000, or $600, every year for 20 years. That's a total of $12,000 contributed by the company. If the pension fund money was invested at an average return of eight percent a year, Earline's personal pension account would have grown to over $27,000 in the 20 years. That would be the lump-sum payment she could take out of the pension fund when she retired.

3. "Integrated" Plans

In the past few years, the popularity of this somewhat devious form of pension plan has grown among employers. When you see how it works, you'll understand why the bosses like it. When a pension plan is integrated with Social Security retirement benefits, it means your actual monthly or yearly pension benefit is reduced by all, or some percentage of, your Social Security check. One type of integrated plan operates by setting up what is called a "benefit goal" for your retirement. This means the plan sets a goal for the amount of money you should have from a combination of pension and Social Security retirement income. The figure the plan arrives at as your benefit goal is usually a percentage of your average pre-retirement income. Your pension amount is then only what is needed to make up the difference between your Social Security benefits and this pre-determined benefit "goal."

Example: Roberto Salazar worked for Pink and Purple Plastics Company, which had an integrated, defined-benefit pension plan which set a benefit goal of 40 percent of the retiree's final salary. Roberto was making $18,000 a year as a mold designer when he retired. His benefit goal, then, would be $7,200 a year, or $600 a month. The company's defined-benefit was $20 a month for each year of service. Since Roberto had 20 years with the company, without "integration" the plan would owe him $400 a month. But Roberto also received $450 a month Social Security retirement benefits. The total of his Social Security and pension benefits would be $850 a month. This would be $250 a month more than the benefit goal, as defined by Pink and Purple. Under their integrated plan, his pension would be reduced by $250 a month to meet the benefit goal. So, instead of receiving a pension of $400 a month from Pink and Purple, Roberto would only get $150 a month from the company pension fund. Isn't it great how the integrated plan works? The company thinks so.

One small--very small--consolation about integrated plans is once they have reduced your pension to "fit" it into the benefit goal along with Social Security benefits, they cannot further reduce your pension amount when Social Security benefits rise because of cost-of-living increases.

The rules and percentages of various integrated plans vary widely. Another common variety is the "offset" plan, which merely reduces ("offsets") your pension benefits by a certain percentage of your Social Security benefits. For example, an offset plan might reduce your pension benefits by 50 percent of your Social Security benefits. If you had earned a $250 a month pension (before the offset), but you received $400 a month from Social Security, your pension would be reduced by $200 (50 percent of the $400 Social Security benefit). You would only actually receive $50 a month from the pension fund.

Check with your own pension plan office to find out if, and by exactly how much, your pension will be reduced through integration with your Social Security benefits.

E. Who Can Participate in a Pension Plan?

Remember, the law does not require an employer to offer a pension plan of any kind. But if your employer does have a plan you must be permitted to participate in it if you are age 25 or older and have worked for the company for at least one year. When you "participate," it simply means your time at the job will be counted toward qualifying for retirement benefits, and the employer must begin making contributions to your pension account (if the particular plan requires such employer contributions). You qualify as having worked one year if you work a total of one thousand (1,000) hours in a 12-month period beginning your first day of work. That's an average of 20 hours a week for 50 weeks.

Though you must be permitted to participate if you meet the age and one-year-of-employment requirements, there are some plans which are limited solely to one category of employee and not to another. For example, some companies have pension plans for employees who are on salary but not for employees who work for hourly wages. This kind of exclusion is perfectly legal, even though it may be neither fair nor just.

As with most rules under ERISA, there are a couple of exceptions to the one-year participation rule. If the pension plan provides for full "vesting" of retirement benefits--meaning you have a right to a retirement pension that cannot be taken away from you because you leave work-- after only three years of employment, then the plan is also permitted to make an employee wait the same three years before being allowed to participate in the plan. ("Vesting" is explained more fully in the following section.)

Another exception to the one-year participation rule is of particular significance for older workers. Before ERISA,

it was a common practice for employers to exclude recently
hired older workers from participating in the company's
pension plan entirely. Now, however, an older worker cannot
be excluded from the plan unless he or she is within five
years of the pension's normal retirement age when first
hired, and the pension plan is the defined-benefit variety
(see Section D, above). In other circumstances, a worker may
not be excluded from participating in the pension plan
because of age.

EXAMPLE: At age 60, Dorothy Constance began working as
a legal secretary for the huge law offices of Richard &
Ellis. The law offices had a pension plan which contributed
5 percent of a workers average salary into the pension fund
for each year of service. Normal retirement age for this
pension plan was 65. Since Dot was within five years of
retirement age when she began work for the law firm, could
she be denied participation in the pension plan? No, she
could not be denied. Since the plan provided for defined
contributions instead of defined benefits, the older worker
exclusion did not apply. Get in there and make sure those
lawyers put you on the pension plan rolls, Dorothy!

F. How Do You Accumulate Pension Credits?

Most pension plans provide that the amount of your
pension at retirement depends on the number of benefit
credits you have accumulated during your years of work with
that particular employer. Once you are participating in the
pension plan, you begin to "accrue" (officially accumulate)
benefits, usually in terms of years of credit. If after you
begin participating in the pension plan, you work 1,000
hours or more during a year, ERISA declares you must accrue
at least partial benefits for that year. Upon retirement, a
defined-benefit plan determines the amount of your pension
by the number of accrued benefits (years of credit) in your
pension account. For example, a defined-benefit plan may
pay $10 per month for each year of credited work; if you
worked for the company for 20 years, you would receive a
pension of $200 per month, assuming the plan is not "inte-
grated" with Social Security benefits (see Section D, above,
for a reminder of how "integrated" plans cut into your pension
check).

G. What Are "Break-in-Service" Rules?

Before ERISA, if you were off work--laid off, disabled, on leave of absence, etc.--for a significant period of time, you could lose all the benefits you had accrued before the "break-in-service," as the time off work is called. The rules under ERISA make it much more difficult for you to lose your accrued benefits. Here's how ERISA protects your accrued benefits:

■ You do not lose your accrued benefits because of a break-in-service if you work over 500 hours for your employer during a year. But while you do not lose previously accrued benefits, your employer does not have to give you credit for that year if you work less than 1,000 hours.

■ Even if you work less than 500 hours in a year, you do not lose your previously accrued benefits unless you are off work as many years (consecutively) as the number of years of accrued benefits you had before the break-in-service. In other words, if you have three years of accrued benefits in your pension plan, you could lose those benefits only if you were off work (worked less than 500 hours in the year) for three consecutive years.

The break-in-service rule assumes you do eventually return to work for the same employer. If you don't return, you will lose the accrued benefits for good and have no right to any pension unless your benefit rights had "vested" before you left work (see below).

H. How Do Pension Benefits Become "Vested"?

When your pension benefits become "vested," it means you have a legal right to receive a pension at retirement based on those benefits, no matter where you work, or don't work, after the benefits have vested. Before ERISA, workers could lose whatever pension benefit they had accrued at one job if they were fired or laid off or if they voluntarily moved to another employer, even if they worked for the first employer for many years. Unscrupulous employers, seeking to avoid paying pension benefits, were known to fire workers just before they reached retirement age, unjustly but legally, ending their claims to pensions.

The vesting rules of ERISA, which declare that once you have worked for the same employer for a number of years you cannot lose your pension benefits, have improved the situation considerably. While ERISA does not dictate the specific rules each pension plan must follow, it has set up mandatory minimum guidelines protecting workers who have spent at least 10 years with one employer. And in some cases, workers who have spent five years with one employer may have some, though not complete, benefit rights.

Under ERISA, a pension plan must meet one of the following vesting schedules. The plan can do better than these schedules, but it cannot do worse:

1. "Cliff" Vesting
(Ten-Year, 100-Percent Vesting)

This is the most common vesting plan. It provides no protection at all for workers who change jobs frequently, but provides excellent protection for long-term employees. Under this type of plan, once you have credit for 10 years of service with one employer, your benefits must be 100 percent vested. One hundred percent vested means you have a right to receive the full amount of benefits normally paid at retirement to someone with the number of years you have with that employer at retirement age. In other words, once you reach 100 percent vested status, you will receive your full pension based on the number of years you worked for that company, even if you leave the company long before retirement age.

Even though your benefits are fully vested after 10 years of service, the benefit <u>amount</u> is based on the number of years of service after you are considered "participating" in the pension plan; and usually it takes one year of service before you are participating in the plan. Thus, in a cliff vesting plan, if you quit work after 10 years, you would be fully vested, but your pension account would only have <u>nine</u> years of accrued benefits. If you had quit the job after only nine years, though, you would not have reached the vesting limit and you would have no pension coming.

Another way of looking at the ten-year, 100 percent vesting rule, assuming for example your company has a defined-benefit plan which pays $10 per month at retirement for each year of accrued vested benefits, is as follows:

Years of Service	Amount of Pension
9	none
10	9 years participating times $10/mo. = $90/mo.
20	19 years participating = $190/mo.

EXAMPLE: Bobbie Jo Emery retired after 23 years with the Let Them Eat Cake Baking Company. Let Them Eat had a cliff vesting pension plan which paid $5 a month for each year of service after participation had begun. Bobby Jo's pension rights vested after ten years with the company. How much was her pension? She had 23 years with the company, but only 22 years after her participation began. Thus she receives a pension of $5 a month multiplied by 22 years, for a monthly total of $110 [unless, of course, her plan is integrated with Social Security benefits, in which case Bobbie Jo might receive little or nothing; see Section D(3) again].

2. "Graded" Vesting

Graded vesting gives some protection to a worker after only five years of service, with increasing benefits for each year after five. Full vesting does not occur, however, until after 15 years of service with the employer. After five years of service, you are 25 percent vested. For each year of service after that, you receive another five percent vested benefits. After 10 years of service, your vesting increases 10 percent per year until you are fully vested after 15 years. Remember that 25 percent vested, for example, means at retirement you would be entitled to receive 25 percent of the full pension someone with your same number of years of accrued benefits would be entitled to if they were fully vested.

Here is another way of looking at the graded vesting plan, assuming a defined benefit of $10 per month for each year of service:

Years of Service		% Vested		Years Benefits		$/Year Service		Pension/Month
5 yrs	=	25%	x	4	x	$10	=	$ 10
10	=	50	x	9	x	10	=	45
15	=	100	x	14	x	10	=	140
20	=	100	x	19	x	10	=	190

The advantage of graded vesting is that a worker gets some pension protection after only five years of service. The disadvantage is it takes 15 years of working for the same employer to become 100-percent vested.

EXAMPLE: Joachim Van Rindt moved to the United States from The Netherlands in 1973 to join his two sons and daughter who lived in the U.S. Joachim began working for Giapetto's Woodworking as a furniture maker, bringing his European craftsmanship to the small furniture company and helping them develop a new line of products. Giapetto's has a graded vesting pension plan paying $10 a month for each year of service. Joachim will turn 65 in 1984 and is considering retiring. What would his pension be? After 11 years of service, Joachim would be 60 percent vested with 10 years of accrued benefits. Thus he would receive 60 percent of 10 years multiplied by $10 a month; that works out to $60 a month. If Joachim waited until age 69 to retire, he would have 15 years of service which would make him 100 percent vested and give him 14 years of accrued benefits for a pension of $140 a month.

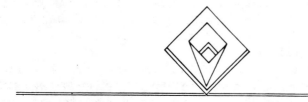

3. "Rule of 45" Vesting

A slight variation is found in Rule of 45 vesting, which is not really a "rule" but just another vesting plan with a little wrinkle to it. What makes the Rule of 45 vesting plan different is it combines the worker's age with years of service to determine when benefits are vested. Under the Rule of 45, your benefits must be 50 percent vested after five years of service if, when you add your age plus your years of service, the total is 45 years or more. And after you have reached this 50 percent vested level, 10 percent vesting is added for each year of work. Thus, you become fully vested no less than five years after meeting the 45 years test.

You can also meet the vesting limits under the Rule of 45 in another way: no matter what your age, you become 50 percent vested after 10 years of service (unless, of course, you had already reached 50 percent vesting under the first method of figuring under the Rule of 45). Again, once you reach the 50 percent vested level, you will get another 10 percent vesting for each additional year of work.

This chart is another way of looking at the alternative methods of becoming vested under the Rule of 45:

Years of Service	and	Age + Service	or	Years of Service	=	Percent Vested
5		45		10		50
6		47		11		60
7		49		12		70
8		51		13		80
9		53		14		90
10		55		15		100

EXAMPLE: Phil Gianapoulos began working for the Kinky Can Company when he was 30 years old. Kinky Can has a Rule of 45 vesting plan. At age 38, Phil became 50 percent vested because his age (38) plus years of service (8) added up to more than 45 years. This means if Phil had quit working for Kinky Can at age 38, many years down the road when he reached retirement age, Kinky Can would have to pay him a pension worth 50 percent of what a worker with a fully vested pension and seven years of accrued benefits would get (remember, only seven years of accrued benefits, not eight, because the first year the worker is not yet participating and thus is not counted for accrual purposes).

If Phil were still with Kinky Can at age 43, he would be 100 percent vested. He had worked five more years, gaining 10 percent vesting each year, after he had reached the 50 percent vested plateau at age 38. So, if Phil quit his job at age 43, he would receive a full pension based on 12 years of accrued benefits (13 years of service minus the first year which doesn't count for accrual purposes).

If the Kinky Can Company pension plan paid a defined-benefit of $10 a month for each year of service, how much would Phil get from Kinky Can at retirement if he quit working for them at age 38? He would receive a 50 percent pension based on seven years accrued benefits. Fifty percent of seven years is three-and-one-half years; $10 for each year would mean a benefit of three-and-one-half times $10, or $35 a month.

And how much would Phil get from Kinky Can if he quit working for them at age 43? He would get $10-a-month for his full 12 years of accrued benefits. That's $120-a-month. Not great after 13 years of work, but what can you expect from the Kinky Can Company?

4. "Year" Vesting

Also called "Class-Year" vesting, this type of vesting is used only with defined-contribution plans. Year-vesting plans provide that employer/employee contributions are vested within five years of the end of the year in which the contributions are made. In other words, contributions made to the pension plan in 1980 would be 100 percent vested at the end of 1985. If you retire, or change jobs, you would have a vested right to all contributions made up to five years before you left that employer.

■■■■■

Under any one of these vesting procedures, the same rules apply regarding how you get credit for a year of service. If you have worked 1,000 hours for the same employer in a given year, that year must be counted as a year of service toward the vesting of your pension benefits. If you have had a break-in-service (less than 500 hours worked in the year) and your benefits were not vested at the time of the break, the pension plan need not count the years before the break in determining when your benefits become vested _if_ the number of years of the break is as great as the number of years of service before the break. However, if your pension benefits had vested before your break-in-service, the years before the break must be credited to your pension account no matter how long your break is (even if you never return to work for that company).

What about your years of service before ERISA went into effect in 1974? If you had a break-in-service before ERISA, the law does not protect your early years. A pension plan may exclude years before a break-in-service if the break occurred before 1974. One other note--your years of service with a company before you reached age 22 need not be credited to your pension account.

I. Do You Have Any Pension Protection?

What happens if your pension plan goes broke? Or your employer goes out of business? Or your employer changes the rules of the plan so your vested benefits are no longer vested under the new rules? Before ERISA, you would have been out of luck. Now you have some protection.

1. If Your Plan is Changed

Once your pension benefits have vested under the existing pension plan, you cannot be deprived of any of those benefits by a change in the plan's vesting rules. (Remember, though, changes in the rules of your pension plan before ERISA went into effect in 1974 may work against you.) If the company you work for is taken over by a new company which continues the existing pension plan, your years of service continue to count and the benefits you receive must be equal to or greater than the benefits you would have received under the old plan.

2. If the Plan Ends or the Fund Goes Broke

In recent years, a number of pension funds have gone broke, either through mismanagement, fraud or over-extension of resources. In the future, it's likely we will be witness to an increasing number of pension plan failures. Under ERISA, there is some insurance against such pension fund collapse. ERISA established the Pension Benefit Guaranty Corporation, a public, non-profit insurance fund, to provide coverage against bankrupt pension funds. Should a pension fund be unable to pay all its obligations to retirees, the PBGC may, under certain conditions, pick up the slack and pay much of the pension fund's unfulfilled obligations. However, the PBGC does not cover all types of pension plans and does not guarantee all pension benefits of the plans it does cover. Only defined-benefit plans are covered (through insurance premiums they pay to the PBGC) and only vested benefits are protected by the insurance. Also, PBGC insurance normally only covers retirement pension benefits; other benefits, such as disability, health coverage and death benefits, are not usually covered.

If you have a question about termination of benefits because of failure of your pension plan, you may write directly to the PBGC, 2020 "K" Street, N.W., Washington, D.C. 20006.

J. How to Claim Your Pension

Although ERISA does not demand one uniform claim procedure for all pension plans, it does establish some rules which must be followed when you retire and want to claim

your benefits. All pension plans must have an established
claim procedure and all participants in the plan must be
given a summary of the plan which explains the plan's claim
procedure. (If you don't have a plan summary, get one from
the personnel or pension office of the company.) When your
claim is filed, you must receive a decision on the claim, in
writing, within a "reasonable time." The decision must
state specific reasons for the denial of any claimed benefits and must explain the basis for determining the benefits
which are granted.

From the date you receive a written decision on your
pension claim, you have 60 days to file a written appeal of
the decision. The details for where and how this appeal is
filed must be explained in the plan summary. In presenting
your appeal, the claim procedures must permit you to examine
the plan's files and records and to submit evidence of your
own. ERISA does not, however, require the pension plan
actually give you a "hearing" regarding your appeal. Within
60 days of filing, the pension plan administrators must file
a written decision on your appeal. If your claim is still
denied, in whole or in part, you then have a right to press
your claim in either state or federal court (see Section M).

K. How Does Working After "Retirement" Affect Your Pension?

If your benefits have vested when you reach the retirement age established by your pension plan (usually 65), you are free to "retire" from a job with the employer who pays your pension and work for someone else, or open your own business, while collecting your full pension. However, if you return to work for the employer who is paying your pension benefits, ERISA permits the employer to suspend payment of your pension for as long as you continue working for that employer. Also, if you are covered by a multi-employer pension plan (such as those through an industry-wide union contract), your pension benefits can be suspended if you return to work for a different employer whose employees are covered by the same pension plan.

L. How Are Retirement Benefits Usually Paid?

There are a number of different ways in which pension plans pay out retirement benefits. Sometimes one plan will offer several options; the worker must choose the form of payment at the time of retirement (and in some instances, before retirement). Normal retirement age is usually 65, though some plans offer early retirement [see Part 5, below].

These are the most common kinds of payment plans:

1. Lump-Sum Payment

Many defined-contribution plans simply pay you the entire amount accumulated in your pension account at retirement. It is up to you to invest or spend that money in any way you see fit.

2. Simple Life Annuity*

Your pension benefits are paid in monthly installments for as long as you live. There is no provision in these simple life annuities, however, to pay pension benefits to your spouse or other person after you die.

---

* "Annuity" simply means a fixed amount of benefits which are paid every year (though most annuities actually pay monthly) for the life of the person who is entitled to it.

3. Continuous Annuity

Some plans offer an annuity which pays monthly installments for the life of the retired worker, and which also
provide a small safety net for the worker's spouse (or other
beneficiary). This means if the worker dies within a speci-
fied time after retirement (in some plans it's five years,
in others 10 years), the monthly annuity will be paid to the
surviving spouse or other beneficiary for the remainder of
the five or 10-year period. If this option is chosen by a
retiring worker, the monthly pension benefits will be
slightly less (usually around 10 percent less) than they would
be under a simple life annuity.

4. Joint-and-Survivor Annuity

ERISA requires any pension plan which pays benefits in
annuity form to offer a worker the choice of a joint-and-
survivor annuity in addition to whatever other form of
annuity is offered. This form of annuity pays monthly
benefits not only as long as the retired worker is alive,
but continues to pay to the worker's spouse for as long as
the spouse lives. If the joint-and-survivor annuity is
chosen by the worker, the pension will be slightly less than
under a simple annuity plan; how much less is determined by
the age of the worker's spouse. The younger the spouse--
meaning the longer the pension is likely to be paid--the
greater the reduction in benefits. The amount of the pension the surviving spouse would receive is usually half of
what the retired worker receives (though some plans provide
for survivor payments of more than 50 percent). Before
choosing one or the other form of annuity, you should find
out exactly what your pension plan would pay under each
alternative annuity; ask the employer's pension administrator to give you the exact figures, in writing, before you
make a decision. When you are nearing retirement age, the
pension administrator will send you a form on which you
choose the annuity you want; if you don't receive a form, or
you fail to let the pension office know what your choice is,
you will automatically receive the joint-and-survivor annuity.

5. Early Retirement ("Pre-Retirement") Survivor Annuity

Many pension plans provide for "early retirement" in
which you may choose to collect a reduced retirement pension
at an age younger than the "normal" retirement age estab-

lished by the plan. Normal retirement age is usually 65, though it may be earlier; early retirement age may range anywhere from 55 to 65.

If your pension plan offers early retirement, it must also offer an early retirement (sometimes called "pre-retirement") survivor annuity. This kind of annuity protects a spouse's right to collect a pension if the worker dies before normal retirement age. For a spouse to collect such an early retirement survivor annuity, the worker must have reached either the company's early retirement age, or have reached an age 10 years before the plan's normal retirement age, whichever is later. (In practical terms, this means the worker must have reached at least age 55). Also, the worker must have signed a form agreeing to take a reduced early retirement pension in exchange for the protection for the spouse of an early retirement survivor annuity. If your employer has an early retirement provision in it's pension plan, you may sign this annuity request form shortly before you reach early retirement age.

Remember, companies offer a number of variations on the above-described pay-out plans. Some of these options have terms more favorable to the worker than those ERISA demands as minimum terms. Check with the pension administrator at your place of employment (or former employer, if that's where you qualify for a pension) when you near early retirement age and again well before normal retirement age. Ask for an explanation in writing of exactly what your benefit options are--and what they would pay--under the different pay-out choices your pension offers.

M. Can You Enforce Your Pension Rights in Court?

The rules of ERISA permit you to file a specific ERISA-enforcement lawsuit in federal court to enforce any rule or provision of the ERISA law or of a pension plan covered by ERISA rules. In particular, you are entitled to file a federal court lawsuit under ERISA:

■ To recover benefits which have been unfairly denied;

■ To change a ruling made by the pension plan that would affect your future benefits (a ruling regarding eligibility, accrual, vesting, break-in-service, etc.);

■ To force the plan to provide information required by ERISA;

■ To correct improper management of the plan or its funds; or

■ To protect any other right established by the rules of your particular pension plan or by ERISA itself.

Now that you know how to make sure that you collect all the pension benefits to which you are entitled, you may also want to know about your right to continue working without being forced to retire, or to work for someone else after you begin to collect your pension. You can find out about your right to keep working by moving on to the next chapter, "Age Discrimination in Employment: Your Right to Work."

Age Discrimination in Employment: Your Right to Work

CHAPTER 12

HIGHLIGHTS

The federal Age Discrimination in Employment Act (ADEA) protects against discrimination not only in hiring and retirement, but in every other employment decision as well, such as promotion, lay-offs, job assignment and wage scale; the ADEA also covers the actions of unions and employment agencies [see Section (B) and (C)].

While the ADEA offers no protection for workers before age 40 or after age 70, nor to people who work for companies with fewer than 20 employees, many states have their own laws which do protect workers in these categories [see Section (D)].

Proving age discrimination in your case may be a difficult task; a number of procedures and suggestions for helping you prove your case are offered [see Section (E)].

The Equal Employment Opportunity Commission (EEOC) may assist you in processing your age discrimination suit, but you must follow specific complaint procedures in order to get the full protection of the ADEA and the assistance of the EEOC [see Section (F) and (G)].

■ ■ ■

A. Introduction

Most of the programs discussed in this book have to do with benefits to which you are entitled when you are no longer working, either because you have retired, or you've become disabled and are unable to work. But what if you're simply not ready to retire from a job you have had for years, even though you're approaching "normal" retirement age? Suppose you decide to leave one job late in your career to seek a different job, or give up your own business to try your job skills working for someone else? Or perhaps you want to move up the ladder on the job you already have, taking on greater responsibility and getting better pay, despite the fact you are nearing an age when retirement would be possible? Are you entitled to keep working? Do you have a right to compete for jobs on an equal basis with younger workers? Can you be passed over for promotion simply because the company wants to "invest" in younger workers?

In many instances, you'll find employers who recognize and reward the skill and experience of older workers; with these employers job security and job mobility are not a problem. Unfortunately, though, there are many occasions when older workers are faced with out-and-out age discrimination on the job. Often, younger workers are unfairly favored, and older workers with more experience, know-how and stability are pushed aside. If you feel you may have been the victim of some form of age discrimination in employment, whether in hiring, firing, lay-offs, wages, promotion, or any other working condition, you'll want to know about the protection afforded you by the federal Age Discrimination in Employment Act (ADEA).

The rules established by the ADEA can be stated fairly simply:

■ Arbitrary age discrimination against workers age 40 to 70, regarding any employment decision, is illegal;

■ The federal law applies to employers with more than 20 employees, as well as to unions and employment agencies;

■ Both public and private employment is covered by the federal law, including state and local governments and their agencies;

■ The federal law is bolstered by separate state laws, some of which extend protection to workers over age 70 and to employers with less than 20 employees.

You can probably tell from the length of this chapter that the question "What is age discrimination" is not answered as simply as these four rules might suggest--some tough problems arise when you try to figure out exactly what "age discrimination" is. A high court justice was once asked to define what was legally "obscene." His famous response was: "I can't define it, but I know it when I see it." In trying to determine whether you have been the victim of age discrimination, you may be faced with a similar problem: how do you prove that the reason your employer (or potential employer) did not hire or promote you, discharged you, or laid you off, was discrimination based on age? Proving someone's reasons for doing something requires you prove what is in the mind of the person making the decision, and getting inside someone's head can be an extremely difficult task.

The discussion in the following sections cannot give you a simple formula to follow in trying to determine whether or not age discrimination has occurred in your employment. The different facts of each case require different interpretations of the law. But this chapter can give you a detailed understanding of the laws pertaining to age discrimination in employment and some suggestions as to how you can apply the law to your work situation in order to decide whether you have been the victim of age discrimination in employment. And if you conclude you have suffered such discrimination, the chapter also explains what procedures you can follow to take advantage of the protection both federal and state laws offer.

B. The Federal Age Discrimination in Employment Act (ADEA)

The first attempts to pass federal legislation barring age discrimination were made in the early 1950s, but little progress was made. By the early 1960s, however, national sensitivity to the evils of discrimination of all sorts was on the rise; prohibitions against age discrimination were included in proposals for the 1964 Civil Rights Act. Although the final version of that law failed to include age as one of the protected categories, a compromise was reached to have the Department of Labor study the problem of age discrimination and report back to Congress.

The inescapable conclusion of the Labor Department study, completed in 1966, was that older workers were significantly discriminated against in employment. In addition, the report concluded that when older workers lost their jobs, they remained unemployed far longer than younger workers, and older workers made up a disproportionately high percentage of "discouraged workers," those people who have given up the search for work. The study also found the assumption about older workers held by most employers--that a worker's productivity declined with age--was just plain wrong. Instead, research indicated older workers are more stable than younger workers; they are equally capable of learning new skills and adapting to new technologies; and their overall mental abilities do not, as a rule, diminish, at least through age 70. The skills or mental ability of some older workers do decline, but such diminishing skill and decline in overall abilities are the exception, not the rule.

The result of the Labor Department study and a growing awareness of the injustice of age discrimination led to the enactment of the federal Age Discrimination in Employment Act in 1967.* The ADEA is the single most important law protecting the rights of older workers. Basically, it provides that workers between the ages of 40 and 70 cannot be arbitrarily discriminated against because of age in any employment decision. This includes hiring, discharges, lay-offs, promotion, wages, other terms and conditions of employment, referrals by employment agencies and membership in and the activities of unions. Perhaps the single most important rule under the ADEA is that there can be no mandatory retirement of a worker until he or she reaches age 70. (When it comes to employment for the federal government, there is no mandatory retirement age.)

Of course, there are a number of exceptions to the broad protection of the ADEA. Here are the most important, and the ones most in need of federal legislative change:

70 or over: The most obvious hole in the law is that it provides protection only until you reach age 70. Once

---

* The Act was amended in 1974 and again in 1978. You can find the complete text of the Act in volume 29 of the United States Codes, Sections 621 to 634. The library citation for the Act looks like this: 29 U.S.C. Sections 621-634. If you do read the law itself, make sure you read a version that includes the 1978 changes.

you reach 70, you receive no protection whatsoever against discrimination in employment because of age, unless you work for the federal government, which has no mandatory retirement. At age 70, you now become the same sort of second class citizen in the working world that almost all older workers were before the federal law was passed. You should be aware, though, that some states have their own laws which might protect workers after age 70. These laws will be discussed a little later in this chapter.

Workers for small companies: Another category of workers left unprotected by the ADEA are those employed by companies which have less than 20 employees. This is an irrational distinction; an older worker is hurt just as much by job discrimination at a little company as at a big one. Again, though, your state may have no such restriction in its age discrimination law, or its law may apply to employers with a smaller number of workers, say 5 or 10.

Executives: Another exception in the ADEA permits the mandatory retirement of "executives or persons in high policy-making positions" at age 65 if they would receive an annual retirement pension from that employer of at least $27,000 a year.

Occupational Qualification Exception: A major exception to the federal age discrimination law is made when age is a "bona fide* occupational qualification" (BFOQ) for a particular job. However, if an employer does set age limits on a particular job, that employer must be able to prove the limit is necessary because a worker's ability to adequately perform that job does in fact diminish after the age limit is reached. A general claim that older workers cannot "handle" the job is not enough to meet this BFOQ standard. The employer must be able to point to specific job performance factors which require particular physical skills known to deteriorate after a certain age. Most of the jobs for which a BFOQ is approved involve the safety of either the public or other workers. For example, a number of transportation systems have an age limit on the hiring of new train or bus operators, arguing the danger to the public inherent in operating a bus or train justifies the occupational qualification. Some of these public transportation limits have been upheld by the courts. On the other hand, an employer or a union could not legally set an age limit on a warehouseman's job. Although that job requires physical work, and some older workers might not be able to handle the job, there is no public or co-worker safety justification for saying that no older person at all should be permitted to try the job.

C. Examples of Protection Under the ADEA

Now, let's illustrate how the ADEA may, or may not, protect you. Here are some typical examples:

EXAMPLE #1: Ted Yablonsky has worked for the Good Fat Meat Packing Company for twenty years. Ted's about to turn 65. Good Fat has informed him that although the company itself has no mandatory retirement rules until a worker reaches age 70, the pension plan in effect when Ted started working, long before ADEA was enacted, requires that he retire at age 65. Accordingly, Good Fat notifies Ted that he will have to retire, with full retirement benefits, at age 65. Does Ted have to retire if he doesn't want to?

The ADEA rules say no. The requirements of the pension plan cannot override federal law, which says Ted has a right

---

*   "Bona fide" means real, legitimate, honest.

256

to keep his job until age 70, as long as he can adequately perform his work. However, the law does permit Good Fat to stop contributing to Ted's pension fund when he reaches age 65, and the company will not have to count his years of service after age 65 in figuring the amount of Ted's retirement pension.

EXAMPLE #2: Janis Valentine is 46. She has been working for Media Hype, Inc., a large advertising agency, for eight years as a "junior" account representative. Recently, three other junior account representatives, all under age 35 and with less experience than Janice, were promoted to account executive positions. This was the third time in two years that younger, less experienced people had been promoted ahead of her. When Janice finally confronted one of the senior vice-presidents about the repeated decision not to promote her, she was told that although her work was excellent and there certainly were no age limits on promotion to account executive, the partners in Media Hype wanted to build up an image of "young, modern-thinking executives," and they also felt their clients preferred young, "dynamic" types working on their accounts. Does Janice have an ADEA age discrimination complaint against Media Hype?

She probably does. Though the company has no "policy" of age discrimination, the effect of what Media Hype has done over time is to deny Janice a promotion solely because of her age. If the company could show that Janice's job performance was poorer than those promoted ahead of her, she would probably lose her claim. In this case, though, Janice had been told her work performance was excellent. Likewise, if younger workers had been leap-frogged over her on only one occasion, Janice would have a more difficult time proving her case. By the way, the comments by the vice-president on the reasons Janice was denied promotion would be important evidence of the age discrimination against her.

NOTE: If Janice were 39 and the exact same things had happened, she would have no protection at all from the ADEA. Remember, the ADEA applies only to persons age 40 to 70. However, she might still have some legal protection if her state's age discrimination law had no such minimum age limit (see Section D, below).

EXAMPLE #3: Toshiro Hayashi is an aerospace technician who has been laid off because his company lost a big government contract. He is 58 years old. Toshiro seeks new work through the Up & At 'Em Employment Agency. Although Toshiro requests a referral to a job offered by an electronics company, the agency only refers him to less skilled, lower-paying jobs. Up & At 'Em tells Toshiro that the electronics firm is looking for people with a different background.

When Toshiro points out that his aerospace experience seems to be perfect for the job specifications at the electronics company, the employment agent tells him the electronics firm is a "growth" company looking for younger people who will stay with the company for many years, and that Up and At 'Em won't refer someone if they know a company wouldn't be interested in a particular "category" of worker.

Toshiro manages to get the name of the electronics company—Short Electric—from another job-seeker, and goes to see the Short people on his own. They tell him that although he is the best qualified person they have interviewed, they will have to teach any new employee how to work on their computer system, and they don't want to invest that much time and energy training someone who won't be around very long. However, since they do need someone soon, they might make an exception for Toshiro if he is willing to take the job for a lower salary than the position had been advertised as paying. That way, the Short people say, they can justify hiring Toshiro as "cost-effective" despite his age. Does Toshiro have an age discrimination complaint against either Up & At 'Em or Short Electric?

Toshiro has a complaint against both. The employment agency cannot refuse to refer Toshiro to a job for which he is qualified just because they don't think the employer wants to see anyone in his "category" if, by using the word "category," they really mean over a certain age. Short Electric has also acted in an unlawful manner by offering the job to Toshiro only if he takes it at a lower pay than they would offer a younger, but no more qualified, worker.

EXAMPLE #4: Rita Orozco has filed a labor grievance against her employer, the Stewrod Company, regarding a job reassignment. Her union filed the grievance on her behalf. As part of the grievance procedure, the union and Stewrod came to a compromise agreement which Rita doesn't think is fair. When she tells her union rep that the compromise with the company is unfair, the rep replies, "That's the best we can do for you." When Rita continues to protest, the union rep tells her "the facts of life," as he puts it. "There are only so many times we can fight hard for individual grievances against any one company," he tells her, "so we've got to pick our spots carefully." The union rep goes on to tell Rita that although her complaint against Stewrod is a perfectly valid one, the union doesn't want to "waste" one of its grievance battles on her because she is 60 years old and only two years away from a company retirement pension.

Rita will just have to take the compromise the union has worked out, he says, and ride out her time until retirement. "It's for the good of the union," the rep sternly reminds her. What does Rita tell him?

After saying some things not printable here, Rita should tell the union rep to get back in there with Stewrod and negotiate a fairer settlement for her. She might also add that if the union fails to do so, they will face a federal age discrimination complaint. She can remind the union rep of Section 623(c) of the ADEA, which prohibits labor organizations from discriminating because of age against a union member in any way that would "adversely affect his status as an employee."*

NOTE: If the union rep had told Rita the union would not press her grievance any further because it felt her grievance was not strong enough to "waste" one of their battles over it, Rita would probably have no age discrimination claim, assuming the union could point to something that backed up their claim that Rita's grievance was weak. In that case, the weakness of her grievance, not her age, would be the reason for the union's action (or lack of action).

"Work keeps at bay three great evils: boredom, vice and need."
Voltaire, *Candide*

D. State Laws Prohibiting Age Discrimination in Employment

In addition to ADEA, more than 40 states have their own laws against age discrimination in employment. An individual working in one of these states can choose to file a complaint under either their state law or the federal law (ADEA), or both. Why bother to file a complaint under state law? In many cases, the state law can provide greater protection than the federal law. For example, a number of states provide age discrimination protection in employment past age 70, where the ADEA stops. Other states provide protection to workers before they reach age 40, while some protect against the actions of employers with less than 20 employees. Even if the protection offered by your state law is the same as that provided by the federal law, you may

---

* Even though a high percentage of age discrimination cases involve female workers, the language of the ADEA is in the masculine form, only.

find that a particular state agency entrusted with the job of investigating and enforcing its own age discrimination law will provide easier, quicker and more aggressive prosecution of your complaint than the overburdened Equal Employment Oppportunity Commission does in enforcing the ADEA.*

If you wish to consider filing a complaint under your state's age discrimination in employment laws, you must first find out if your state has an agency empowered to process such a complaint. Unfortunately, there are several states which have age discrimination laws, but no state agency to enforce them. In these states you must rely on the federal law and/or a private law suit to enforce your rights. If your state does have an enforcement agency, you can find it through your state's labor commission (or department), state employment office, "fair employment" commission, human or civil rights agency. If these sources don't get you to the agency in your state which handles state age discrimination complaints, the local office of the federal Equal Employment Commission will be able to direct you to the right agency in your state.

Though procedures vary from state to state, most agencies require that you first file a written complaint, usually on a form the agency provides. Then the agency will contact your employer and try to "mediate" your complaint in some way. This will involve trying to get your employer's side of the story. At this point, if the agency decides your complaint is not valid, or cannot be proved, it may decide not to do anything further. If, however, it decides both your complaint and the employer's reasons for its actions have some validity, the agency may try to work out a compromise between you and the employer. If a voluntary compromise cannot be reached--because one or both sides will not agree to a reasonable resolution of the problem--the agency will hold a "hearing" (like a "trial") in front of an administrative judge or board at which you can be represented by an attorney or other legal representative. The decision from that administrative hearing can then be challenged by either you or the employer in the state courts.

E. How Do You Prove Age Discrimination?

It's one thing to claim you are the victim of age discrimination in employment; it's another to prove it. Fortunately, if you have what seems to be a valid complaint,

---

* Procedures followed by the Equal Employment Opportunities Commission (EEOC) are discussed in detail in Sections F and G, below.

either the federal EEOC or your state's age anti-discrimination agency will do much of the formal evidence-gathering for you during the course of their investigation of your charges. However, you must do some of the crucial evidence-gathering before either the federal or state agency gets involved. There are several reasons why you have to do this initial work:

1. The first reason is purely practical--the more information you present to the investigating agency when you file your complaint, the more interested they will be in investigating. The EEOC and the state agencies have very limited budgets and staff with which to make investigations. They simply won't be interested in vague claims of age discrimination which cannot be documented.

2. Some of the crucial facts in your case may only be available at the time the "acts" of discrimination are occurring. If you wait for the EEOC or state agency to discover these facts for you, they may have "disappeared"-- memories fade, information gets garbled, and employers have an opportunity to change their stories or cover up unseemly evidence.

3. Finally, don't forget the old adage that "If you want something done well, do it yourself." You are more familiar with the inner goings-on of your workplace than anyone sent from an outside investigating agency. And in many situations, you will be better able to identify and collect useful information than any outside investigator would be.

■ ■ ■ ■ ■

What kinds of things can be used as evidence of age discrimination?

Company Policy

The most obvious are statements of company policy, either written or verbal, which indicate arbitrary discrimination because of age: such things as job descriptions, work rules, personnel pamphlets, company notices or anything else--preferably in writing--which either directly indicate or imply that company policy favors younger workers or treats older workers unfairly. Also important are individual statements by supervisors, personnel administrators or other members of management concerning the reasons for their decisions regarding conditions of your employment. If any of these statements are in writing, save them and note when and from whom you received them. If you have not received any written reasons for the job decision you feel is discriminatory, make a written request for a statement of the company's reasons.

Comments by Management

In many cases, employers and their managers are too crafty to put in writing their discriminatory reasons for making an employment decision. In such cases, you may still be able to document your grievance with verbal statements by supervisors or other management people concerning unwritten company policy or undocumented reasons for a particular action involving your job. Such verbal statements can be valuable if made in the presence of a third person who could verify what you heard. Make notes of what was said, as accurately as possible, as soon as you can after the statement is made; also note the time and place the statement was made, who else was present, and the conversation surrounding the crucial statement. If others heard the statement being made, try to get them either to write down what they heard (and have them sign it) or have them sign your written version of the statement, indicating that it accurately reflects what they heard.

NOTE: When you approach co-workers about helping you with your age discrimination complaint, either by giving statements of their own experiences or by backing up your story of what has occurred, you may run into the common reaction: "I don't want to get involved." People may be afraid they will lose their own job or suffer in some other way because of having created bad blood with the company. You may be able to persuade them to help you by reassuring them the ADEA law which prohibits age discrimination also specifically prohibits retaliatory actions by the company or union against anyone who "has made a charge, testified, assisted, or participated in any manner in an investigation, proceeding, or litigation" under the ADEA. That protection is included in Section 623(d) of the Act. By the way, this same provision also protects you against further actions by the company because of your claim.

Two Areas of Proof:

Of course, in some instances, your employer will not have actually stated the reasons why you did not get a promotion, were laid off, did not get a particular job, or were transferred to a job you don't want or cannot adequately perform. In this situation, your task in proving age discrimination is even tougher. You've got to gather information which proves two things. First, you must prove there were no valid reasons why you did not get the particular job, promotion, etc.; and, second, that the person who did get or stay on the job was both younger and less qualified than you.

The following suggestions may help you out:

1. Start by making an honest evaluation of your own status with the company. Write down all the things pertaining to your training, education, experience and work record which would tend to qualify you, or disqualify you, for the job or promotion in question. Note such things as how long you've been working for the company; how many years experience you have in the type of work in general; any particular training or education which would qualify you for the job; the quality and reliability of your recent job performance; any problems you have had with management or with fellow workers, etc.

2. Try to gather as much information as you can about the person(s) who did get the job or promotion, or who did not get laid off when you did. Are they younger than you? Do they have less experience or training for the job? Do they have less seniority with the company than you do? Have any other workers close to your age been hired or promoted to these jobs? What is the ratio of older workers to younger workers in such job categories? Are younger workers as well as older workers being laid off with you? Did a job you wanted remain open for awhile after you had applied for it and before a younger person was hired or promoted to fill the slot?

These are the kinds of things to find out about and write down while putting together your "package" of evidence to back up your age discrimination claim. The more evidence of this kind you can present to the agency which investigates your age discrimination in employment claim, the greater your chance of having that agency take your claim seriously and do a thorough job for you.

<u>REMINDER</u>: Some occupational requirements are legal: there are times when a particular job category may in effect discriminate against older workers because the particular requirements of the job favor younger workers. Examples might be where perfect eyesight is required or where a great amount of physical exertion is needed. The fact that many more young workers hold such jobs than do older workers may appear to be evidence of job discrimination, but it does not necessarily prove illegal age discrimination. Age discrimination laws prohibit only arbitrary (meaning without good reason) discrimination. If the job criteria which favor younger workers are an accurate measure of what the job truly requires, there is no unlawful discrimination. However, if an employer used perfect eyesight or great lifting strength, for example, as job criteria when the jobs did not really require such eyesight or strength, unlawful age discrimination may have occurred.

F. How to File an Age Discrimination in Employment Complaint

Once you are convinced you have been the victim of age discrimination in employment, whether you alone have been discriminated against or what has happened to you is part of a pattern of discrimination against many others in your company, you must carefully follow the procedures established by the ADEA in order to insure you can get all the protection to which you are entitled. Here's how to proceed:

Step 1. File a Complaint with Your Employer

Follow the company's own internal grievance procedures.

Filing an Age Discrimination Charge

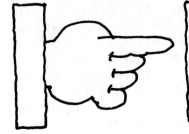

BEFORE YOU FILE
- EVALUATE YOUR STATUS
- GATHER INFORMATION
- ORGANIZE PAPERS
- CONSIDER ASSISTANCE

FILE A GRIEVANCE WITH YOUR UNION **AND** FILE A COMPLAINT WITH YOUR EMPLOYER

CONTACT THE FEDERAL EQUAL EMPLOYMENT OPPORTUNITY COMISSION **AND** THE EQUIVALENT STATE AGENCY

- DISCUSS YOUR PROBLEM
- DECIDE WHO IS MOST RESPONSIVE

INTERVIEW

THE FOLLOWING STEPS ARE DONE BY THE AGENCY.

FILE A " CHARGE" WITH THE FEDERAL AND THE STATE AGENCY.

CONCILIATORY MEETING WITH EMPLOYER.

FORMAL INVESTIGATION

AGENCY FILES A LAWSUIT ON YOUR BEHALF **OR** YOU INITIATE A PRIVATE LAWSUIT

The personnel office will be able to tell you what, if any, procedures they have. This may seem futile, sort of like asking a hungry lion to give you back your leg, but it is important for two reasons. First, when the company's management takes a look at what has happened, they may decide to change the corporate mind and give you the job you want. This may be a lot easier than going through formal discrimination charge procedures. Second, even if the company denies all wrongdoing and refuses to change its decision, or to offer you a compromise, you haven't wasted your time because to qualify for protection by the ADEA and the courts, you must first formally complain to the company. In legal lingo, this is called "exhausting your remedies," and though it may indeed be exhausting, the ADEA law requires you to do it.

Step 2. File a Grievance with Your Union

If you belong to a union and your job, or the job you applied for, is covered by a union contract, file a grievance with the union at the same time you file your complaint with the company. Some unions are excellent when it comes to aggressively protecting the rights of their older workers. They may have particular staff workers ready to help you gather evidence--or may already have evidence of discrimination against other workers by the same company--helpful in proving your case. Sometimes there is even a union legal fund that can help you with the cost of investigating and prosecuting your complaint.

Step 3. Decide Whether to File a Complaint First with EEOC or with Your State Agency

At the same time you file company and union grievances, contact the EEOC and the state agency which handles age discrimination complaints in your state. If the rules and procedures of the state law seem more favorable to you than the ADEA criteria, or if the state agency indicates it will prosecute your case faster or more aggressively than the EEOC, file your complaint with the state agency shortly before you file your charge with the EEOC. Usually, the agency that receives the complaint first will handle the case; the other agency will wait to see the result of the first investigation. If you are in doubt as to which complaint to file first, contact both the state agency and the EEOC in your area and

266

discuss the problem with them informally (but in person so they won't too easily shuffle you to the other agency). They will usually tell you which agency could better handle your complaint. The answer will vary from state to state, depending on the rules of the state agency, the workload of the respective agencies and the experience one or the other agency may have with your employer, etc.

Step 4. File a Second Complaint with the EEOC or State Agency

Even if you decide the EEOC can better handle your complaint, you must also file a separate complaint with the state agency, if your state has such an agency. Filing complaints in both federal and state agencies is a requirement for being able to go to court under the ADEA. Protect your right to sue in court later on, should it become necessary, by filing complaints with both the state and federal agencies.

If you file your complaint with the state agency first, you must also file a "charge" with the local office of the EEOC. Even if you want the state agency to handle the investigation and prosecution of your complaint and have filed first with them, you must also file a complaint, called a "charge,"* with the EEOC in order to be permitted to file a lawsuit under the ADEA if such a lawsuit becomes necessary later on.

IMPORTANT: Time Limits: Ordinarily a charge with the EEOC must be filed within 180 days of the date of the discriminatory act you are complaining about. State laws will have their own time limits. The days are counted from the date you received the notice from the employer of the action--refusing to hire or promote you, laying you off, etc.--about which you are complaining. If there is no specific date you can pinpoint as the date on which the discriminatory act took place--as in the case of a long-term refusal to promote or transfer--file your charge as soon as you have gathered the information that convinces you that you have been the victim of age discrimination.

Your charge with the EEOC must be in writing, and it must give the basic information you are complaining about, but it does not need to be in any particular form or contain any magic words. Just write a letter (send it by registered

---

* The company may call it an "appeal;" your union may call it a "grievance;" the state agency may call it a "complaint;" EEOC calls it a "charge." Don't be confused. It all refers to the same thing--you speaking up for your rights.

mail and always keep a copy) giving the name and address of your employer, your name and address, your job description and a description of the job or work condition that was denied you, along with the dates of any actions by the employer indicating discrimination and a brief description of why you believe the action was discriminatory. You will have an opportunity at a later time to explain your charges in greater detail. Keep your initial charge simple. For an example of a "charge" letter, see the following section, using Janice from Example #2 back in Section C as our letter-writer.

G. EEOC Procedures Enforcing the ADEA

1. Initial Interview

When you file a charge with the EEOC,* you will be notified by mail to make an appointment to see a case-worker/investigator who specializes in age discrimination matters. During this interview, the EEOC worker will ask you questions about the details of your charges, take a look at any written evidence you may have, and discuss what you would like to have happen as a result of your complaint. Bring with you copies of any written statements of company policy or actions, as well as any written notes of verbal statements or any other information which you believe might help prove your case. The EEOC worker will put copies of these documents in a file it will keep on your case. Also, bring with you the names and addresses of any witness who can back up your story of what has happened to you at work. In addition, try to write out a list of events, in chronological order, which apply to the charge you are making and how any appeal has been handled by the company and your union. Also bring the evaluation you made of your own work history and training. All these things will help the EEOC worker get a clearer picture of what has gone on.

The following is a sample "Charge" letter to EEOC:

---

* Don't feel like you're the only one having age discrimination problems that have to go to the EEOC for solution. More than 11,000 age discrimination charges were officially filed with the EEOC in 1982.

Janice Valentine
14 February Lane
Asbury Park, Texas

June 22, 1983

Equal Employment Opportunity Commission
2500 Federal Building
Asbury Park, Texas

Re: Age Discrimination in Employment Charge
Employer: Media Hype, Inc., 1234 Slick Lane, Asbury Park,
           Texas.

To Whom It May Concern:

This letter is written as a formal "charge" of age discrimination in employment, in violation of the federal Age Discrimination in Employment Act, against Media Hype, Inc. of Asbury Park, Texas. The facts pertaining to this charge are as follows:

1. I am employed by Media Hype, Inc. as a junior advertising account representative. I have been employed by Media Hype for eight years. I am 46 years old.

2. Over the past two years, eight other junior account representatives have been promoted to account executive positions while I have been passed over for such promotions. The last set of promotions were made during the week of June 1, 1983. All eight of the persons promoted ahead of me were under age 35 and have less experience in advertising and less seniority with Media Hype than I have.

3. On June 7, 1983, I spoke with Harold Hype, managing vice-president of Media Hype, Inc. When I asked him about the promotions of younger, less-experienced workers, he told me that although my work was excellent, the younger workers had been promoted because the company wanted to build an image of young, "dynamic" types as executives. I was told, in effect, that my age, and not my job performance, was the reason I had not been promoted.

4. On June 10, 1983, I filed a written appeal with Media Hype, Inc. under the provisions of their personnel policy. As of the date of this letter, I have received no written response to my appeal.

Please contact me as soon as possible regarding action on this charge.

Very truly yours,

Janice Valentine

2. "Conciliation"

After your initial interview, the EEOC will contact your employer to ask that information presenting the company's side of the story be submitted. The EEOC will also set up a "conciliation" meeting. At this meeting, an EEOC specialist--maybe the same EEOC worker you spoke to at your interview, but perhaps a different employee of EEOC--will sit down with you and a representative from your company and try to work out a compromise solution to your complaint. Many age discrimination complaints are settled at this stage. Sometimes the company will want to avoid further investigation by the EEOC, or they may simply want to avoid further hassle. In other situations, they may see that they would be in worse shape if they fight you, and lose, in a clear-cut case of age discrimination than if they compromised. Similarly, you may want to settle the case at this stage if the compromise arrived at substantially satisfies you. In some circumstances, you may want to accept a compromise you're not crazy about in order to avoid a full-fledged age discrimination case. These cases can take a long time and even if you have a good case, there is always the chance of losing. And sometimes you will be able to reach a compromise because the EEOC conciliator will suggest settling the dispute in a way that neither you nor your employer had thought of.

If your case is not settled at the first conciliation meeting, more sessions may be scheduled. You or the company may need more time to gather information or to consider various possible compromises. The EEOC worker may also do some preliminary investigating before the next conciliation meeting.

3. Formal Investigation

If several conciliation meetings do not result in a compromise settlement, the EEOC will begin a full investigation of your charges (assuming they consider your charge to have some merit). This investigation may take weeks or months. At the conclusion of the investigation, the EEOC may have developed more information with which to convince the employer to settle your case.

4. U.S. Justice Department Lawsuit on Your Behalf

If no settlement is reached after a full investigation, and the EEOC has found that there has been age discrimination, the EEOC may refer the matter to the United States Department of Justice (U.S. Attorney) for them to consider filing a lawsuit in federal court on your behalf against the employer. But don't hold your breath. In 1981, for example, there were about 10,000 charges filed with the EEOC; yet the Department of Justice filed less than 100 lawsuits to enforce the ADEA. The Justice Department claims their limited budget for age discrimination matters forces them to choose only those cases in which there is both a good chance of winning and in which the decision by the courts would have an impact on a large number of workers. Under present funding, they assert they cannot afford to underwrite individual age discrimination lawsuits, no matter how gross the age discrimination violations have been, unless the ruling would affect many other workers as well. If they do file a lawsuit on your behalf in federal court, it will take precedence over any private lawsuit or any lawsuit by a state agency in state court. But if the Justice Department does not take your case, that doesn't mean you can't pursue it on your own or with the help of your state agency (see below). When the Justice Department decides not to sue on your behalf, they will send you a "right to sue" letter which permits you to go to court on your own to enforce the ADEA.

"It is work which gives flavor to life."
Amiel, *Journal*

H. State Agency Files a Lawsuit on Your Behalf

If the Department of Justice does not file a lawsuit on your behalf in federal court, your state agency may decide to file a lawsuit on your behalf in state court to enforce the provisions of your state's age discrimination laws. The odds on whether your state agency will do this depend on the strength of your case, on the provisions of the age discrimination law in your state, and on the budget and inclination of the agencies empowered to enforce the law in your state.

I. Filing a Private Lawsuit to Enforce Your Rights Under the ADEA

In most cases, the U.S. Department of Justice will not file a federal lawsuit on your behalf. However, you are fully entitled to file a federal court or state court lawsuit on your own behalf to enforce the protections of the ADEA or state law. There are some rules to be aware of: You may not file a federal court lawsuit until at least 60 days after you have filed a complaint with both the EEOC and with your state agency, if your state has one (and you must file both); the lawsuit must be filed within two years from the date of the alleged discriminatory action. You may also be able to file a lawsuit in state court to enforce your state's age discrimination laws. Each state has its own rules about time limits and procedures. Even if your state agency does not file a suit for you, they may give you some information and assistance regarding when and how to file a lawsuit on your own.

Help in deciding if it's wise to file a lawsuit, whether to file in state or federal court, and assistance in prosecuting any lawsuit you do file, can be obtained from private attorneys or from organizations which provide legal help to seniors. Though private lawyers cost money, as we all know, there are a number specializing in age discrimination suits who are willing to take them on "contingency" basis. This means they will wait to get paid from the final court award or settlement of your case, and will not take any fee if you do not win something from the lawsuit. This contingency arrangement is usually dependent, however, on the lawyer believing you have a "good case," meaning a good chance of winning at least part of what you ask for. The lawyer may also require that you pay some money in the beginning to help defray the expenses of preparing the lawsuit. More and more lawyers are accepting age discrimination suits under such contingency fee arrangements because in an ADEA lawsuit you are now entitled to have a jury hear your case--usually more sympathetic to your situation than a federal judge--and you may be entitled to what are called "liquidated damages" (usually double what you have actually lost) if you win the lawsuit at trial. In addition, if you win, the other side can be required to pay your attorney fees.

NOTE: Help in Choosing a Lawyer: In addition to the normal considerations when choosing a lawyer--do they seem helpful and interested in your case? Are their fees reasonable?--you should make certain that the lawyer you choose to handle your age discrimination case is experienced in that particular field. Where do you start to find a lawyer with experience in age discrimination cases? One place is the

272

lawyer's referral panel of the local bar association in your community. But you must make it clear to the referral person that you want to be referred only to those lawyers who specialize in age discrimination cases.

Another way in which you may be able to find a lawyer who specializes in age discrimination cases is to contact senior citizens organizations in your community, as well as state and federal offices on aging. Because so many age discrimination matters involve older women, the National Organization for Women (N.O.W.) and the Commission on the Status of Women often are in contact with lawyers who handle both age and sex discrimination cases. Contact a local office of one of those agencies and ask for a referral to an experienced lawyer.

Yet another way to find lawyers who handle age discrimination cases is to visit the clerk's office of the United States District Court nearest you. Ask the clerk how many age discrimination cases are pending in the court at that time, and ask for the names of the plaintiff's (the person complaining about age discrimination) lawyer in each case. Some of the clerks will be very helpful in this, others may hand you the files and tell you to find the names of the lawyers yourself. Remember, you want to contact the lawyer whose name appears above the title "Attorney for Plaintiff."

When you finally reach a lawyer or lawyers, make sure to get specific answers from them about their experience in handling age discrimination matters.   If the lawyer is experienced in the field of age discrimination, seems interested in your case, and willing to push hard to enforce your rights and is someone you feel you can work with, go ahead with your case, and good luck!

About the Authors

Joseph L. Matthews has been an attorney since 1971. From 1975 to 1977 he taught at the law school of the University of California at Berkeley (Boalt Hall). He presently writes and practices law in San Francisco. Mr. Matthews' previous book for Nolo Press is AFTER THE DIVORCE.

■ ■ ■

Dorothy Matthews Berman is Program Director at a senior citizens center in the Los Angeles area. She has been involved in work with seniors in various capacities since 1973. Mrs. Berman and Mr. Matthews are mother and son.

NOLO PRESS Self-Help Law Books

BUSINESS & FINANCE

How To Form Your Own California Corporation

By attorney Anthony Mancuso. Provides you with all the forms, Bylaws, Articles, minutes of meeting, stock certificates and instructions necessary to form your small profit corporation in California. It includes a thorough discussion of the practical and legal aspects of incorporation, including the tax consequences.
California Edition. $21.95

The Non-Profit Corporation Handbook

By attorney Anthony Mancuso. Completely updated to reflect all the new law changes effective January 1980. Includes all the forms, Bylaws, Articles, minutes of meeting, and instructions you need to form a nonprofit corporation in California. Step-by-step instructions on how to choose a name, draft Articles and Bylaws, attain favorable tax status. Thorough information on federal tax exemptions which groups outside of California will find particularly useful.
California Edition $19.95

The California Professional Corporation Handbook

By attorneys Mancuso and Honigsberg. In California there are a number of professions which must fulfill special requirements when forming a corporation. Among them are lawyers, dentists, doctors and other health professionals, accountants, certain social workers. This book contains detailed information on the special requirements of every profession and all the forms and instructions necessary to form a professional corporation. $21.95

Billpayers' Rights

By attorneys Honigsberg & Warner. Complete information on bankruptcy, student loans, wage attachments, dealing with bill collectors and collection agencies, credit cards, car repossessions, homesteads, child support and much more.
California Edition $9.95

The Partnership Book

By attorneys Clifford & Warner. When two or more people join to start a small business, one of the most basic needs is to establish a solid, legal partnership agreement. This book supplies a number of sample agreements with the information you will need to use them as is or to modify them to fit your needs. Buyout clauses, unequal sharing of assets, and limited partnerships are all discussed in detail.
California Edition $15.95
National Edition $15.95

Plan Your Estate: Wills, Probate Avoidance, Trusts & Taxes

By attorney Clifford. Here in one place for the first time people can get information on making their own will, alternatives to probate, planning to limit inheritance and estate taxes, living trusts, and providing for family and friends.
California Edition. $15.95
Texas Edition $14.95

Chapter 13: The Federal Plan to Repay Your Debts

By attorney Janice Kosel. This book allows an individual to develop and carry out a feasible plan to pay his or her debts in whole over a three-year period. Chapter 13 is an alternative to straight bankruptcy and yet it still means the end of creditor harassment, wage attachments and other collection efforts. Comes complete with all the forms and worksheets you need.
National Edition $12.95

Bankruptcy: Do-It-Yourself

By attorney Janice Kosel. Tells you exactly what bankruptcy is all about and how it affects your credit rating, your property and debts, with complete details on property you can keep under the state and federal exempt property rules. Shows you step-by-step how to do it yourself and comes with all forms and instructions necessary.
National Edition $12.95

Legal Care for Software

By Dan Remer. Here we show the software programmer how to protect his/her work through the use of trade secret, trade-work, copyright, patent and, most especially, contractual laws and agreements. This book is full of forms and instructions that give programmers the hands-on information to do it themselves.
National Edition $19.95

Small-Time Operator

By Bernard Kamoroff, C.P.A. Shows you how to start and operate your small business, keep your books, pay your taxes and stay out of trouble. Comes complete with a year's supply of ledgers and worksheets designed especially for small businesses, and contains invaluable information on permits, licenses, financing, loans, insurance, bank accounts, etc. Published by Bell Springs Press. National Edition $ 8.95

We Own It!

By C.P.A.s Kamoroff and Beatty and attorney Honigsberg. This book provides the legal, tax and management information you need to start and successfully operate all types of coops and collectives. $ 9.00

FAMILY & FRIENDS

How To Do Your Own Divorce

By attorney Charles Sherman. Now in its tenth edition, this is the original "do your own law" book. It contains tear-out copies of all the court forms required for an uncontested dissolution, as well as instructions for certain special forms--military waiver, pauper's oath, lost summons, and publications of summons.
California Edition $ 9.95
Texas Edition $ 9.95

The People's Guide to Calif Marriage and Divorce

By attorneys Ihara and Warner. This book contains invaluable information for married couples and those considering marriage on community and separate property, names, debts, children, buying a house, etc. Includes sample marriage contracts, a simple will, probate avoidance information and an explanation of gift and inheritance taxes. Discusses "secret marriage" and "common law" marriage. California Edition $12.95

How To Adopt Your Stepchild

By Frank Zagone. Shows you how to prepare all the legal forms; includes information on how to get the consent of the natural parent and how to conduct an "abandonment" proceeding. Discusses appearing in court, making changes in birth certificates.
California Edition $14.95

After The Divorce: How To Modify Alimony, Child Support and Child Custody

By attorney Joseph Matthews. Detailed information on how to increase alimony or child support, decrease what you pay, change custody and visitation, oppose modifications by your ex. Comes with all the forms and instructions you need. Sections on joint custody, mediation, and inflation.
California Edition $14.95

The Living Together Kit

By attorneys Ihara and Warner. A legal guide for unmarried couples with information about buying or sharing property, the Marvin decision, paternity statements, medical emergencies and tax consequences. Contains a sample will and Living Together Contract.
National Edition $ 8.95

Sourcebook for Older Americans

By attorney Joseph Matthews. The most comprehensive resource tool on the income, rights and benefits of Americans over 55. Includes detailed information on social security, retirement rights, Medicare, Medicaid, supplemental security income, private pensions, age discrimination and much more.
National Edition $10.95

A Legal Guide for Lesbian/Gay Couples

By attorneys Hayden Curry and Denis Clifford. Here is a book that deals specifically with legal matters of lesbian and gay couples. Discusses areas such as raising children (custody, support, living with a lover), buying property together, wills, etc. and comes complete with sample contracts and agreements. National Edition $12.95

RULES & TOOLS

The People's Law Review

Edited by Ralph Warner. This is the first compendium of people's law resources ever published. It celebrates the coming of age of the self-help law movement and contains a 50-state catalog of self-help law materials; articles on mediation and the new "non-adversary" mediation centers; information on self-help law programs and centers (programs for tenants, artists, battered women, the disabled, etc.); articles and interviews by the leaders of the self-help law movement, and articles dealing with many common legal problems which show people "how to do it themselves" without lawyers. National Edition $ 8.95

Author Law

By attorney Brad Bunnin and Peter Beren. A comprehensive explanation of the legal rights of authors. Covers contracts with publishers of books and periodicals, with sample contracts provided. Explains the legal responsibilities between co-authors and with agents, and how to do your own copyright. Discusses royalties negotiations, libel, and invasion of privacy. Includes a glossary of publishing terms. $14.95

The Criminal Records Book

By attorney Siegel. Takes you step-by-step through all the procedures available to get your records sealed, destroyed or changed. Detailed discussion on: your criminal record--what it is, how it can harm you, how to correct inaccuracies, marijuana possession records & juvenile court records. Complete with forms and instructions. $12.95

California Tenants' Handbook

By attorneys Moskovitz, Warner & Sherman. Discusses everything tenants need to know in order to protect themselves: getting deposits returned, breaking a lease, getting repairs made, using Small Claims Court, dealing with an unscrupulous landlord, forming a tenants' organization, etc. Completely updated to cover new rent control information and law changes for 1981. Sample Fair-to-Tenants lease and rental agreements. California Edition $ 9.95

Everybody's Guide to Small Claims Court

By attorney Ralph Warner. Guides you step-by-step through the Small Claims procedure, providing practical information on how to evaluate your case, file and serve papers, prepare and present your case, and, most important, how to collect when you win. Separate chapters focus on common situations (landlord-tenant, automobile sales and repair, etc.). $ 9.95

How To Change Your Name

By David Loeb. Changing one's name is a very simple procedure. Using this book, people can file the necessary papers themselves, saving $200-300 in attorney's fees. Comes complete with all the forms and instructions necessary for the court petition method or the simpler usage method. California Edition $10.95

Fight Your Ticket

By attorney David Brown. A comprehensive manual on how to fight your traffic ticket. Radar, drunk driving, preparing for court, arguing your case to a judge, cross-examining witnesses are all covered. California Edition $12.95

Legal Research: How To Find and Understand the Law

By attorney Steve Elias. A hands-on guide to unraveling the mysteries of the law library. For paralegals, law students, consumer activists, legal secretaries, business and media people. Shows exactly how to find laws relating to specific cases or legal questions, interpret statutes and regulations, find and research cases, understand case citations and Shepardize them.
National Edition $12.95

Protect Your Home With A Declaration of Homestead

By attorney Warner. Under the California Homestead Act, you can file a Declaration of Homestead and thus protect your home from being sold to satisfy most debts. This book explains this simple and inexpensive procedure and includes all the forms and instructions. Contains information on exemptions for mobile homes and houseboats.
California Edition $ 7.95

Marijuana: Your Legal Rights

By attorney Richard Moller. Here is the legal information all marijuana users and growers need to guarantee their constitutional rights and protect their privacy and property. Discusses what the laws are, how they differ from state to state, and how legal loopholes can be used against smokers and growers.
National Edition $9.95

Landlording

By Leigh Robinson. Written for the conscientious landlord or landlady, this comprehensive guide discusses maintenance and repairs, getting good tenants, how to avoid evictions, recordkeeping, and taxes. Published by Express Press.
National Edition $15.00

How To Become A United States Citizen

By Sally Abel. Detailed explanation of the naturalization process. Includes step-by-step instructions from filing for naturalization to the final oath of allegiance. Includes study guide on U.S. history & government. Text is written in both English & Spanish. $9.95

The Unemployment Benefits Handbook

By attorney Peter Jan Honigsberg. Comprehensive information on how to find out if you are eligible for benefits, how the amount of those benefits will be determined. It shows how to file and handle an appeal if benefits are denied and gives important advice on how to deal with the bureaucracy and the people at the unemployment office.
National Edition $ 5.95

Don't Sit in The Draft

By Charles Johnson. A draft counseling guide with information on how the system works, classifications, deferments, exemptions, medical standards, appeals and alternatives.
National Edition $ 6.95

Computer Programming for The Complete Idiot

By Donald McCunn. An excellent introduction to computers. Hardware and software are explained in everyday language and the last chapter gives information on creating original programs.
$6.95

Write, Edit and Print

By Donald McCunn. Word processing with personal computers. A complete how-to manual including: evaluation of equipment, 4 fully annotated programs, operating instructions, sample application. 525 pages. $24.95

California Dreaming: The Political Odyssey of Pat and Jerry Brown

By Roger Rapoport. Here for the first time is the story of the First Family of California Politics from the Gold Rush to the 1980s. Based on more than 200 interviews, access to papers previously unavailable to scholars, lengthy talks and travels with Pat and Jerry Brown and their family. $ 9.95

IN A LIGHTER VEIN . . .

29 Reasons Not To Go To Law School

A humorous and irreverent look at the dubious pleasures of going to law school. By attorneys Ihara and Warner with contributions by fellow lawyers and illustrations by Mari Stein. $ 4.95

Order Form

QUANTITY	TITLE	UNIT PRICE	TOTAL

Prices subject to change

☐ Please send me a
catalogue of your books

Tax: (California only) 6½% for Bart,
Los Angeles, San Mateo & Santa
Clara counties; 6% for all others

Name_____

Address_____

_____

SUBTOTAL _____

Tax _____

Postage & Handling $1.00

TOTAL _____

Send to:

NOLO PRESS
950 Parker St.
Berkeley, CA 94710
or

NOLO DISTRIBUTING
Box 544
Occidental, CA 95465

Table of Contents

Acknowledgements

Many thanks go to Stephanie Harolde and Ralph Warner for their knowledgeable and patient editorial work on the manuscript. Thanks, too, go to Toni Ihara for a design which makes the book both attractive and easy-to-read for seniors, and to Linda Allison, whose drawings and flow charts enliven these pages.

Special thanks go to the National Council of Senior Citizens in Washington, D.C., and particularly to Janet Myder of that organization, for many helpful suggestions on the manuscript; to Bob Kovash and Tom Burtscher of the Health Care Financing Administration for their review of the chapters on medical coverage; to John Percy and Fred Young at the Office of Information of the Social Security Administration; to Edith Manley for her article on age discrimination in the PEOPLE'S LAW REVIEW (Nolo Press); and to Amy and Toshiro Ihara, D.J. Soviero, San Francisco attorney and specialist in the area of age discrimination, and Marilyn Griffin, Assistant Director for Program Services, Martin Luther King Junior Family Health Center for their careful reviews of the entire manuscript.

UPDATE SERVICE & LEGAL DIRECTORY

Our books are as current as we can make them, but some-times the laws do change between editions. You can read about any law changes which may affect this book in the **NOLO NEWS**, a 12 page newspaper which we publish quarterly.

In addition to the **Update Service**, each issue contains a directory of people-oriented lawyers and legal clinics avail-able to answer questions, handle a complicated case or process your paperwork at a reasonable cost. Also featured are comprehensive articles about the growing self-help law movement as well as areas of the law that are sure to affect you.

To receive the next 4 issues of the **NOLO NEWS**, please send us $2.00.

Name_____

Address _____

_____

Send to: **NOLO PRESS, 950 Parker St., Berkeley, CA 94710**